1 FUNDAMENTAL SKILLS AND CONCEPTS

FUNDAMENTAL 1 SKILLS AND CONCEPTS

Language Arts Lessons
for Grades 1–3

Dorothea M. Ross, Ph.D.
University of California, San Francisco

Sheila A. Ross, Ph.D.
Palo Alto Medical Research Foundation

Fearon Teacher Aids
a division of
Pitman Learning, Inc.
Belmont, California

Editorial director: Roberta Suid
Adapted from the *Pacemaker Primary Curriculum*
by Glen Harvey, Ph.D.
Editor: Kevin Mayford Cox
Production editor: Zanae Jelletich
Designer: Susan True
Cover designer: Susan True

ISBN-0-8224-0291-2
Printed in the United States of America.
1.9 8 7 6 5 4 3 2 1

Contents

Contents . . .

Introduction

Fundamental Skills and Concepts 1 is designed for the child who has difficulty grasping specific concepts or mastering skills in language arts. Many children at the primary level have difficulty developing proficiency with the basic skills and concepts that provide the foundation upon which the remainder of the school curriculum is based. If these fundamental skills and concepts are not mastered, children find the school curriculum increasingly difficult and fall further and further behind their peers in achievement and ability. *Fundamental Skills and Concepts 1* has been developed to supplement the regular primary grades curriculum and provides new ideas, activities, games, lessons, teaching routines, and seatwork to augment and facilitate the teaching of fundamental skills and concepts.

Fundamental Skills and Concepts 1 is divided into four sections: reading, spelling, printing, and listening. (Arithmetic is contained in a separate volume, *Fundamental Skills and Concepts 2: Arithmetic Lessons for Grades 1–3.*) Each section contains a variety of suggestions for supplementing the normal primary curriculum in order to provide the necessary remedial work. For example, the *reading section* has been subdivided into the following subsections: letter recognition, phonetics, reading words, sample reading lessons, reading improvement, reading tests, rhyming, and a reading list with sample discussion topics. All seatwork (reading sheets, reading tests, printing sheets, and so forth) are located at the back of the volume on perforated sheets, facilitating removal and photocopying.

Although *Fundamental Skills and Concepts 1* has been designed for the child in need of remedial work, the material is presented in such a manner that it can be used to augment lessons designed for an entire class. It can also be used by a teacher or instructional aide with an individual child or a small group of children. Numerous games, activities, teaching routines,and seatwork have been discussed in detail to enhance the multifaceted nature of the text in order to maximize its usefulness.

General Procedure

To be effective in using *Fundamental Skills and Concepts 1,* the teacher should follow this procedure:

1. When a child manifests a learning difficulty, determine all the major sections (such as reading, spelling, and printing) and subsections (such as letter recognition and phonetics) that might be used to supplement the child's regular textbook and workbook.

2. Isolate the particular problem as much as possible. For example, if a child is having difficulty reading, determine if the problem is one of phonetics, letter recognition, or particular consonants or vowels.

3. Skim the entire section(s), including all subsections, determined appropriate to the learning difficulty. Once familiar with all the material available pertaining to a particular section, select appropriate procedures, activities, and seatwork.

4. Since there is considerable overlap in reading, spelling, and printing, skim all three sections covering these areas before beginning remedial teaching. Do not hesitate to combine materials from various sections when useful.
5. Slowly work through the selected routines, lessons, activities, and seatwork, giving as much individual help as necessary, paying careful attention to problem areas, and stressing comprehension and mastery rather than rote performance.
6. If the child is still exhibiting difficulty, repeat appropriate routines and activities, supplementing them with related material from the volume. Carefully note the child's learning problems in order to isolate the precise difficulty. Once determined, focus teaching efforts on remedying the specific problem.
7. At times a child may understand a particular concept or may have developed some facility with a skill, but now he or she requires additional practice. In such cases the teacher may determine that extended individual attention or lessons are unnecessary, but that additional seatwork or practice through games would be beneficial. Always select activities and seatwork appropriate to the child's ability.
8. Activities, games, and seatwork from the various sections may be used to supplement the everyday classroom routine even when remedial work is not required. This volume has been designed so it can be used as a resource to increase the teacher's classroom repertoire.

Procedure Rationale

Much of the material in *Fundamental Skills and Concepts 1* can be presented in the context of the small group, with five children participating in the lesson. The small group teaching situation facilitates the acquisition of mediational skill (organizing and storing information for late retrieval and use). To understand the process through which this occurs, it is necessary to be familiar with some of the basic principles of observational learning. *Observational learning* is learning that occurs in the absence of any direct instructions to learn. For example, when a child *spontaneously* adopts a mannerism of a TV star, or cheats as a result of seeing another child cheat, or climbs a ladder after seeing an adult go up the ladder, we say that observational learning has occurred as a result of the child seeing a symbolic peer or adult *model* performing a specific activity. Observational learning can occur simply as a result of seeing a model perform, but the learning is enhanced if the observer sees the model *rewarded* (the peer model cheats and gets a perfect score on the test),or if the model is a *high status or powerful* person (adult), or if factors in the environment serve to direct the observer's *attention* to the model (the TV show is exciting or the TV star gets impressive rewards for behavior).

In the small group teaching situation, intentional training is combined with highly explicit modeling procedures, attention-directing activities, and appropriate reinforcement procedures. Consider a typical reading lesson: The children are playing a table search game in which the goal is to be the first to turn up an *s*. Child A picks up a *g*, and is unable to identify it. The teacher says that it is a *g*, asks the child to hold it up and name it (one-to-one intentional training),and gives praise (social reward) for naming it correctly. Child A then *observes Child B* go though the same general sequence except that Child B names the letter correctly and is rewarded with praise, and sometimes the teacher comments that Child B found a *g*. Subsequent children repeat this general sequence. Attention is focused on the game because each child wants to find the goal letter. The child who finds it wins a star (symbolic reward). Thus Child A is familiarized with the learning task through frequent *active participation* combined with *intentional training* and is also provided with a series of opportunities to *observe peer models* participating in nearly identical sequences and to *verbalize these observed events* overtly or covertly.

Supplies and Rewards

From the beginning, the children are praised whenever there is justification. In addition to praise, they earn stars for good effort, behavior, or work, and receive many prizes to take home.

Prizes. Rewards are an essential part of the program. Keep on hand an assortment of poker chips to be awarded as prizes. Accumulated poker chips can be exchanged at a later time for a special privilege or treat.

Coins and Tokens. Handling and recognition of coins is an important part of the arithmetic program. Coins, especially pennies, are used as tokens in the teaching of game skills. Keep a box of coins, starting with two rolls of pennies, a roll of nickels, and a roll of dimes (total value, $8), and add other coins and bills as needed. Count the money before each exercise or game in which money is used, and be certain that all of the money is returned to the box when the activity is completed.

Also put together an assortment of such things as checkers and washers for times when the lessons require that good answers be rewarded with tokens.

Lesson Preparation

This program requires the teachers to do lesson preparation in the form of reading over each day's lessons carefully in advance and being sure that all of the materials needed for each lesson are ready and that the general procedures for the lesson are known. The teacher does *not* try to learn or memorize the lesson, but has the lesson book at the table and reads from it or refers to it whenever necessary.

Every day each teacher should go over each lesson that will be taught the next day, check that the necessary supplies are in the box for each subject's lessons, get out accompanying seatwork sheets if any, and briefly practice the games. After reading the entire lesson, teachers may select from the *Equipment* list only those supplies needed for the learning activities to be carried out. Particular attention should be given to letter, word and flash cards. A single set of 52 letter cards should be kept ready for recognition activities. And a careful reading of each lesson will suggest when the teacher must prepare pairs, multiples or a variety of letter and word cards.

Seatwork Format

When the children do independent seatwork, they work on single sheets directly related to the lessons. Most periods of work are between 15 and 20 minutes.

Some pages of seatwork have an instruction box at the top of the page. The instruction box shows the child what to do and whether to use crayon or pencil. The teacher must complete the right side of the box in the way that the child should complete the page. The child is taught to look first at the left side of the box to see what the task is and then at the right side to see how the task is done. The child should do the task exactly as the teacher has done it; for example, if the teacher has used a red crayon, the child should use a red crayon. Note that often a seatwork sheet can be completed in several different ways (and so can be used several times) if the teacher varies the way in which he or she completes the instruction box.

Introducing Seatwork

Explain that at the top of the page there is a box, and in the box it shows you what to do. Tell children that their names are at the top of the page; show them the instruction picture on the left and the completed picture on the right. On the chalkboard display an exact replica of the top part of the setwork sheet. Now give each child a crayon. Ask the children to *tell* you what they are going to do before beginning.

Marking Seatwork

Consider the page completed if a child has attempted to follow the instructions, has used the correct crayon color or has attempted to do the task as it is set out in the sample at the top of the page. Try to help the children improve their skill at the task, for example, by guiding their hands to get them started. But do not expect more than the child is capable of at this point.

Mark each page and return it to the child to correct, or if the page is completely messed up, give the child a duplicate page to do over. Point out that the child did not do it the right way and can try it again. You want to establish right from the beginning that work must be completed and errors must be corrected before new work is started.

Mark the seatwork on a daily basis. If you let it pile up, the child will be working on new work the next day only because none of the old work has been marked and cannot be corected. If there are corrections to be made, set out the seatwork for the child to begin as soon as he or she arrives the next morning.

Scorecard Format

The teacher should make scorecards for the children. Each child should always have a scorecard to keep at the desk or bring to the small table.

The first scorecards should have eight spaces ruled in pencil with room at the top for you to print the child's name. Quickly increase the number of spaces so that by the end of the year the cards have forty or more spaces. Keep scorecards ruled up so that you always have some blanks on hand.

Whenever a child answers or behaves well, he or she may win a star, which you pencil in one square. In some lessons, give tokens for good answers or behavior and then at the end of the lesson give a star to the child who has the most tokens.

Introducing Scorecards

Display the scorecards. Draw a scorecard on the board. Explain that each square must have a star in it in order to complete the card. Demonstrate on the board. Hold up a completed scorecard. Tell the children that as soon as they have a completed card, they will win a prize, which they may take home to keep. Show some sample prizes. Give each child a blank scorecard with the child's name printed on it to put on his or her desk. Explain that stars are given for good seatwork, for good line behavior, and so forth.

General Game Skills

Much of the material in *Fundamental Skills and Concepts 1* is presented in a game format. Teach one game skill at a time, starting with hands on knees between turns. As soon as the children sit down, they should put their hands on their knees while you set out game materials and explain the activities. Unless they are asked to help, they should not touch anything on the table until their turns. Be very firm about this rule right from the beginning, and reward with praise and stars those players who know the game skill of hands on knees. Do not try to teach the next game skill until the children really know this one. Instead, tell the children what to do (for example, one turn each, clockwise play) but do not drill or scold for not remembering a game skill that has not yet been taught.

The game skills that should be taught over a long period of time in any of the programs involving games are:

1. Hands on knees when not playing.
2. Listening when the game is being explained.
3. Playing in turn; knowing when it is one's turn.
4. Paying attention between turns.
5. Taking only one turn at a time.
6. Touching the game only when it is one's turn.
7. Following rules.
8. Losing with reasonable grace.
9. Accepting decisions of the game controller.
10. Handling game materials carefully.
11. Accepting that the game is over.

Establish the *rules of play* so that once the game begins, the rules are adhered to. When a game is over, the rules may be changed for the next game; for example, the player may receive three tokens instead of one for a correct answer. As the children become used to following rules of play, encourage them to decide on the rules for a particular game. For example, the winner might decide on the rules for the next game: who will be first, how many tokens to take, penalties, and so forth.

When the children know how to take turns, understand that play is clockwise, and know their turns, do not say a child's name when it is his or her turn. Instead, say the item (or whatever the turn consists of) and expect the child to be attending. If not, the next child should have the turn.

Copying

Help in copying is given mainly during seatwork correction and help periods. The principle to stress in all copying training is that the child should break the whole in parts and do one part at a time, temporarily ignoring the remaining parts. The child should look at the point where *one line begins* and put the pencil at about the same point on the blank space. Then look at the original to see where the line goes and move the pencil accordingly. The child would follow the same procedure for the next part of the design, then compare the work with the original and make changes if the two do not look the same.

In the beginning, the aim would be to have the child identify and put in each part of the design although the proportions may differ from those of the original. It is important that the child acquire a strategy for attacking copying tasks. As children become more proficient at breaking the whole into parts and doing one part at a time, emphasis on correct proportions can be gradually introduced.

Lessons

Reading

This first section reinforces reading skills from letter recognition through reading aloud. Some lessons suggest using reading markers (cardboard strips to be placed underneath a word, phrase or sentence). Teachers may prefer to ask children to isolate words with an index card, ruler, or by some other technique more familiar to them.

As teachers read through other lessons, the following should be kept in mind. With the exception of lessons in which stories are read, every lesson should begin with the Alphabet Drill. However, it is important to avoid a drilling procedure in other games and activities. If children do not know an answer, tell them almost immediately, ask them to repeat it, and then go on with the game.

LETTER RECOGNITION

Alphabet Drill

Purpose: To teach the alphabet by rote and letter recognition.
Equipment: Letter cards, paper and pencil for each child, chalkboard.
Seatwork: Reading Seatwork 1–4.
Procedure: Print 52 letter cards, one letter per card for uppercase and lowercase letters. With the exception of lessons in which stories are read, every lesson should begin with the alphabet drill. Begin with lowercase letters. Once these are mastered, use the drill to teach uppercase (capital) letters.

1. Go through the entire alphabet with lowercase letter cards at the beginning of the lesson. With this procedure the child becomes familiar with the letters and starts learning the alphabet by rote.
2. Start with three cards—*a, b,* and *c.*
3. State: "The alphabet *begins* with *a* [show *a*], *b* [show *b*], *c* [show *c*]."
4. Ask one child to repeat this after you as you show the three cards again.
5. Begin again with *a,* and show every letter in the alphabet quickly, naming it clearly with no child participation.
6. When you get to *z,* pull out the last three cards, and say, "The alphabet *ends* with *x* [show *x*], *y* [show *y*], *z* [show *z*]."
7. Ask one child to repeat this as you show the three cards again.
8. Using all six cards (*a, b, c, x, y, z*) say, "The alphabet *begins* with *a, b, c.* The alphabet *ends* with *x, y, z.*" Show each card as you say the letter.
9. Each day add one letter. Add *d* then *w,* then *e* then *v,* and so on until you get through the entire alphabet.

The advantage of this method is that the child learns to say the alphabet from different points within the twenty-six-letter series instead of overlearning the beginning of the alphabet and being weak on the last half.

10. After the alphabet drill stress recognition of the letter chosen for that day.
11. Demonstrate printing the letter on the chalkboard, and ask the children to print it. Be sure the children use the correct sequence of movements when printing the letter.

12. Reading Seatwork 1–4 and similar teacher-made seatwork can be used to supplement the alphabet drill and the letter teaching routines if the children are able to print the letters of the alphabet. Do not use seatwork of this type until children are able to print all the letters of the alphabet.

Letter Teaching Routine—Lowercase Letters

Purpose: To teach letters.
Equipment: Letter cards, pencil for each child, chalkboard.
Seatwork: Use appropriate printing seatwork.
Procedure:

1. Show the children the letter selected, tell them the name of the letter, and ask them to say it.
2. Demonstrate printing the letter on the chalkboard. If a letter is very similar to another letter, demonstrate the difference, and give some practice in recognition of the spatial differences (*b, d*) and the visual differences (*m, n*).
3. Play a table search game using letter cards. Ask the children to select from among a number of cards with the letter being taught and a number of cards with a letter that is quite different.
4. Ask the children to practice printing the letter. (Use appropriate printing seatwork and teacher-made printing seatwork).
5. Ask the children to practice printing the letter on the chalkboard.

Letter Teaching Routine—Uppercase Letters

Purpose: To teach recognition of uppercase letters.
Equipment: Letter cards, ABC book, chalkboard.
Seatwork: Use appropriate printing seatwork.
Procedure:

1. Start with *A*.
2. Hold up a lowercase *a* letter card, and ask the children to name the letter.
3. Show them the uppercase form of the letter.
4. Display an *ABC* book that shows both forms to supplement your teaching of the letter.
5. On the chalkboard write one or two names that have the phonetic value of *A* that you are teaching, for example, Anne or Andy, to demonstrate the letter in a word.

Additional Procedures:

1. Play *Which Two Go Together?* Ask the children to find pairs of uppercase and lowercase letters from a set of letter cards. One point is awarded for each matched pair.
2. Play *Capitals*. The teacher holds up a lowercase letter, and the children search simultaneously for the uppercase letter that matches the lowercase letter.
3. Play *Quick! What Letter?* Quickly display letter cards, asking the children to identify the letters you hold up.
4. Demonstrate Printing. Have the children practice printing the letters, using seatwork sheets and the chalkboard.

Letter Review One

Purpose: To give practice in letter recognition.
Equipment: Letter cards, picture cards, tokens, paper and pencil for each child.
Procedure: The alphabet drill (see p. 3) should be used prior to letter review routines. Play a table search game. Include teacher-made picture cards of familiar objects.

1. Place the picture cards facedown on the table, and ask the children in turn to identify the letter or picture on the card picked up. (The first letter of the objects pictured is the letter being reviewed.)
2. The goal can be either to be the first player to find a particular letter or to find the most of a particular letter.
3. Award tokens.
4. It is important not to use drill in the games. If children don't know the name of the letter or picture, tell them almost immediately, ask them to say it, and go on with the game.

Additional Procedures:

1. Play *Quick! What Letter?*
    - Hold up a letter card, and point at a player.
    - Ask the child to identify the letter quickly or lose a turn.
    - Award tokens.
2. Play *Guess What?*
    - The teacher displays samples of three letters.
    - Each child writes one of these letters on a sheet of paper, then turns the paper over. (Note that all children write their letters at the same time.)

- The teacher guesses which letter each child has written. For a correct guess the teacher wins a token from the child. If wrong, the teacher loses a token. For variety, the teacher may write and the children guess.

Letter Review Two

Purpose: To give practice in letter recognition.
Equipment: Letter cards, pennies.
Procedure: The alphabet drill (see page 3) should be used prior to letter review routines. Play *Bingo.*

1. Give each child two different letter cards. No two children should have identical pairs.
2. Ask each child to identify the two letters.
3. Explain that the task is to find two matching letters in a table search game.
4. Each time children find a matching letter, they place it under the card it matches.
5. As soon as a child has two matching letters, he or she calls "Bingo."

Additional Procedure: Play *Pass It On.*

- Everyone at the table has pennies and one letter card except the teacher, who has the letter being reviewed and the card to be passed on (*i*, for instance).
- Each player in turn must draw one card from the person on his or her right. The object is to avoid the *i* card.
- The child on the teacher's left starts the game by drawing one of the teacher's two cards.
- Players should be encouraged to keep poker faces and to try different strategies for getting rid of the *i* card.
- Once a player has touched a card in the preceding player's hand, he or she must take the card.
- At intervals stop the game; the child with the unlucky letter must give everyone else a penny.

Letter Review Three

Purpose: To give practice in letter recognition.
Equipment: Letter cards (several cards for each of any five letters being reviewed).
Procedure: The alphabet drill (see page 3) should be used prior to the letter review routines. Play *Find Five Letters,* a table search game.

1. The winner is the first person to find all five letters named by the teacher and to place the letter cards on the table in alphabetical order.
2. There are several variations: Players may be allowed to find the letters in any order, or they may be required to find them in alphabetical order. They may pick up a card and replace it if they already have that letter, or they may keep the card and use it for trading. Children may pick up cards in turn or simultaneously with the other children. In addition children may pick up cards in turn from a center pack, or the teacher may deal each child five cards, one of which is discarded before another is chosen from the center pack.

Additional Procedure: Play *Look Alikes.*

- Introduce this game by talking about pairs of shoes, houses, and other objects that are very similar but not identical in all respects; for example, two shoes from a pair are not interchangeable.
- Set out at least five cards, two of which are look-alikes and one that is completely different. Use letters easily confused spatially (*p, q*) and visually (*m, n*).
- In this game the child tries to find the pairs of look-alike letters.

Sample Lesson One

Purpose: To give practice in letter recognition.
Equipment: Letter cards, picture cards.
Procedure: Play a table search game using teacher-made cards with pictures of familiar objects and some letter cards with the lowercase letters *o* or *s* on them (or any lowercase letters). The first letter of objects pictured would be *o* or *s.*

1. Ask the children to identify the picture cards first. Then show them the *o* and *s* cards.
2. To help children remember the letter names, point out the similarity between *s* and a snake, and ask them to make an "s" sound. Tell them that snakes often make a hissing sound.
3. Show the shape of your mouth when you say "Oh," and ask the children to say it.
4. Alternate the *o* and *s* cards, and ask the children to name them.
5. Mix the *o* and *s* cards with other letter cards. In this game the *o* and *s* cards should be the most valuable cards.

6. Place all the letter cards facedown on the table. Ask the children, in turn, to draw a card. The winner can be the first child to find an *o* and an *s,* to find the most *o*'s or the most *s*'s, or to find the first or most appropriate pictures. Vary the letters and pictures that are needed to win.
7. Immediately tell the names of any letters children can't remember. During any game there should never be drill on the letters or the names of pictures. Games should be fast, fun, and exciting; they are not drill sessions. After you tell the child the name of any card, ask him or her to say it once after you.
8. Each child must name each card found.

Use the general procedure described here whenever you play a table search game with specific letters. Once the children have played games with letters, pause at those letters in the alphabet drill (see p. 3) and see if the children can identify the letters. In this way they will become familiar with the place of each letter in the alphabet.

Sample Lesson Two

Purpose: To give practice in letter recognition.
Equipment: Letter cards and five pennies for each child.
Procedure: Play *Find the (name of letter).*

1. Each child has *s, o,* and *p* cards and five pennies.
2. Children put their cards facedown on the table, and the teacher tries to guess which card is a specified one.
3. After a correct guess the teacher wins a penny from the child. If the teacher is incorrect the child receives a penny. The winner is the player with the most pennies.
4. In guessing, the teacher should say, "Is this card the *p*?" and point clearly to one card. The child must say, "No, it's an *o* (or *s*)," or "Yes, it's a *p*."

Sample Lesson Three

Purpose: To give practice in letter recognition.
Equipment: Letter cards, pennies.
Procedure: Play *Quick! What Letter?*

1. The teacher holds up a letter card and points at a child, who must answer quickly.
2. If the child answers correctly, he or she receives a penny.
3. The first child to receive five pennies wins.

Sample Lesson Four

Purpose: To give practice in letter recognition.
Equipment: Five pennies and two letter cards for each child.
Procedure: Play *Guess Which Hand?*

1. Note which letters present problems for the children. Ask each child to name the two letters when you hand out two letter cards.
2. Review left and right, and ask the child to put one letter in the left hand, the other in the right.
3. The teacher must guess, "You have the *h* in your left hand and the *e* in your right."
4. The child then shows the letters.
5. The child wins a penny if the teacher is incorrect and loses a penny if the teacher is correct.
6. Note that the word *right* should not be used to signify a correct guess because it will confuse the child about left and right hands. Say, "Is it an *h*? It *is.* I win a penny." You may use the word *wrong,* however.

Sample Lesson Five

Purpose: To give practice in letter recognition.
Equipment: Letter cards.
Procedure: Play *Bingo.*

1. Give each child two different letter cards. No child should have the same two letters as another child.
2. Ask each child to identify the two letters.
3. Explain that the task is to find two matching letters from the cards lying facedown.
4. Each time the children find one, they place it under the card it matches.
5. As soon as a child has two matching letters, he or she calls "Bingo."
6. This introductory procedure should move along rapidly because the children must hold up and identify the cards they find and replace them on the table if they cannot use them. Since all other players will be watching, any child with good place memory will soon locate the cards needed.

7. If the children have any difficulty with letter cards, begin with picture cards. When they are proficient with the two-card procedure, move up to three or more cards.

Sample Lesson Six

Purpose: To give practice in letter recognition.
Equipment: Letter cards.
Procedure: Play *Pickup Bingo.*

1. Give each child two (or three) letter cards. No two children should have the same set of cards.
2. Ask each child to identify the letters and to review the two or three cards needed so that he or she knows what cards to keep.
3. The task is to find matching letters from the cards lying facedown on the table.
4. All players simultaneously pick up one card at a time and replace it if they do not need it.
5. As soon as a child has matched his or her letters, he or she calls "Bingo."
6. You may wish to play the game first with picture cards.

Sample Lesson Seven

Purpose: To give practice in letter recognition.
Equipment: Magic slate or chalkboard.
Procedure:

1. Use your magic slate or chalkboard to review straight lines, curves, lines going up above a line, lines going down below a line, curves to the right, and curves to the left.
2. Use any of the letters the children know to demonstrate these lines.
3. Emphasize that *p* goes down below the line while *h, l,* and *t* go up.
4. Take two letters at a time that differ greatly, such as *s* and *h.*
5. Print them on your magic slate or chalkboard; then erase them. Put in a baseline to print on, and tell the children to watch and to raise their hands as soon as they know which of the two letters you are printing.
6. Stop as soon as a child's hand is raised. Let the child tell you how he or she knows which letter you are printing. Supplement what is said with demonstration and explanation.
7. As the children become more proficient, use pairs of letters that must go quite a way before the children can be certain which they are, such as *l* and *t.*

Sample Lesson Eight

Purpose: To give practice in letter recognition.
Equipment: Letter cards, pennies, timer (optional).
Procedure: Play *Pass It On.*

1. Each child has the same card, for example *w.*
2. The teacher has two cards, such as *w* and *g.*
3. The child on the teacher's left picks one card and then turns to let the next child to the left draw a card.
4. The object is to avoid getting the second letter (*g*) and, if you do get it, to pass it on. Encourage children to maintain a poker face throughout so that no one knows where the unlucky letter is.
5. At intervals stop the game. The child with the unlucky letter must give everyone else a penny. It makes the game more exciting to have a timer sound the end of an interval.

Sample Lesson Nine

Purpose: To give practice in letter recognition.
Equipment: Letter cards.
Procedure: Play a big table search game in which the children play against you in trying to find all the letters reviewed to date. Set out letters five at a time, starting with *a* through *e.* You should have about three of each of the five letters. (See Sample Lesson One, p. 5, for more details on table search games with specific letters.)

PHONETICS

Word Recognition through Phonetics—General Routine

Purpose: To begin teaching word recognition through phonetics.
Equipment: Letter cards, paper and pencil for each child, magic slate or chalkboard.

Procedure:

1. Teach phonetic values for the letters as they sound in the following:

a—cat	*j*—jam	*r*—red
b—bit	*k*—keg	*s*—sat
c—cat	*l*—let	*t*—tan
d—dig	*m*—man	*u*—cut
e—pet	*n*—net	*v*—van
ee—see	*o*—hot	*w*—wet
f—fan	*o*—no	*x*—x-ray
g—get	*oo*—pool	*y*—yes
h—hen	*p*—peg	*z*—zip
i—pin	*qu*—quick	

2. Start with the letter *a*. Explain that *a* is the name of the letter, but some of the sounds the letter makes do not sound like *a*. As an example of this concept, mention that *xylophone* is the name of an instrument, but the sounds a xylophone makes are quite different from the sound of the word *xylophone*.
3. Teach the children to say "a" (sound as in *cat*) when you point to *a* and "t" (sound "tuh" as in *tan*) when you point to *t*.
4. Hold up an *a* card and a *t* card, and ask the children to practice the sounds. Ask the children to say them closer and closer in time until they have blended them into a single sound, "at."
5. As soon as the children recognize *at*, say and then write some short sentences and phrases so that they see and hear the word in a meaningful context. Use phrases such as *at school, at the dentist's*, and *at four o'clock*.
6. Now teach *c* ("kuh" as in *cat*) and *m* ("muh" as in *man*), and use blending to teach *cat* and *mat*.
7. Give out paper and pencils for children to write the words, after demonstrating on your magic slate or chalkboard.
8. Differentiate between the concepts of reading, writing, and spelling.
9. One way to emphasize the sound values of letters is to use incomplete sentences: "I am thinking of an animal that says 'meow.' It is my 'kuh' ____________ (cat)." As you say "kuh," write a *c* on the board. Then point to the *c*, say "kuh" and ask a child who has raised his or her hand what the word is. Ask the child to spell the word.

Basic Blending Routine

Purpose: To facilitate reading complete words through blending sounds.
Equipment: Letter cards.
Procedure:

1. In teaching the word ending *at*, start by establishing the sounds that the two letters make separately, "a" and "tuh."
2. Hold the two cards six inches apart, and ask the children to say the sounds separately several times.
3. As you bring the cards closer together *in space*, ask the children to say them closer together *in time* until the cards are adjacent to one another and the children have blended the two sounds into a single sound, "at." Note that there are two distinct steps—sounding out the "a"–"tuh" and putting the sounds together. The children will be able to do this independently after they have had some experience with it.

Word Teaching Routine

Purpose: To teach regularly spelled, regularly pronounced words.
Equipment: Paper and pencil for each child, magic slate or chalkboard.
Procedure:

1. Teach the phonetic sounds of the letters, using many words beginning with that letter as examples of the sound. (See Word Recognition through Phonetics, pp. 7–8.)
2. Blend the smallest number of letters (*a*–*t*) into one sound "at." (See Basic Blending Routine, this page.)
3. Use blending to teach a longer sound or word (*cat, mat*).
4. Use the longer word in a meaningful sentence and in a meaningful phrase that you write on your magic slate or chalkboard. Have the children generate a sentence to show that they understand the meaning of the word.
5. Spend some time teaching recognition of the word by flash card procedures.
6. Ask the children to write the word. It is important that they understand the distinction between reading, writing, and spelling.
7. Give frequent one- and two-word spelling tests.

READING WORDS

Word Reading Routine

Purpose: To teach regularly spelled, regularly pronounced words.
Equipment: Magic slate or chalkboard.
Procedure:

1. Write down the vowel *a* on your magic slate or chalkboard and ask the children to tell you what letter it is.
2. Tell them that this letter makes more than one sound, and the sound they are going to learn today is "a" as in *mat, can, pad, apple,* and *and.*
3. Use incomplete sentences and clues to elicit words that have the "a" sound: "Your mother is a woman, and your father is a ___________."
4. Write some of the words you elicit on your magic slate, saying, "This is how you write *man,*" and "*Man* is spelled *m-a-n.*"
5. Print the end consonant on your magic slate, and ask the children to name it.
6. Tell children the sound made by the letter, such as "tuh" as in *hit, cut, hot, it, at, rat,* and *set.*
7. Use incomplete sentences and clues to elicit words with the "tuh" sound.
8. Print on your magic slate some of the words you elicit, emphasizing the concepts of reading, spelling, and writing as you do.
9. Use the blending procedure to teach the children to read the two letters as a unit. (See Basic Blending Routine, p. 8.)
10. Teach the beginning letter. Follow the same procedure of printing a letter, having the children name it, giving the sound of the letter, eliciting words with that sound, writing some of the words, and finally blending the letter into the word. (See Beginning Letter Routine—Consonants, below.)

Beginning Letter Routine—Consonants

Purpose: To give practice with beginning consonants.
Equipment: Chalkboard.
Procedure:

1. On the chalkboard write the lowercase form of the letter being taught. Ask the children to name it and to tell you what sound it makes.
2. Ask a child to write the uppercase form on the chalkboard.
3. Say some words familiar to the children which begin with the letter being taught.
4. Elicit more difficult words beginning with the letter by using incomplete sentences.
5. Say sentences or word strings and ask the children to tell you the *h* ("huh" as in *hen*) word. Be sure that the other words are clearly contrasting in sound.

Additional Procedures:

1. Play *Round the Table.* One child, then the next, and so on, says a word that begins with the designated consonant. The game ends when no one can think of another word.
2. Play *One of These Words Doesn't Belong.* Give the children a four-word series with three words beginning with the designated consonant and one that does not.

Word Games

Teach the following games and play them occasionally in reading lessons as a change from the procedure in the word reading routine (see this page).

Purpose: To give practice in reading words.
Equipment: Word flash cards, tokens, magic slate or chalkboard, coins.
Procedure: Play *Magic Word.*

1. This is a table search game in which teacher-made word flash cards are used. One flash card is designated the winning card.
2. Children should pick up cards in turn and read them. (If children don't know a word, tell them. Don't drill. A game should be fast and fun.)
3. Children discard the cards in a pile in front of them.
4. The winner is the child who finds the designated card.

Additional Procedures:

1. Play *Word Rounds.*
   - The teacher flashes cards, and the children name them.
   - If the children go for a complete round

without making an error, they win pennies from the teacher; if not, the child who misses loses pennies.

- The object of the game is for the children to clean the teacher out. If they do, they each win a prize, which should be something of immediate value, such as a small edible or a privilege, not merely a star on the scoreboard.
- Arrange the letter cards so that those having difficulties receive easier words. Do not permit children to ridicule or criticize others for making mistakes. Point out that everyone makes mistakes.

2. Play *Change a Word.*
   - The teacher writes a word on the magic slate. The child's task is to change it to another word by changing one letter.
   - Give practice with this before you play a game.
   - Don't play in turns; the game will go faster if the children raise their hands.
   - Give a token for each correct answer. The winner is the child with the most tokens.
3. Play *Guess What Word?*
   - The teacher writes two letters of a three-letter word on one magic slate and then writes the whole word on a second magic slate, which is placed upside down on the table.
   - The first child to guess the word wins a token. The winner is the child with the most tokens.

SAMPLE READING LESSONS

Sample Lesson One

Purpose: To teach *a* as in *cat.*
Equipment: Letter cards, pennies, magic slate or chalkboard.
Seatwork: (The teacher can provide appropriate seatwork if desired; use spelling lists of words containing *a* as in *cat* and reading selections with numerous *a* words.
Procedures: Letter Recognition.

1. Play letter recognition table search games. (See Letter Recognition, Sample Activities One and Nine, p. 3, for game procedures.)
2. Play *Quick! What Letter?* in which the teacher holds up a letter card and points to a child. The child must answer quickly or will be told the answer. (See Letter Recognition, Sample Activity Three, p. 3 for game procedure.)
3. Play *Pass It On* in which everyone at the table has two cards except the teacher, who has three, including the penalty card which is the card to be passed on. The player on the teacher's left starts the game by drawing one of the teacher's three cards. Going around the table, each player draws from the person on his or her right. When the teacher says "Stop," the player with the penalty card pays a penny to each of the other players. (See Letter Recognition, Sample Activity Eight, p. 3, for game procedure.)
4. Play *Bingo* using cards handmade from index cards and press-on letters. In the early letter recognition lessons, use a card with only one row of three letters. In subsequent lessons make the cards progressively more difficult, up to two rows of four letters. (See Letter Recognition, Sample Activity Five, p. 3, for game procedure.)

Additional Procedures:

1. Sound Identification and Reading Words. Use the following procedure to establish the essential idea that letters have names and make sounds.
   - Select three familiar musical instruments, such as drums, sticks, and bells. Ask the children what the *names* of the instruments are. Now ask them to listen to the *sounds* the instruments make. Point out that the sound a drum makes is very different from its name. Go over this with each instrument.
   - Follow the same procedure with animal names and sounds.
   - Display a toy car. Establish that the sound of a car (ask the children to give imitations) is very different from its name.
   - Display the letter *a,* and ask the name of the letter. Tell the children that this letter makes several sounds. The first sound they are going to learn is "a" as it sounds in *man.*
   - Repeat this procedure with *t,* "tuh" as in *cat.*
   - Ask the children to say the word "a"–"tuh" as you hold up the cards. Start

with the cards well apart; then put them closer together until they have blended into the word *at*.

- Use *at* in a sentence. Print *at* on the magic slate or chalkboard, and ask the children to spell it. Point out that when you spell, you use the letter names, *a–t*.
- Review *at* several times. Then tell the children that you will teach them how to read some more words. Teach the words *bat, cat, fat, hat, mat, pat, rat,* and *sat*. Give a clue for each word (for example, "Something you use to hit a baseball"), and ask the children to name it.
- Ask the children to sound out each word. Give practice in word recognition and spelling. Talk frequently about the difference between spelling words and reading words.

2. Play *Quick! What Sound?* The teacher holds up a letter card, and the child says the phonetic sound.
3. Play *Round the Table*. The teacher holds up one letter card for several times in a row and then attempts to catch someone by presenting a different card.
4. Play *Listen*. The teacher says a series of words beginning with the same phonetic sound and then says a word that begins with a different sound. Children must raise their hands, put down a token, or otherwise indicate recognition of the new sound. Before you play this game, show the letter, then write it, sound it out, and read a word beginning with that letter.
5. Word production. Use questions, incomplete sentences, and direct assistance in helping the children to think of a word beginning with a specific letter.
6. Spelling. Frequently give one- and two-word tests, oral and written. Also conduct spelling bees.

Sample Lesson Two

Purpose: To review *at* words (*bat, cat, fat, hat, mat, pat, rat, sat*).
Equipment: Letter cards, chalkboard.
Seatwork: (The teacher can provide appropriate seatwork if desired.)
Procedure:

1. Print *at* on the chalkboard. Using the letter cards, ask the children to sound it out.
2. Display a *b*, and ask the children to first sound, then read, and then spell *bat*.
3. Continue through the list until all the words are on the board. Point to different words, and ask the children to read them. If children don't read a word correctly, tell them what it is, and ask them to say it as you point to it. Then ask them to sound it out. Give immediate help if they can't sound it out.
4. Use the words in sentences as you ask the children to read them: "Jane hit the ball with her __________ [point to bat]." Ask the child to read the word to which you are pointing. Use interesting sentences: "My __________ [cat] caught a __________ [rat] and put it on the __________ [mat]." "My __________ [rat] does not wear a __________ [hat]."
5. Give practice with *a, the, see,* and *I*. Sometimes ask the children to sound out regularly spelled words. At other times ask them to say what *at* says as a unit, then sound the consonant and blend it in.
6. Use additional sentences for *at* words: John went out to play baseball with his ball and __________ (bat). I heard a meow. It was my __________ (cat). If you eat too much you will get __________ (fat). In cold weather you should wear a __________ (hat). Wipe your feet on the door __________ (mat). Give the dog a friendly __________ (pat). The dog will catch the __________ (rat). This is my chair; yesterday at dinner I __________ (sat) in it.
7. Show the children how the basic words fit into bigger words. Give clues and let the children tell you the bigger words: *batter, catch, fathead, cattle, hatch, latch, match, matter, patch, patter,* and *Saturday*.

Sample Lesson Three

Purpose: To teach *s* as an end letter for verbs and noun plurals.
Equipment: Chalkboard.
Seatwork: Reading Seatwork 5–6.
Procedure:

1. On the chalkboard, print sentences beginning with *I*: *I sit on the chair. I see the pig. I set the table.*
2. Ask the children how each sentence would change if you were talking about your mother, whom you may refer to as *Mother* or as *she*.

3. Establish that usually an *s* is added to the verb.
4. Establish the above orally, and stress the change in sound from *sit* to *sits.* Ask the children how to spell *sits.* Demonstrate the spelling on the chalkboard. Use unfamiliar verbs in addition to verbs the children can spell.
5. Proceed to noun plurals. Print on the board, "1 pig, 2 __________," and ask the children to spell the plural. Use the term *plural,* and tell the children that when you talk about two of something, you usually add an *s.*
6. Ask the children to write the noun plurals on Reading Seatwork 5. Assign Reading Seatwork 6.

Sample Lesson Four

Purpose: To review regularly spelled, three-letter *it* words.
Equipment: Chalkboard, newsprint.
Seatwork: (The teacher can provide appropriate seatwork if desired.)
Procedure:

1. Print *i* on the chalkboard, and ask the children to tell you what letter it is.
2. Say that this letter makes more than one sound. The sound they are going to learn is "i" as in *sit, it, itchy, fit, mitten, city,* and *hit.*
3. Use incomplete sentences to elicit words with the "i" sound (such as *bit, ditch, pin, kitten, city, fill, quit,* and *spit*).
4. Write some of the words, including *city,* on the chalkboard.
5. Write *t* on the chalkboard, and ask the children to tell you what letter it is.
6. Say that this letter makes a "tuh" sound as in *hit, bat, cut, mitt, let, basket, slit, tent,* and *can't.*
7. Use incomplete sentences to elicit other words with the "tuh" sound.
8. Use a blending procedure to teach the children to say *it.* Note that this is a two-step procedure: sounding out the "i"–"tuh" and putting the sounds together.
9. Read aloud the words from 2 or 3 above, stressing the "it" whenever it occurs.
10. Next teach the beginning letter. Follow the same procedure of writing down the letter, having children name it, giving the sound of the letter, eliciting words with that sound, writing some of the words, and finally blending the letter into the words.

In this lesson *it* was taught first, then longer words were introduced with *it* in them, and then still longer or more complex words were introduced. This is a pyramid approach to reading. It helps the child to hear the vowel-consonant sound "it" in many words.
Additional Procedures:

1. Phonetic Values. Teach the phonetic values in regularly spelled words found on p. 8.
2. Capitals. As you review *it* words, use names such as *Mitch* to demonstrate uppercase letters. Review the high-frequency words *I, see, a,* and *the* with short sentences containing *it* words. Emphasize uppercase letters and periods when you put the sentences on the chalkboard.
3. Reader Words. Take every opportunity to familiarize the children with words from their readers. Clearly display the words, and draw attention to them with questions. Only use words that are regularly spelled. Emphasize the beginning letter. These words will be designated as *reader words.* The word reading routine can be summarized as follows (see also Word Reading Routine, p. 9).
   - If any part of the word is regularly spelled, as *it* in *city,* teach that part with the word reading routine.
   - Emphasize the beginning sound. If it is not a sound the children know, say that it is a new sound for the letter, and give some common words as examples. With *city* give words such as *ceiling, cellophane, Cindy, central, cedar,* and *celery.*
   - Print the word on the chalkboard, and ask the children to say it. Then use it in a sentence. Leave it on the board, and return to it during the lesson.
   - Review it often in subsequent lessons. This is essentially a look-and-say method, and for success this method requires frequent exposure, repetition, and meaningful use.
4. Dictating Stories.
   - To familiarize the children with the reader words and to develop their descriptive language skills, ask your group to dictate one- or two-sentence stories about topics related to the reader words or about interesting or exciting events that occur in your area.

- Always give the story a title. Print the story on a big piece of newsprint.
- When you have finished printing the story, read it to the children. Then ask the children to read it to you. The entire activity should take only a few minutes.
- In one of these lessons, you might write about the first day of school. Save the stories; later in the year the children will be able to read them with little or no help.
- As you write a story, talk about uppercase letters at the beginning of names and sentences. Call attention to periods, question marks, plurals, and possessives.

Sample Lesson Five

Purpose: To review all regularly spelled and high-frequency words learned to date.
Equipment: Tokens, word flash cards, chalkboard.
Seatwork: Appropriate reading tests (see Reading Test Seatwork 28–45). (The teacher can provide other appropriate seatwork if desired.)
Procedure: Vowels. (A knowledge of vowels is prerequisite to playing some of the games.)

1. Print the lowercase alphabet on the chalkboard.
2. Say that there are twenty-six letters in the alphabet and that five have a special name, *vowels.*
3. Circle each of the five vowels, and write them on the chalkboard again.
4. Show that vowels are often the middle letters in three-letter words. Put *p* ____ *t* on the board five times; then show *pat, pet, pit, pot,* and *put* by changing the vowel. Note that *put* is a new *ut* pronunciation; you have been teaching "ut" as in *hut.*

Additional Procedures:

1. Play *Missing Vowel.* In this game you put consonant-blank-consonant on the board, and give a clue. The first child to supply the correct missing vowel wins a token. For example, you might use *m* ____ *t* with the clue "Something to wipe your feet on."
2. Play *Hotword.*
   - Ask the children to think of the first and last halves of the alphabet. Print the alphabet, clearly divided into halves, on the chalkboard.
   - In this game you put the first or last letter of a three-letter word on the board, and the children use questions to identify it.
   - If the children get the word in less than twelve questions, they each win a token. If not, they each lose a token.
   - Encourage elimination questions: "Is the middle letter a vowel?" "Is the first letter in the first half of the alphabet?" Note that it is more efficient to identify the vowel first.
   - Use the phrases, "You're cold," "You're getting warm," and "You're red hot."
3. Play *Rhyme Sounds.*
   - The teacher says a first line ending in a regularly spelled word, and the children see how many lines they can add. For example, the first sentence might be "There once was a boy named Pat." The next lines might end in *bat, cat, that, fat,* and so on.
   - Keep a record of the rhymes for each round, and encourage the children to try to beat their own records.
4. Play *Flashwords.* (This game allows you to give intensive practice in high-frequency words as well as other words that do not lend themselves well to other games.)
   - Ask the children to identify words on cards.
   - Keep a tally on the board for each round, and encourage the children to try to beat their records.
   - The teacher should use signs (*yes, no, stop, go*) as much as possible to facilitate the game.
   - Review any words that are missed.
5. Use appropriate reading tests.

Reading Seatwork 7–8 can be used to give practice in reading words, making up sentences, spelling, and printing.

READING IMPROVEMENT

Oral Reading Routine

Purpose: To improve oral reading ability.
Equipment: Tape recorder.
Seatwork: Appropriate reading seatwork.
Procedure: Tape Recording.

1. Choose a reading sheet (Reading Seatwork 9–27) that the children enjoyed, and ask each

child to read the sheet while you record it on tape. Record children's names and the date before they read.

2. After each reading, leave enough space for a second recording of the same sheet.
3. Later in the year, when the children are reading more smoothly, have each child record the sheet again. Then play the tape to show the children how much they have improved.

Additional Procedure: Reading Improvement.

- Practice phrasing: Teach the children to read smoothly—*in the woods,* not *in . . . the . . . woods.*
- Practice expression: When children read *Ned is mad,* the tone of voice should express anger.

Phrase Reading Routine

Purpose: To teach phrase reading.
Equipment: Word cards, markers.
Seatwork: Reading seatwork can be used if desired.
Procedure:

1. Insist that the children read in phrases: *a can,* not *a . . . can.*
2. Give the children practice by printing the words to be read on flash cards.
3. Point out that you do not have one word in your extended left hand and the other in your extended right hand. The words are close together and are to be read as such.
4. Illustrate the difference between the children's reading and their conversation by asking questions that the children can answer with short sentences or phrases. Spend sufficient time on this. In order not to produce word-readers, reading by word should be prevented before it begins.
5. Use the phrase reading routine every time the children read orally. Also, make certain children use markers correctly.

Reading Sheets Routine

Purpose: To give practice in silent and oral reading.
Equipment: Markers.
Seatwork: Reading seatwork.
Procedure: Use reading seatwork to achieve a high level of competence in word recognition, speed, and phrase reading rather than word reading. Many of the reading sheets give practice in reading the high-frequency, irregularly spelled words.

Before you introduce a reading sheet, discuss the topic and review some of the words, particularly the high-frequency, irregularly spelled words. Be sure that the children use their markers correctly and use the following procedure for all reading sheets:

1. Review any words that may cause difficulty before you distribute the sheet.
2. Distribute the sheet and markers, and see that the markers are used properly.
3. Allow children to read the sheet silently.
4. Ask them what words they don't know, line by line, and review the words.
5. Help children to read aloud in turn.
6. Review difficult words again.
7. Assign the sheet for seatwork and homework.
8. Check children's reading of the sheet in the individual test periods.

READING TESTS

Reading Test (Seatwork 28–37) Instructions:

The reading tests are word-recognition tests to be given in reading periods. Explain the test with examples on the chalkboard. For example, use the following instructions for Reading Test Seatwork 28: "Find Box 1. Look for the word *pup.* Underline *pup.*" Insist on good test behavior. Watch closely to see that the children work on the correct box. If there is any doubt about their ability to read the box numbers, put each number on your magic slate, hold up a number card, or point to each box on your sheet as you give the item. Arrange the chairs at the table to minimize copying from others.

Reading Test (Seatwork 38–44) Instructions:

Print a sample box on the board, and show the children that they must look at the picture in the box and find the word that names the picture. Demonstrate the process of looking at the picture, thinking of its name, reading the list of words in the box, and underlining the correct word. The teacher may use test results as a guide to reviewing.

RHYMING

Sample Lesson One

Purpose: To introduce rhyming.
Equipment: Blocks, boxes, tape recorder (optional).
Procedure: Terms.

1. Discuss the difference between the meaning of *the same* (identical) and *almost the same.*
2. Use identical blocks and boxes to establish the meaning of the word *exactly:* "Everything about one is just like the other." Show that you can't tell two dimes of the same minting apart because "One is just like the other."
3. Discuss letters, children, shoes, houses, and any other look-alike topics. After you have discussed this subject thoroughly, talk about things that sound alike, for example school bells and telephone bells. Other examples include the piano and xylophone, voices of two children, barking of two dogs, tapping and hammering, and cutting paper and tearing paper. You might record some of these sounds on tape and play them. For contrast, record some sounds that differ sharply as well as those that are identical.

Additional Procedures:

1. Block Sequences.
   - Build three-block sequences for the children to compare. (Remember to work from the children's left to right.)
   - Start with two identical sequences, such as red, yellow, blue, and establish that they are exactly the same. Set the identical pair off to one side where the children can easily refer to them.
   - Now set up a sequence of green, blue, and orange blocks.
   - As you start the next sequence, tell the children to watch and see if it is the same.
   - Place a green block, and say, "It begins the same. It begins with green just like this one [point to finished sequence]."
   - Place a blue block, and say, "It's still the same, isn't it? This one [point to finished sequence] starts green–blue and so does this one [point to two blocks]."
   - Add a red block, and ask the children, "Does it end the same?" Establish that the ending is different. Repeat this procedure several times. (You must define beginning and ending operationally; the *first* thing you do, the *last* block you put down, the *first* sound you say, the *last* sound, and so forth. Give examples of beginning and ending during table search games by saying "You go first. You begin." "You are the last to look. This is the end of the game.")
   - Use different beginnings (various colors) and identical endings (same colors).
2. Sentences.
   - Say a short sentence, such as "My pig's name is Tom."
   - Tell the children to listen to see if the next sentence is the same.
   - Say, "My pig's name is Dick."
   - Ask the children if the sentences were the same and, if not, what was different. Establish that they begin the same but end differently. Repeat this general procedure with different beginnings but identical endings.
3. Word Series.
   - Use pairs of three-word series that may be identical (ABC–ABC), or begin the same but end differently (ABC–ABX), or begin differently but end the same (XBC–ABC).
   - Use familiar one-syllable words, such as *cat, dog, cow,* and *pig.*
   - Ask the children to tell you what was the same, what was different, and whether the beginning or the ending differed.
   - Now use two-word series in which *most* have a different beginning but the same ending.
   - Ask the children to say how the series began and how it ended.
   - Examples of two-word series include: *big-mouse, big-house; blue-house, glue-house; green-pail, green-mail; boy-mouse, toy-mouse; yellow-hair, yellow-pair;* and *ice-milk, nice-milk.*
   - Make certain the children understand that the beginnings differ, but the ends are the same, or vice versa. Use some identical pairs as a contrast.

- As soon as the children are proficient at identifying the beginning as different and the end as the same, stop using two words and begin using pairs of single two-syllable words, such as *looking-cooking, baking-making, higher-flyer, single-jingle, paper-taper,* and *yellow-fellow.* In each case emphasize the beginning letter sound. Help the children to sound the beginning of the word and the part that is identical in both words.

4. Rhyming Words.
   - Continue to give practice in identifying different beginnings and same endings using one-syllable words such as *big-pig, look-cook, make-bake, back-sack, fill-pill, can-man, soap-rope,* and *now-cow.*
   - After you have spent some time on this, tell the children that when one word ends the same as another word, we say that the two words rhyme: *big* rhymes with *pig, cat* rhymes with *mat,* and so on.
   - Now give the children easy words, such as *cat, star,* and *sky,* and give clues about words that rhyme: "Tell me a word that rhymes with *star.* Your daddy and mommy drive one. It has four wheels, and you go places in it."
   - Use additional pairs for giving clues: *rat-cat, mouse-house, how-cow, lake-cake, bone-cone, log-dog, wag-bag,* and *lock-clock.*

Sample Lesson Two

Purpose: To give practice in rhyming.
Procedure: Rhyming Words.

1. Use sets of three words, two that sound very similar and one that is clearly different (for example, *school, pool, car; bike, like, man; bat, ring, cat;* and *two, twenty, zoo*).
2. Vary the different word's position in the series.
3. Ask the children to tell you which two words sound the same and which word is different.

Additional Procedures:

1. Nursery Rhymes. Say some rhymes such as "Jack and Jill," "Humpty Dumpty," "One, Two, Button My Shoe," and "Little Miss Muffet." Help children pick out the rhyming words. Discuss the meaning of *rhyme.*
2. Basis of Sound-Alikes. Occasionally write words such as those with the *at* endings to show that the reason these words sound alike is that they have some of the same letters in them. *Do not,* however, introduce the idea of different letter combinations making the same sounds.
3. Generating Rhyming Words.
   - Tell the children that you will say a word, and that they must give a color (list the colors) that rhymes with it. (Treat black and white as colors.) Use the following and any others that occur to you: *quack (black); light (white); glue, two (blue); clown, town (brown); bed (red); marshmallow (yellow); play (gray); bean, queen (green).*
   - Follow the same procedure with numbers: *fun, run, sun (one); blue, glue, you (two);* and so on.
   - Follow the same procedure with animals: *bat, mat, pat, sat (cat, rat); fog, log (dog, frog, hog); fair, care (bear, mare); two, blue, glue (kangaroo); habit (rabbit); fig, big (pig); meow, how (cow); box, socks (fox).*

Sample Lesson Three

Purpose: To give practice in rhyming.
Equipment: Paper, pencils, and pennies for each child, chalkboard.
Procedure: Play *One of These Words Doesn't Belong.*

1. Use similar sounds as the variable.
2. Give the children a four-word series with three words that rhyme and one that does not.
3. Ask the children to identify the word that does not belong.

Additional Procedures:

1. Play *Round the Table.*
   - The teacher names an ending such as *at,* and the children in turn add rhyming words. (List the children's rhymes on the chalkboard.)
   - Any child who can't think of a rhyme gives each of the others a penny.
   - Occasionally display the alphabet to help the children think of words.
2. Two-Line Rhymes. Help the children make up two-line rhymes, such as "There was a green snake/Who fell into a lake."

3. Rhyme Race. Distribute pencil and paper, or ask the children to work at the chalkboard. Say a word, and ask the children to race to write down a rhyming word.
4. Rhyming from Word Stems. Give children lined paper with two word stems at the top, such as *at* and *in,* and have them make up rhyming words. Review this task carefully first. Use it whenever time is assigned to rhyming.

READING LIST

Storybooks should be used regularly in the reading program. The criteria for selecting a particular book to add to the reading list included: evidence of a clearly stated message related to the socialization of children; use of clear language and effective illustrations; development of story lines that children in primary grades would enjoy; and the availability of books (books that are in print and are likely to be found in public or school libraries). If teachers are unable to obtain any of the books, alternates should be selected on the basis of the criteria listed above. Check on the availability of paperback books before buying hardcover editions.

The storybooks on this list differ in length and in difficulty of content. The teacher is encouraged to utilize the more difficult stories to extend each child's level of concentration. At other times a shorter, less complex story may be more appropriate. It is the responsibility of the teacher to modify the story content as needed to match the children's level of comprehension and attention span.

Before reading a story to the children, teachers should read it over themselves, considering the discussion topics, the vocabulary, and how the pictures can be used during discussion. The reading of the story to the children should be preceded by a short, lively discussion, including vocabulary words, without allowing the discussion to become a drill.

Read the story enthusiastically but not too quickly. Change a particular word only if the children will not understand it. Do not stop to discuss the story as it is read. Discourage questions during the reading; stopping to answer questions may cause some children to lose the thread of the story.

Hold the book so that all the children can easily see the pictures. Encourage them (before and after reading the story) to ask, name, and describe rather than to point or touch. Their verbal skills will be reinforced if they are required to use language.

Listening to stories helps to increase each child's vocabulary, broaden general knowledge, lengthen attention span, and give practice in listening. Keep in mind, however, that unless listening to stories is enjoyable for the children, it is unlikely that they will become readers.

1. *Andy and the School Bus.* Jerrold Beim. New York: William Morrow, 1947.
Discussion.

- Talk about children wanting to go to school and having to wait until they are a certain age.
- Discuss waiting for something to happen, such as a holiday or a birthday.
- Bring up problems with cars: breakdowns, running out of gas, and engine failure. Point out that often the driver can fix the problem.
- Discuss offering a favor and receiving a favor from someone in return.
- Read the story, changing ***next term*** to ***next year*** or ***next September.*** Turn through the book, and look at the pictures of the seasons, talking about seasons and about the duck, Sam.

2. *Things to See.* Thomas Matthiesen. New York: Platt & Munk, 1966.
Discussion. This lesson is designed to increase the child's ability to identify common objects. Help the children identify each object; say what it is used for and what it is made of (if this is appropriate).

- If the picture is of a toy, ask the children to name some other toys. Ask them to name other animals, other modes of transportation, and so forth. Help them to express their ideas in sentences. Try to have on hand any unusual object, such as a trumpet, to demonstrate. Later the children can select single objects from more complex pictures.
- Work through the book slowly, using extra lessons if necessary.
- Consider putting a small boat in a pan of water to demonstrate floating. Have a rock, too, to show that not everything will float.

- Occasionally, give the children clues about the picture coming next, and let them guess.
- Talk about each picture (in terms of structure and function where appropriate), and ask each child to make up a sentence about each picture. You may have to give lots of help on this.
- Ask the children to repeat the whole sentence once, after you have helped them. One technique is to ask questions using the words and to have the children answer them.

3. *We Were Tired of Living in a House.* Liesel M. Skorpen. New York: Coward, McCann & Geoghegan, 1969.
Discussion.

- Talk about the advantages of living in a house.
- Ask the children about other places where it might be fun to live. Point out that people could live in tents, on boats, and in caves.
- Tell them to listen to see what happens when some children and their dog and cat decide to try living in other places.
- After you have read the story, review the difficulties that occurred.

4. *ABC: An Alphabet Book.* Thomas Matthiesen. New York: Platt & Munk, 1968.
Discussion. Follow the same procedure as used in *Things to See* (see 2, p. 17).

- Focus on any one picture only as long as the children are talking freely and responding to your questions. (You probably will need two lesson periods to complete the book.)
- When you are finished, ask the children what pictures they liked best. This provides an opportunity to test their recall of the pictures.
- If they cannot remember any pictures, flip quickly through the book, ask them to name the pictures, and ask them again which pictures they liked or which one they liked best.
- Whenever possible, use actual objects to extend the discussion of the pictures. It will often be impossible to obtain an identical object. For example, if you have a picture of a car and a toy car, they are likely to have different colors and designs.

5. *Make Way for Ducklings.* Robert McCloskey. New York: Viking, 1941.
Discussion. This story is about the problems that two ducks have in finding a suitable place for raising their offspring.

- Discuss how ducks are born from eggs.
- Talk about how to find a home that would meet the children's needs.
- Discuss the concept of island. Use a pan to construct a small island of pebbles, clay, and twigs.
- Talk about what a mother duck would have to teach her babies.
- Read the book.
- When you have finished, let the children look at the pictures. Discuss the difficulties that the ducks had getting to the island.
- Emphasize kindness to animals. Note that the ducks thanked the police officer.
- Emphasize the safety lesson in teaching the ducklings to walk in a line. Talk about when and why children walk in lines.

6. *5A and 7B.* Eleanor Schick. New York: Macmillan, 1967.
Discussion. This is a story about two small girls who live in an apartment block. Each of them wants a same-age friend very badly, and in the end they meet and become friends. Discuss the concept of friends.

- Ask: "Why should friends be about the same age?" "What do you do with friends?" "How do you make friends?" "Where might you meet friends?"
- Discuss apartment and city living, particularly if your pupils are primarily suburban children.
- Ask: "Why was there an elevator in the apartment house?" "Why weren't the children playing out on the street?"

7. *A Letter to Amy.* Ezra Jack Keats. New York: Harper & Row, 1968.
Discussion.

- Talk about fights and disagreements among friends and discuss accidents and misunderstandings as causes. Some of the children may give examples of accidents, such as collisions, which cause fights because one child doesn't recognize the accidental nature of the collision.

- Talk about birthday parties, invitations, and receiving invitations by mail.
- Read the story. After you have finished, look at the pictures, and talk about storms.
- Discuss apologies.

8. *One Dark Night.* Edna M. Preston. New York: Viking, 1969.
Discussion.

- Read this book as if it were Halloween, starting with the words "One dark Halloween. . . ."
- Interpret all the characters as being children in costume on their first Halloween.
- Point out how different things seem at night and when you are alone.
- Talk about surprises and Halloween costumes and masks.
- Just before you reach the end of the story, ask the children to guess who made the squeak.

9. *A Tree Is Nice.* Janice M. Udry. New York: Harper & Row, 1956.
Discussion.

- Look at trees, and discuss how they are useful to us by providing shade, beauty, and windbreaks. Don't talk about wood products here unless a child suggests them.
- Discuss all the ways you can play in and around trees, such as playing in tree houses, climbing, swinging, and hiding.
- Talk about shelter.

10. *Is It Hard? Is It Easy?* Mary McBurney Green. Reading, Mass.: Addison-Wesley, 1960.
Discussion.

- Talk about *hard* and *easy* in terms of children's activities, such as baseball, reading, and swimming.
- Emphasize that some things that are hard now will be easy later.
- Note that some things are hard to do alone but easy to do with someone.

Vocabulary: Explain *hard, easy, skipping, palm of hand, seesaw (teeter-totter);* substitute *forward roll* for *somersault,* or use both terms.

11. *Nobody Listens to Andrew.* Elizabeth Guilfoyle. Chicago: Follett, 1957.
Discussion.

- Talk about listening when people speak. Discuss the problems that occur in class when children don't listen.
- Ask what you should say when you don't hear what someone says ("Pardon." "Pardon me." "I'm sorry, I didn't hear you.").
- Note when you read the book that, in general, people don't listen to Andrew because they are doing something else. Ask the children what they would do if they wanted people to listen and no one would.
- Tell children to listen to the story and see what Andrew does (he shouts).
- After you have read the story discuss the roles of the police department, the fire department, the dog catcher, and the zoo.

12. *When Will It Snow?* Syd Hoff. New York: Harper & Row, 1971.
Discussion.

- Talk about winter. Ask: "Where do the birds go?" "What happens to the leaves?" "How do we dress?" "What is on the ground?" "What things are fun to do in winter?"
- After you read the book, turn through it again, and talk about each picture noting the signs of cold weather. Talk about holidays in the winter.

Vocabulary: Explain *now, soon, smoke, cave* (talk about animals who sleep all winter), *sled, more blankets.*

13. *The Snowy Day.* Ezra Jack Keats. New York: Viking, 1962.
Discussion.

- Discuss snowflakes. Cut some snowflakes from paper, and have them on hand.
- Talk about snow, blizzards, what people do when it snows, street cleaners, melting snow, slides, sleighs, toboggans, snowballs, and snow figures.
- Read the book; then review using the pictures, and talk about snowsuits, footmarks in snow (like footmarks in sand, new lawn, new cement), making tracks, sliding, and making snow figures.

14. *Josie and the Snow.* Helen E. Buckley. New York: Lothrop, Lee & Shepard, 1964.

Discussion. This is the story about a child who spends a happy day playing in the snow with his family. Emphasize joys of outdoor play and family fun.

- Demonstrate cutting out a snowflake.
- Note the rhymes.

15. *Noisy Nancy Norris.* L. A. Gaeddert. New York: Doubleday, 1971.
Discussion. Make certain that children understand what is meant by an apartment block, especially if you are in a suburban setting where the children never see apartment blocks.

- Discuss the theme that there is a time and place for noisy play, but the place is not an apartment building. In discussing this, point out what it would be like in a school if the class next door made a tremendous amount of noise.
- Point out the need for cooperation within rooms as well as between rooms in a school.
- Mention the playground as a place for noisy play.

16. *I'm Hiding.* Myra C. Livingstone. New York: Harcourt Brace, 1961.
Discussion.

- Talk about hiding yourself. Discuss the game of "Hide and Go Seek," emphasizing that when you try to put yourself where others cannot see you, you *hide yourself.*
- Discuss the places in the room and in the playground where you might hide.
- Turn through the book talking about each picture.
- Demonstrate hiding by placing small objects under paper cups. Define *hiding* as putting something where other people cannot see it. Point out that if children look, they may or may not find it, but the hider knows where it is.

17. *The Secret Hiding Place.* Rainey Bennett. Cleveland: William Collins, 1960.
Discussion.

- Talk about the number of people in the children's houses, the noise level, and the lack of space. Mention places children can go when they want to be by themselves; for example, they could climb a tree and sit where no one can see them. They could find an empty box and get in it. They could go away from the house.
- Discuss the concepts of hiding and secrets.
- Read the book. Change any words that you feel are too difficult, or define them as you read.

18. *Rudolph, the Red-Nosed Reindeer.* Robert L. May. Chicago: Follett, 1964.
Discussion. This story is about a reindeer who is different and who uses his different appearance to help out in an emergency. Use your judgment about changing vocabulary.

- Emphasize Rudolph's supposed inferiority and the fact that a difference turned out to be an asset.

19. *How Santa Claus Had a Long and Difficult Journey Delivering His Presents.* Fernando Krahn. New York: Delacorte Press, 1970.
Discussion. Talk about Christmas, Christmas trees, and presents being delivered.

20. *The Remarkable Egg.* Adelaide Holl. New York: Lothrop, Lee & Shepard, 1968.
Discussion. The purpose of this story is to provide experience with the concept of responsibility. The story has a surprise ending. After you read the story, ask the children if they were surprised.

- Discuss the nest-building process.
- Share the excellent pictures of bird's eggs with the children.
- Note the solution to the problem.
- Discuss what would happen if people found a strange baby in their house.

21. *Evans Corner.* Elizabeth Starr Hill. New York: Holt, 1967.
Discussion.

- Talk about the importance of having a place of your own even if it is small.
- Discuss sharing.

22. *Excuse Me! Certainly!* Louis Slobodkin. New York: Vanguard, 1959.
Discussion.

- Talk about being polite. Find out what the children think being polite means.
- Use doll play to dramatize the difference between surliness and politeness. Show two dolls walking toward each other and then

colliding. Make the collision clearly the fault of one doll who says, "Watch where you're going, stupid!" Have the other doll reply rudely. Then demonstrate the same interaction with both acting courteously. Try to convey how good manners smooth everyday living.

- Read the book. The pictures are clear, and there are no hard words.
- Follow the reading with a discussion of each incident. Emphasize that Willie finds that being polite is pleasant.

23. *Thank You, You're Welcome.* Louis Slobodkin. New York: Vanguard, 1957.
Discussion.

- Give each child a snack. Note which ones say "Thank you." Talk about thanking people when they do or say something nice.
- Use doll play materials to emphasize polite and impolite interactions. Show a doll snatching something from another doll and running away; then demonstrate what should have happened.
- Use a series of doll play interactions to demonstrate both "Thank you" and "You're welcome." Discuss the meaning of these two phrases again after you have read the book.

24. *Push Pull, Empty Full: A Book of Opposites.* Tana Hoban. New York: Macmillan, 1976.
Discussion.

- Talk about each picture.
- Ask the children to tell you when they push and pull, and when it is good to have something empty or full. Have demonstrations using objects or actions.
- Discuss other opposites such as new–old, soft–hard, clean–dirty, and noisy–quiet.

25. *Who Took the Farmer's Hat?* Joan L. Nodset. New York: Harper & Row, 1963.
Discussion.

- Discuss the need for birds to have nests and what shape a nest should be. If possible, have an old straw hat on hand.
- After you have read the story, point out that the bird didn't know that the hat was a hat. Talk about what the other animals and insects thought the hat was.
- Emphasize the kindness of the farmer in not disturbing the nest and the reasons a farmer needs a hat.
- Talk about wind and what it does.

26. *Humpty Dumpty.* Rodney Peppe. New York: Viking, 1976.
Discussion. After you have read the book, tell the children that Humpty Dumpty broke.

- Ask: "What breaks that cannot be put together again?" Use questions and clues to elicit such responses as drinking glasses, reading glasses, and thermos bottles.
- Set up a wall of large wooden blocks, and place a container, such as a Pyrex baking dish, against the wall on the floor.
- Tell the children that you are going to put Humpty Dumpty on the wall. They will see him fall and break, but first they must tell you what Humpty was (an egg). (Use an egg with a face painted on it.)
- Put the egg on the wall, and let it fall into the baking dish and break.
- Let the children handle pieces of eggshell. Show them an unbroken egg for comparison, and tell them how difficult it would be to put a broken egg together again.
- Use simple pictures and talk about the sequence of events in *Humpty Dumpty.*

27. *The Valentine Party.* Pamela Bianco. New York: Lippincott, 1964.
Discussion.

- Talk about Valentine's Day, and Valentine cards, boxes, and hearts. Have a few cards on hand for the children to examine.
- After you have read the story, show the pictures, emphasizing the ways Cathy's friends tried to keep her from knowing about the party. Emphasize two examples of Cathy's inappropriate behavior: (a) going uninvited to a party, and (b) wanting to have everything an older sibling has.
- Discuss the concept of surprises. Point out how Cathy's friends tried to keep the party a surprise.

28. *Harry the Dirty Dog.* Gene Zion. New York: Harper & Row, 1976.
Discussion. Before beginning to read, cover the

essential vocabulary—words that must be understood to appreciate the story.

- Discuss baths. Ask the children how they get dirty and how their dogs or cats get dirty. Talk about why dogs do not like baths, and about dog tricks, such as shaking hands.
- Discuss heating and the burning of fuel, then show the children a small lump of coal.
- Discuss the procedure of putting coal into a basement through a chute.
- Read the story enthusiastically but not too quickly. So that the children will not lose the thread of the story, discourage questions during the reading.
- Hold the book so that all children can see the pictures easily.
- When you have finished, ask the children to tell you the parts of the story that they liked.

29. *The Shy Little Girl.* Phyllis Krasilovsky. Boston: Houghton Mifflin, 1972.
Discussion.

- Start by talking about being shy in operational terms, for example, "When you can't get started playing with other children." (Shyness will be a difficult idea for children to grasp because they aren't used to verbalizing such subtle feelings. It would be hard for them to label any feeling, such as being ill at ease or uncomfortable.)
- Tell the children that this story is about a girl named Anne who doesn't have any friends in her class. She doesn't think anyone would like her, so she never tries to make friends. Instead she plays by herself or with her cat. Ask them to listen to see how Anne gets a friend.
- Read the story.
- In the discussion try to show that Anne didn't like herself very much, so she thought other people wouldn't like her either.

30. *Day and Night.* Roger Duvoisin. New York: Alfred A. Knopf, 1959.
Discussion.

- Start with a discussion of people who stay up all night (night nurses in the hospital, police officers, airplane personnel).
- Next discuss animals who stay out at night (mention owls). Tell the children that this is a story about an owl and a dog who become good friends because of something the dog does for the owl.
- Explain that owls can see well at night.
- Note that even though the dog and the owl were friends, they could not see each other often. The story tells how they created a problem in their effort to see each other and how the problem was solved.

31. *Harry by the Sea.* Gene Zion. New York: Harper & Row, 1965.
Discussion.

- Start by talking about going to the beach, beach umbrellas, sand castles, waves, seaweed [show a jar of seaweed], and sea monsters.
- Establish that the sun is hot and the water is cold.
- Read the story. Emphasize the part that describes Harry's search for his family.
- When you have finished reading the story, ask the children to tell you specific things they liked about the story. Turn to the pages where those pictures are, and discuss them.
- Include as many vocabulary words as you can.

32. *The Hare and the Tortoise.* Paul Galdone. New York: McGraw-Hill, 1962.
Discussion.

- Start by discussing races. Emphasize excitement.
- Talk about overconfidence, persistence, and trying hard.
- Use your judgment about changing words and spend time looking at the pictures as you read the story.
- Note that the hare thought he was more clever because he was faster.

33. *The Fire Cat.* Esther Averill. New York: Harper & Row, 1960.
Discussion.

- Start with a discussion of what fire fighters do. Try to mention helping those in distress, such as cats in trees and people locked out of their homes.

- Tell the children to listen to see what happens when the cat has a chance to be good.
- Read the story, and then ask questions about it.

34. *Oscar Otter.* Nathaniel Benchley. New York: Harper & Row, 1966.
Discussion. The theme of this story is that it pays to listen to your parents. Children who don't may get into trouble. Sometimes they are lucky, as Oscar was.

- Talk about animals that live in our forests (beaver, moose, mountain lion, fox). Discuss the beaver in some detail.
- Talk about slides, about sliding down hills, and about how young animals love to play just as children do.
- After you read the book, note that Oscar learned his lesson.

35. *The Several Tricks of Edgar Dolphin.* Nathaniel Benchley. New York: Harper & Row, 1970.
Discussion. One of this story's themes is that you should obey your parents. Emphasize this, and remind the children of *Oscar Otter* (see 34 above).

- The second theme of the book is concerned with problem solving. Talk about problems, and use the words *solving* and *solve.*
- Ask the children to listen to see what problem Edgar has because he doesn't do what his mother tells him to do.
- Ask them to listen to see how Edgar solves his problem all by himself.

36. *Harry and the Lady Next Door.* Gene Zion. New York: Harper & Row, 1960.
Discussion.

- Talk about sounds the children dislike.
- Discuss sounds you don't like to show the children that adults dislike some sounds, too.
- Ask the children what they would do about a noise they didn't like (remove themselves, remove the noise if it couldn't be stopped, stop the noise, block their ears).
- Make a tape of some of the sounds in the book. Any recording of a soprano singing operatic selections will illustrate the lady's singing.
- Explain that Harry doesn't like the noise that comes from the house next door.
- Play the tape, and ask the children what kind of "noise" it is. Identify the noise as the sound of a lady singing.
- Tell the children that Harry tries a lot of ways to show the lady how he wants her to sound.
- Read the story, playing the tape softly as you do.
- If you can't finish this book in one session, try to stop at a logical place, such as page 27 (end of "Harry's First Try") or page 39 (end of "Harry's Second Try").
- If you have to stop before the end, try to inject a "to be continued" excitement into the carry-over.
- After you've read the story, ask the children what ways Harry used to show the lady next door how she should sound.
- Emphasize how Harry was helped by the frogs. Discuss people being afraid of frogs.
- Discuss Harry's taking the lady's music.

37. *Frederick.* Leo Lionni. New York: Pantheon, 1966.
Discussion. The message transmitted in this story is that happy thoughts are almost as important for well-being as the material necessities of life, such as food and water.

- Talk about animals getting ready for winter, especially really cold, snowy winters.
- Ask the children if they have ever seen squirrels burying nuts. Discuss storage of food for winter. Point out that we don't have to do that because the stores are usually open every day, but animals have a food supply shortage in winter. They must gather food while it is available.
- Talk about field mice living in barns where food is available all winter. Ask: "What happens if the barn is empty?"
- Ask the children if they ever think of nice things when they're in bed at night before they go to sleep. Ask them to talk about things they think about.
- Ask them what nice thing they could imagine if (a) they were coming home from the store, and they were cold and wet; (b) they were very, very hot; or (c) it was almost their birthday.

- When you read the book, substitute *what you store for the winter* for *supplies* and *flowers* for *periwinkles*. Omit *granary*, and substitute *empty* for *abandoned*.

38. *No Roses for Harry*. Gene Zion. New York: Harper & Row, 1958.
Discussion.

- Discuss presents and how you feel when you don't like a present.
- Ask the children if they have ever received clothing that they did not like. Tell them that in this story Harry gets something to wear that he does not like.
- Discuss birds' nests. Talk about how they are built.
- Ask what would make them soft and comfortable for baby birds.
- Read the story.
- Ask why Harry did not like his sweater [show picture] and why he liked the second one better.

39. *The Cat Who Thought He Was a Tiger.* Polly Cameron. New York: Coward, McCann and Geoghegan, 1956.
Discussion. Use additional books with suitable animal pictures.

- Point out that there is a group of animals that has similar characteristics and that cats and tigers are both in this group.
- Try to establish that tigers always have stripes. Cats that have stripes are called tiger-striped cats.
- In this story the cat thought he was a tiger because he had stripes while none of this brothers and sisters had stripes.

40. *Swimmy*. Leo Lionni. New York: Pantheon, 1963.
Discussion. The basic themes are aggression, loneliness, and problem solving. The secondary themes are ability to enjoy the world around us, making the best of things, and seeking out friendships rather than waiting for friends to materialize.

- Start with a discussion of bigger animals, birds, and fish who eat smaller animals. Point out that smaller animals eat animals smaller still.
- Discuss loneliness. Talk about lonely jobs, such as a forest-fire lookout staffed by a single person.
- Talk about sea life, shells, and types of fish.
- Read the story. Use your judgment about what words to change. As you read the story, point out the beauty under the sea and how cold and lonely Swimmy looks when he is alone.
- After you have read the story, discuss other groups that move in strict formation as the fish did, such as airplanes, birds, parades.
- Emphasize that the success of Swimmy's idea depended on all the fish taking part. Point out that sometimes a group of people can do something together than one person could not do alone.

41. *The Tale of Peter Rabbit.* Beatrix Potter. New York: Western Publishing, 1970.
Discussion. The theme of this story is the price of disobedience.

- Discuss rabbits and what they like to eat, why farmers (like Mr. MacGregor) don't like rabbits, and how to make rabbit pie.
- Read the story. Be sure that the children are able to see the excellent illustrations.
- Discuss the story in a general way.

42. *The Little Wood Duck.* Brian Wildsmith. New York: Franklin Watts, 1973.
Discussion. The theme in this story is the rejection of someone who is different. Note the unkind remarks the others made and the misery it caused the duck.

- Point out that the duck swam in circles because of circumstances completely beyond his control.
- Emphasize the kindness of the owl.
- Discuss natural enemies in the animal kingdom.

43. *Crictor.* Tomi Ungerer. New York: Harper & Row, 1969.
Discussion. The themes are kind acceptance of someone who is different, versatility in adjusting to a new environment, and kindness repaid.

- Start with a discussion of snakes. Ask how many of the children have seen harmless water and garter snakes.
- In reading the story, omit *French* and change *Madame* to *Mrs.*

- After the reading, flip through the book, noting ways the environment was made to accommodate the snake, such as the O-shaped box, the sweater, and the length of the bed.
- Spend some time talking about receiving gifts graciously. Note that a snake was probably not what Madame would have chosen.
- Discuss desirable and undesirable reactions to presents.
- Note that Madame's initial horror disappeared when she gave Crictor a change and came to know him.
- Point out how Crictor tried to be a help in his new environment.

44. *The Brave Cowboy.* Joan Anglund. New York: Harcourt Brace, 1959.
Discussion.

- Spend some time talking about dreams, daydreaming, and enjoyable events that are approaching.
- Encourage the children to imagine and discuss exceptionally nice things that could happen in connection with school but have never happened in the past.
- Talk about things you wish would happen to you but in all likelihood will not happen. Use *Frederick* (see 37 above) as an example.
- Explain that you are going to read a story about a boy who likes to pretend he is a cowboy.
- Talk about cowboys. Try to elicit discussion about Indians, coyotes, guns, holsters, rattlesnakes, mountain lions, stagecoaches, covered wagons, and sheriffs.
- Point out the black and red pictures. Explain that black is real and red is pretend.
- As you read the story, discuss the red pictures and try to convey that pretending is fun.

45. *The Small Lot.* Eros Keith. New York: Bradbury, 1968.
Discussion.

- Talk about the differences in the number of places for children to play in the city versus the suburbs.
- Use miniature houses and green paper to demonstrate the difference between a city street and a suburban street.
- Emphasize that in the city the children have only the street or the sidewalk on which to play if there are no vacant lots.
- Use the houses to demonstrate a vacant lot.
- Talk about playing house and playing catch. Point out that in playing house you pretend, while in playing catch you do not pretend. Emphasize that both kinds of games are fun.
- Tell the children that this book is about two city boys who have a small vacant lot to play on. If someone decides to buy the lot and build on it, they would have no place to play.
- Tell the children to listen to see how the boys solve their problem.
- As you read, emphasize the imaginary games the boys play.

46. *The Lion in the Meadow.* Margaret Mahy. New York: Franklin Watts, 1969.
Discussion. The messages here are that events sometimes get out of hand when you start making things up and that not only children make things up.

- Tell the children that you are going to read them a story about making things up.
- Ask what other pretending stories you've read. (Have *The Brave Cowboy* and *The Small Lot* on hand; see 44 and 45.)
- Tell the children to listen to *Lion* and think about who was making up a story. After reading the story have a discussion about what was made up and about the problems that result when you make things up.
- Mention that adults do not always tell the truth.
- Note that in *Lot* and *Cowboy* the children were making things up for their own amusement only, but in *Lion* it was a different situation.

47. *The Smallest Boy in the Class.* Jerrold Beim. New York: William Morrow, 1949.
Discussion. The story is about being different in a supposedly undesirable way and how a boy tries to cope by making other things about him unusually big.

- Talk about individual differences and preferences in terms of such things as size, hair color, and eye color.

- Discuss name-calling.
- Talk briefly about goats and what they eat.

48. *The Hating Book.* Charlotte Zolotow. New York: Harper & Row, 1969.
Discussion.

- Talk about what *hating* means. Note that we use the word *hate* quite freely; for example, we say we hate foods.
- Talk about friendships, fights, misunderstandings, advantages of frank discussions, how hating doesn't make you feel good, making up, and how both sides are reluctant to take the first step in making up.
- After you have read the book talk about the cause of the fight and how it could have been averted easily.

49. *One Kitten for Kim.* Adelaide Holl. Reading, Mass.: Addison-Wesley, 1969.
Discussion.

- Discuss giving versus trading.
- As Kim makes each trade discuss whether his parents will be likely to prefer a kitten or what he is bringing home (fish, parrot, rooster, puppy, chameleon).
- Let the children discuss the questions unanswered in this book: Does Kim keep what he has? Does he give them away for more trades?

50. *The Strange Disappearance of Arthur Cluck.* Nathaniel Benchley. New York: Harper & Row, 1967.
Discussion.

- Talk about what action families should take if one of the young children is missing.
- Emphasize the resources and helpfulness of the police in locating missing persons.
- Be sure that the children understand what *missing* means.
- Discuss animals and how the mother watches over her children just as human parents do.
- Bring out *Make Way for Ducklings* (see 5 above), and remind the children of the mother care there.
- Talk about owls and the advantage of sharp eyes and being able to fly while looking for a missing chick.

Vocabulary: chicken, unusual, horror, outcry, duck, rooster, crowing, helpful, owl, disappeared, fox, perch, pack rat, farmhouse, cheep, crate, children's zoo, popular.

51. *The Boy Who Cried Wolf.* Katherine Evans. Chicago: Albert Whitman, 1960.
Discussion.

- Talk about false alarms and why they are dangerous.
- Emphasize that persons found giving a false alarm will be punished.
- Distinguish between harmless jokes, irresponsible mischief, and legal offenses.
- Talk about sheep, wool, flock, the enemies of sheep (wolves, wild dogs, careless hunters), why sheep need someone to watch them, and the responsibility of a sitter or person on a job.

52. *Cinderella.* Beni Montresor. New York: Alfred A. Knopf, 1965.
Discussion.

- Discuss the role of the underdog in a group. Talk about how the underdog feels when treated unkindly by most of the group.
- Talk about fairies and magic.
- Make it clear that this is a story that someone dreamed up—it is not a true story or likely to have happened. It is important that the children grasp the idea of fantasy. Do not belittle fantasy, but try to help the children understand the difference between fantasy and real-life stories.
- After you read the story, discuss the sequence of events. Note Cinderella's forgiveness and generosity.

53. *How Many Kids Are Hiding on My Block?* Jean Merrill and Frances G. Scott. Chicago: Albert Whitman, 1970.
Discussion.

- Talk about dreams and pretending.
- Remind the children of *The Brave Cowboy* and *The Small Lot* (see 44 and 45 above).
- Read *How Many Kids Are Hiding on My Block?*
- Talk about Hide and Go Seek.
- Ask where children might hide in an area near small stores when the rule is that you can't hide inside a house or a store.

- Discuss the kind of stores found in such an area and why the rule is a good rule.
- Note the ingenuity of the hiding places the ten children select.

54. *The Magic Wallpaper.* Frank Francis. New York: Abelard-Schuman, 1970.
Discussion. This is one of a series of books about imagining, daydreams, and dreaming.

- Have some samples of wallpaper on hand. Some of the wallpaper should contain realistic pictures.
- Talk about wallpaper and the advantages of papered walls.
- Discuss dreams. Encourage the children to discuss different kinds of dreams they have had.
- Point out that often you dream about something you've seen.
- After you read the book, discuss the sequence of events that led to the dream.

55. *What Do You Say, Dear?* Sesyle Joslin. Reading, Mass.: Addison-Wesley, 1961.
Discussion.

- Discuss manners, politeness, and rudeness.
- Talk about not knowing what to say or do.
- Read the book, asking the children what they would say for each situation. They will soon grasp the idea that the responses are common courtesies.
- Accept any reasonable answers as correct.
- The children should not be led to think that there is only one right answer in a social situation.

56. *Two Is a Team.* Lorraine and Jerrold Beim. New York: Harcourt Brace, 1974.
Discussion.

- Talk about teams, and play one or two games, such as table search games, in which your group is divided into two teams.
- Discuss the concept of teams from two viewpoints: (a) in terms of sports like baseball in which one person simply could not play the game alone, and (b) in terms of two or more people voluntarily working together toward some goal.
- Discuss cooperation, responsibility for damages in an accident, fights, making up, and group processes such as group decision making.

57. *The Fox Went Out on a Chilly Night.* Peter Spier. New York: Doubleday, 1961.
Discussion.

- Talk about responsibility and animals being responsible for their children. Children who have had cats with kittens should be able to contribute examples of caretaking and safekeeping.
- Point out that domestic animals have their food provided for them by their owners, but wild animals must find their own food.
- Emphasize that wild animals know no boundaries and, when they take food that belongs to humans, they are not stealing in the sense that humans steal.
- Read the book once so that the children get some feeling for the rhythm of the song, then review, looking at the pictures and discussing them.
- Note details in the pictures that tell you it is autumn.

58. *Thin Ice.* Jerrold Beim. New York: William Morrow, 1956.
Discussion.

- Talk about signs. Why is it important to pay attention to signs?
- Discuss the kinds of dangers, such as swimming, skating, and construction, that require signs.
- Talk about the effect of thinking something is too hard when it really isn't, or thinking that you can't do something when you really can.

59. *Peter's Chair.* Ezra Jack Keats. New York: Harper & Row, 1967.
Discussion. This is the first of two stories about jealousy (see 60 below).

- Talk about being jealous, how it feels, when it happens.
- Discuss losing poorly as a form of jealousy.
- Let the children talk freely about times when they have felt jealous.
- Talk about what made you feel jealous when you were a child.
- Discuss running away—the disadvantages, the reasons why children do it, and the effects on the parents.
- Read the story; then discuss the idea that parents do not have a fixed amount of love

to share, that there is room for all, and that having brothers and sisters offers advantages.

60. *Benjy and the Barking Bird.* Margaret B. Graham. New York: Harper & Row, 1971.
Discussion. This is the second of two stories about jealousy. In discussing jealousy, remind the children of *Peter's Chair* (see 59, p. 27).

- Talk about jealousy in terms of someone else doing something better than you can or someone getting more attention than you do.
- Discuss guests and privileges they receive simply because they're guests.

61. *What Mary Jo Wanted.* Janice M. Udry. Chicago: Albert Whitman, 1968.
Discussion.

- Talk about the pleasure, problems, and responsibility of having a dog.
- Discuss the leash law (if there is one in your area), dog catcher, humane society, and lost and found ads. (Bring a newspaper and read a few ads to the group.)
- Ask those who have dogs to describe them as young puppies.
- Discuss the similarity of needs of a human baby and a puppy.
- Tell the children to listen to the story to see if Mary Jo was responsible.

62. *Katie Goes to Camp.* Eleanor Schick. New York: Macmillan, 1968.
Discussion.

- Talk about the summer vacation and what the children will do.
- Tell children that you are going to read them a story about what two children do during the summer.
- Discuss summer camp, going on the train with responsible adults other than the children's parents, advantages of independence, pleasures of summer camp, and writing letters home.
- When the story is finished, talk about why Katie needed her doll at first and why she didn't need it later.

63. *The Plant Sitter.* Gene Zion. New York: Harper & Row, 1976.
Discussion.

- Talk about going away, vacations, and the responsibility of the home owner for lawn care, home maintenance, and care of pets while away.
- Discuss plants and their need for water.
- If possible, display two plants—one that has been watered regularly and one that has not. Point out that indoor plants need human care because they do not benefit from rain.
- Discuss earning money by baby-sitting, and introduce the idea of plant-sitting. The theme of the story is that a good idea got out of hand. Talk about this problem.

64. *Andrew's Amazing Boxes.* Unada. New York: Putnam, 1971.
Discussion.

- Talk about cartons big enough to climb into, and ask what games you could play with them.
- Have a big carton on hand.
- When you read the book, describe the story children as being the same age as those in your class.

65. *The Egg Tree.* Katherine Milhous. New York: Charles Scribner, 1950.
Discussion. Just before Easter have an Easter egg hunt, and read *The Egg Tree.*

- Talk about Easter egg hunts.
- Try to get decorated eggs or pictures of them to show to the children.
- Note that Katy did not give up and that she showed her appreciation to the Easter Bunny by scattering flower petals for him.

66. *The Sugar Pear Tree.* Clyde Robert Bulla. New York: Thomas Y. Crowell, 1961.
Discussion.

- Talk about trees, gardens, and greenhouses.
- Discuss the problems of keeping any kind of garden in an apartment as compared to the ease of growing a garden in the suburbs or in the country.
- Talk about compositions and prizes.

67. *The Little House.* Virginia L. Burton. Boston: Houghton Mifflin, 1978.
Discussion.

- Ask what happens to houses that are in the way of highways and freeways.
- Talk about house-moving, and look at the pictures in *The Little House.*

Spelling

Spelling consists of writing letters in a left-to-right sequence that corresponds to the sequence in which sounds are quickly uttered in a word. To learn to spell the child must learn to identify the phonemes in a word in the order in which they are spoken. For example, the phoneme heard at the beginning of dog is "duh" (*not* the grapheme "de"). To spell, the child must know the beginning sound of a word (*phoneme*) and the letter used to write the sound. (*grapheme*).

TEACHING SOUNDS ROUTINES

Beginning Sounds Routine

Purpose: To teach identification of beginning sounds.
Equipment: pictures and/or objects.
Procedure:

1. Display teacher-made pictures or objects (their names beginning with the sound being taught).
2. Ask the children to name the pictures or objects.
3. Ask them to listen as you point to each picture or pick up each object, saying its name. Say the endings distinctly so that children will not confuse similar words, such as *cap* and *cat.*
4. Ask them to listen as you say the beginning sound for each picture or object.
5. Have the children say each word, and ask, "What was the first sound you made when you said the word?"
6. Present another list of words (such as *cut, cabin, can, camera,* and *candle*), and establish that all of these begin with the same sound.
7. Ask the children to think of other words that begin with this sound. Use incomplete sentences to elicit additional words (such as *cab, cabbage, call, card, carry, canary, canoe, camera, camp,* and *captain*).

Additional Procedure: Play *One of These Sounds Doesn't Belong.*

- In this game you say four words, three with the same beginning sound and one with a beginning sound that is clearly different. The children must identify the word that doesn't belong.
- When you introduce the game, talk about things that are the same, that belong together.
- Ask the children to tell you which word does not belong in the following series: (a) *shoe, foot, sock, candy;* (b) *tree, leaf, king, branch;* and (c) *school, teacher, moon, school bus.*
- Explain that words that begin with the same sound belong together when you play the game with sounds.
- Say, "All of these words except one begin with the 'kuh' sound. Which word doesn't begin with 'kuh'? Which word doesn't belong here?" Then say the series: *cat, carry, camera, acorn, camp.*

Second Sounds Routine

Purpose: To teach identification of second sounds.
Equipment: Pictures and/or objects.
Procedure:

1. Display pictures or objects (their names contain the sound being taught).
2. Ask the children to name the pictures or objects.
3. Ask them to identify the beginning sound in each word.
4. Children should listen as the teacher says each word; says each sound separately; identifies each sound as beginning, middle, or end; and demonstrates blending. (Blend "kuh"–"a"–"n" into *can.*) It is very important that separation of the elements in the word be followed by blending into one unit.
5. Tell the children to listen while you say some words that have different beginnings but the same middle or second sound.
6. Use clues and incomplete sentences to help the children think of other words that have the correct second sound. Short vowels will be the sounds taught for most of the year.

End Sounds Routine

Purpose: To teach identification of ending sounds.
Equipment: Pictures and/or objects.
Procedure:

1. Display pictures or objects (their names ending in the sound being taught).
2. Ask the children to name the pictures or objects.
3. Ask them to identify the beginning and second sounds in each word.
4. Ask the children to listen as the teacher says the word clearly; sounds out each part separately; and identifies the beginning, middle, and end sounds.
5. Say some words that have different beginning and middle sounds but end in the same sound. Ask the children to tell you what sound they hear last.
6. Now use some words ending in a different sound to contrast with the above.
7. Ask the children to think of words ending in the sound being taught.

Letters-for-Sounds Routine

Purpose: To teach spelling words.
Equipment: Pictures and/or objects, chalkboard.
Procedure:

1. Review the sound being taught, such as "muh," using the appropriate spelling sheet or words, objects, and pictures.
2. Write each word on the chalkboard. Say the word, sound it out, and teach the letter for each sound.
3. Erase the chalkboard. Go through each word on the word list, and ask the children what letter to write down for the beginning sound. If appropriate ask for the second sound.
4. Say the last sound. If it is one the children know, they must tell you what letter to write.

Review Routing—Consonants

Purpose: To review the consonants.
Equipment: Paper and pencil for each child, chalkboard.
Procedure:

1. Write the letter on the board, and ask the children to identify it.
2. Establish what sound the letter makes.
3. Ask the children to name words beginning with that letter.
4. Ask the children to spell several of the words they suggest.
5. Write the words on the chalkboard.
6. If the children can't spell the words, sound out the words, and ask the children to give the letter for each sound.
7. Ask the children what letter goes with the sound you are teaching.
8. Ask the children to think of more words beginning with the letter. Write them on the chalkboard.
9. As words are suggested, emphasize the blending sounds—"ma" as in *man,* "me" as in *met,* "mi" as in *mitt,* "mo" as in *Molly.*
10. If the letter has been taught as an end sound, elicit words that end in it. Write the words on the chalkboard as the children spell them.
11. Give out paper and pencil, and dictate three words beginning or ending with the letter for the day, for example, *mad, met,* and *Sam.*

12. Play at least one appropriate game in each review lesson. Use as many lessons as needed to review each letter.

TEACHING NEW WORDS

High-Frequency Words Routine

Purpose: To teach high-frequency, irregularly spelled words.
Equipment: Word flash cards, paper and pencil for each child, magic slate or chalkboard.
Procedure:

1. Say the word. Ask the children to use it in a sentence.
2. Write the word on your magic slate or chalkboard, and spell it for the children.
3. Ask them to spell the word by reading it from your magic slate.
4. Ask them to say the word, close their eyes, and spell it.
5. Ask the children to write the word.
6. Repeat the five previous steps.
7. Print the word on a flash card and mix it with cards of the regularly spelled words. Test the children with the flash cards.

New Words Routine

Purpose: To introduce and teach new words.
Equipment: Paper and pencil for each child.
Procedure:

1. Pronounce the word carefully, giving vowels and consonants their correct sound values.
2. Explain the meaning of the word, or ask the children to define it.
3. Ask one child to use the word in a sentence.
4. Ask one or two children to spell the word without looking at the word list.
5. Ask the children to write the word on a blank sheet of paper.

Learning-to-Spell Routine

Purpose: To teach how to spell new words.
Equipment: Marker, pencil.
Seatwork: Appropriate spelling seatwork.

Procedure: State steps 1–7 as directions for children to follow.

1. Place the marker under the word, and look at the word.
2. Say the word aloud softly; then spell it while looking at the sheet.
3. Look at the word again to see how it is spelled.
4. Close your eyes, and pretend that you are looking at a TV program with this word on the screen. Try to "see" the word.
5. Look at the word on the sheet again; then spell the word softly without looking.
6. Cover the printed word with your marker, and write the word in the space on the sheet.
7. Check your writing of the word. If you did not get it right, erase it, and try again. Check it again.

Follow the above routine with each of the words. After children have printed the first three words, ask them to tell you the steps in the routine. Encourage them to spend as much time as they need on step 5. Children should be confident about the spelling of a word before they write it.

TESTING ROUTINES

Test-Study Routine (for words with a vowel-consonant common ending)

Purpose: To test ability to spell.
Equipment: Paper (prepared) for each child.
Seatwork: Spelling Seatwork 8 (or appropriate spelling seatwork for the words being tested).
Procedure:

1. Tell the children that they are going to have a test of words that all end the same (in this case with *et*).
2. Give out dittoed sheets of paper with the numbers 1–10 in the margin, beside each number a blank, and then *et.*
3. Explain that you will say the word and that the child should fill in the first letter. The advantages of this method are that the test can be given quickly and, more important, that the child is aware that only the first letter of each word is different.
4. Correct the test (see the correcting test routine, p. 32).

5. Review sounds for which there are errors.
6. Give out Spelling Seatwork 8 with instructions to focus on error words.
7. In the next spelling period review the meaning of each word, and ask for sentences.

Spelling Test Routine

Purpose: To test ability to spell.
Equipment: Lined sheet of paper with numbers in left margin, double-spaced, and pencil for each child.
Procedure:

1. Give a test on the spelling seatwork of your choice.
2. Give each child a lined sheet of paper with the appropriate numbers in the left margin, double-spaced.
3. Ask the children to print their names in the top right-hand corner.
4. Explain how to use the numbers as guides for writing.
5. Give the test.
6. Use clear instructions, such as: "First, next to the *one,* write *and,*" or "Find the number *one* on your paper. Write *and,*" or "The first word is *and.* Write *and* on the line where the *one* is."

Correcting Test Routine

Purpose: To correct spelling tests.
Equipment: Markers.
Procedure:

1. Distribute markers.
2. Say the first word, and ask the children to place their markers under that word.
3. Spell the word slowly.
4. Watch to see that the children mark their work correctly.
5. If any child has made an error, say the word, and spell it again.
6. Repeat this procedure for each word.
7. Show the children how to count their correct words and to use the total as a numerator over a denominator (the last number on the page).
8. Emphasize that most study time should be spent on words missed but some time must also be spent reviewing the words that were spelled correctly.

SAMPLE LESSONS

Sample Lesson One

Purpose: To give practice spelling and to have each child hear each word said and spelled several times.
Equipment: Tokens.
Procedure: Play *Stop That Word.*

1. Before the game starts, demonstrate mistakes to give the children practice.
2. The teacher says a word, such as *cat,* turns to the child on the left, and spells the word.
3. The child says the word, turns to the child on the left, and spells the word.
4. If the word can be sent around the group and back to the teacher without error, each child in the group wins a token.
5. The children must listen each time the word is spelled. If a word is misspelled, the other children should say, "Stop that word." The first child to stop the word wins two bonus tokens if he or she can spell the word correctly.
6. The child who misspelled the word then starts the word going around again by spelling it correctly, and the word must return to him or her. The advantage of this procedure is that the child who misspelled the word has to say and spell the word twice, once when it starts around the table again and once when it returns. The teacher should ask, "Is it spelled right?" or "Did we get it all the way around without making a mistake?"
7. It is very important that the children say the words before they spell them because it helps them associate sounds with specific letters.

Sample Lesson Two

Purpose: To give practice in spelling rhyming words.
Equipment: Paper and pencil for each child, tokens.
Procedure: Play *Rhyming Words.*

Review rhyming. The children should know what rhyming means, but to be sure, demonstrate it with "Jack and Jill" and other familiar rhymes. Emphasize that rhyming words are ones whose end sounds are the same. (Do not say "words that go together.")

1. The teacher says, "Spell (or write down) a word that rhymes with *man.*" (The advantage

of writing is that each child participates on each word, but oral spelling is usually preferable because it's faster.)

2. The child must say the word before spelling it.
3. If the children are unable to supply rhyming words in turn around the table, let any child suggest a rhyming word, such as *can.* Then say to another child, "*Can* rhymes with *man.* Spell *can.*"
4. Award tokens.

Additional Procedure:

- When the children are proficient at this activity, try this variation. Say a word, such as *log.*
- Ask the children to listen while you say three words, only two of which rhyme with log. For instance, use *dog, cat, fog,* and ask the children to tell you the word that does not rhyme.
- Ask one child to spell *cat.*
- Award tokens.

Sample Lesson Three

Purpose: To give practice in spelling.
Equipment: Tokens, pencil and paper for each child.
Before the Game:

- Give the children practice in responding to true-and-false items. Explain what *true* and *false* mean. (The children will be more familiar with *true* than with *false.*)
- Hold up a picture of a cat, and say, "This is a horse. True or false?"
- When the children are proficient with pictures, shift to statements: "We come to school here every Saturday and Sunday."
- Then use words spelled correctly, followed by words that are blatantly misspelled (dog—m–m–o–s), and finally words with one incorrect letter (dog—d–i–g).
- Always start with a few correct and incorrect statements to give some practice in true-and-false responses.

Procedure: Play *True or False?*

1. In this game the teacher says a word, spells it, points to one child, and asks "True or false?"
2. The child must respond "True" if the word was spelled correctly and "False," if it was misspelled.
3. The adult confirms "True" without spelling the word again. If, however, the word was misspelled, the child who says "False" must then spell it correctly to win a token.
4. If a child says a word was spelled correctly when it was not, a token is forfeited.
5. Any child who disagrees should quickly raise a hand. The first child to raise a hand receives the first chance to correct the answer and to win two bonus tokens.
6. You can vary this game by giving children pencils and paper and requiring them to mark down *T* or *F* for each word spelled. Give the correct answer immediately after each word. Don't ever let a word go by misspelled without making the error known and spelling it correctly twice.

Sample Lesson Four

Purpose: To give practice in spelling.
Equipment: Word cards, tokens.
Procedure: Play *Find a Word.*

1. Small cards with one word on each are spread out facedown on the table.
2. The word to be found is named and spelled. Each child in turn picks up a card and reads it.
3. The child who finds the right word wins two tokens.

Additional Procedure:

- A variation of this game is to name a word and deal each child three cards, which are kept facedown on the table.
- When all the cards have been dealt, each child picks up his or her cards and looks for the word.
- The child who has the card wins two tokens.
- Let the children pick the word for the next round.

Sample Lesson Five

Purpose: To give practice in spelling.
Equipment: Paper and pencil for each child.
Procedure: Play *Make a Word.*

1. Distribute paper and pencils, and ask the children to write words according to your instructions. Note that the writing must be legible. (If you can give the children magic slates, they will be able to write faster and will enjoy the novelty of erasing by lifting the page.)

2. Start with easy tasks, such as a three-letter word that begins with *c*, ends with *at*, *an*, and so forth.
3. Ask each child to say the word and then to spell it.
4. Check each word. Give a token for each correct word.
5. You can use this activity as a silent exercise in which children write words and you correct them, or as a race in which each player tries to be the first to write down three words ending in *at*, or beginning with *c* ("kuh"). Or give clues about the word, and have the child first identify the topic and then write the word. Tailor the activity to the children's ability.

Sample Lesson Six

Purpose: To give practice in spelling.
Equipment: Flannel board, a chalkboard, or magic slate.
Procedure: Play *Incomplete Words*.

1. The child's task is to fill in the missing letter in a word that is written on a flannel board,chalkboard, or magic slate. It is important that all children in the group be able to see each word.
2. When a child supplies the missing letter (which should be the middle or end letter in a three-letter word until children become proficient), have him or her say the word.
3. At times suggest an alternate letter, or ask the children if they can think of one.
4. If the children know the vowels, tell them that in a three-letter word that begins and ends in a consonant, the middle letter is always a vowel.

Sample Lesson Seven

Purpose: To give practice in identification of beginning sounds.
Equipment: Magic slate or chalkboard.
Procedure: Play *One of These Words Doesn't Belong*.

1. In this game the teacher says four words, three with the same beginning sound and one with a beginning sound that is clearly different. The children must identify the word that doesn't belong.
2. Tell the children what letter they would say first if they were spelling that word, and write the word on your magic slate or chalkboard, emphasizing the letter you write first.
3. Make a habit of using this game when the spelling words begin with the same letter.

Sample Lesson Eight

Purpose: To give practice in spelling.
Equipment: Crossword puzzles
Procedure:

1. Cut out crossword puzzles from the newspaper.
2. Ask the children if they know what a crossword puzzle is, and then show them. Point out that it is made up of words going across other words.
3. Talk about the clues and the concepts of *down* and *across*.
4. Demonstrate with two-word puzzles on sheets of paper. Use very obvious clues, such as, "The down word has three letters [point to three squares] and is a four-legged animal that barks." "The across word has three letters. The middle letter is *o* [point to space with *o* in it], and it is a short word that means the same as police officer." [Fill in *dog* and *cop*.]
5. Complete more two-word puzzles using *cat-man, big-pin, hen-leg,* and *cup-bug*. Give explicit clues and encouragement.
6. If the children grasp the idea, give each child a sheet of paper and ask them to write in the words themselves.

Sample Lesson Nine

Purpose: To give practice in spelling.
Equipment: One large sheet of paper or chalkboard.
Procedure: Play *Chains of Words*.

1. Ask the children to suggest and spell a three-letter word.
2. Write it in the center of a large sheet of paper or on the chalkboard.
3. Suppose the word is *cat*. The children's task is to add on words using these letters; for example, going down from *c* you could have *can*. Going down from the *t* in *cat*, you could have *tag*,*tug*, or *the*. Next you might add *ten*, using the *n* in *can*.

4. You will have to give the children clues. It is preferable, but not essential, to use words the children can spell. The important thing is to keep the game going briskly so that it is fun. The goal is to have words in chains all over the page.

SPELLING SEATWORK INSTRUCTIONS

1. Use the New Words Routine (see p. 31) and the Learning-to-Spell Routine (see p. 31) or Test-Study Routine (see p. 31) in teaching Spelling Seatwork 1–17.
2. Use Spelling Seatwork 18–21 (and similar sheets) when you teach *endings* to words. Sheets of this type can also be used in teaching rhyming (see Rhyming, pp. 15–16).
3. Spelling Seatwork 22–45 can be completed independently. Do not assign these sheets unless the child is capable of spelling all the words correctly. It is important to check the sheets for unfamiliar words before assigning them.

Printing

Printing activites are used in conjunction with the other subjects in the curriculum. Spelling words and reading words can be used extensively. The children should be able to print the date on the chalkboard each day and complete other printing tasks in connection with the day's routine. All children should have a turn at this extra printing, provided they can print legibly and neatly. As often as possible, encourage the children to use the printing skills they are practicing to reinforce the utility of good printing. Although the printing on chalkboard will not always be neat, the children learn more from active participation than from passive observation of the teacher's superior printing (often completed when the children are absent).

The lessons begin with a printing test (Printing Seatwork 1), which should be repeated twice later in the year to show children the progress they have made. In addition, every two weeks all children should be given back their practice sheets for that period to be arranged chronologically. The child then selects the sheet he or she thinks is best, and puts it in a storage folder. Each child will need two file folders, one for the daily work and one for the selected samples of best work in each two-week period. Spend some time helping the children evaluate their work. The children often need help with standards for self-evaluation, and the folders provide an excellent oppportunity for practice. In the latter half of the year conduct two printing competitions, one of which may be judged by upper elementary helpers.

For printing practice use demonstrations, skywriting, practice at the chalkboard, practice on lined paper, seatwork, and competitions.

Most lessons require each child to have one or more lined practice sheets (Printing Seatwork 3), an extra-soft round lead pencil, a ruler, and the daily folder. The teacher should have on hand a magic slate, newsprint, and a felt pen for sample printing, and a stiff piece of cardboard or easel to hold the newsprint so that the children can see the teacher's movements while printing. Note: Supplies are listed under sample lessons only if they differ from the above.

The children should not use erasers. If a mistake is made, it should be crossed out neatly with one horizontal line. Most of the practice should be done on lines that are 3/4-inch apart with a center guideline. There should be a 3/8-inch space below the lower line. At the beginning of the year, if this spacing is too difficult, use practice lines that are 1-inch apart with center guidelines and a 1/2-inch space below the lower line. For chalkboard practice, use lines that are 3 1/2-inches apart.

To make the transition to cursive writing as easy as possible, stress making each letter—except *i, t, j,* and *k*—without lifting the pencil off the paper. Watch the children closely as they practice, and continue the emphasis on making each letter with a continuous movement.

TEACHER-MADE PRINTING SEATWORK

The printing seatwork section includes four sheets; additional sheets (ditto masters) must be made by the teacher. All of the teacher-made single lowercase letter dittoes and single uppercase letter dittoes should be similar to Printing Seatwork 4. All dittoes having two or more letters are teacher made (see sample blank form, p.160). The printing seatwork sheets are described as follows:

Printing Seatwork

1. lowercase and uppercase letters from *a* to *z*, numerals from 1 to 33, days of the week
2. months of the year and their abbreviations
3. a plain sheet of lines to match the lines drawn on Printing Seatwork 1
4. lowercase *a*
5. lowercase *d*
6. lowercase *g*
7. lowercase *q*
8. lowercase *c*
9. lowercase *a, d, g, q, c*
10. lowercase *l, b*
11. lowercase *h*
12. lowercase *k*
13. words printed in a column on the left edge of the page: *had, bad, cab, dad, gag, a;* opposite each word is a line on which the children will print
14. lowercase *l, b, h,* and *k*
15. words to copy on ruled lines: *lad, glad, clad, lack, black;* opposite each word is a line on which children will print
16. lowercase *m*
17. lowercase *n*
18. lowercase *r*
19. lowercase *u*
20. lowercase *e*
21. lowercase *f*
22. lowercase *i, j*
23. lowercase *o, p*
24. lowercase *e, f, i, j, o, p*
25. lowercase *s*
26. lowercase *t*
27. lowercase *v, w*
28. lowercase *s, t, v, w*
29. lowercase *x, y, z*
30. lowercase *m, n, r, u*
31. months to copy (Starting below the line for the child's name, rule twelve lines. At the left edge, print *September* on the first line, *October* on the fourth line, *November* on the seventh line, and *December* on the tenth line.)
32. special days to copy, along with their dates, following the form in 31: Halloween, October 31, 19____; Thanksgiving, November ____, 19____; Christmas, December 25, 19____; New Year's Day, January 1, 19____
33. uppercase *A*
34. uppercase *D*
35. uppercase *G*
36. uppercase *Q*
37. uppercase *A, D, G, Q, C*
38. uppercase *L*
39. uppercase *B*
40. uppercase *M*
41. uppercase *T*
42. uppercase *W, S*
43. uppercase *F*
44. days of the week (Rule 14 lines. Print *Monday* on the top line at the left edge, *Tuesday* on the third line, and so forth.)
45. uppercase *H*
46. uppercase *K*
47. uppercase *N*
48. uppercase *R, U*
49. uppercase *E, O*
50. uppercase *I, J*
51. uppercase *E, O, I, J, P*
52. uppercase *V, X*
53. uppercase *Y, Z*
54. lowercase letters printed in three columns; opposite each letter is a space in which the children can write the uppercase letter; ruled lines at the bottom of the page for extra practice
55. uppercase letters printed following the form in 54, opposite each letter is a space in which the children can print the lowercase letters
56. two envelope-shaped rectangles, one above the other
57. uppercase *L, B, M, T, W, F*
58. uppercase *H, R, S, N, U*
59. uppercase *V, X, Y, Z*
60. printed paragraphs for the children to copy on another line sheet; examples:

- The mother bakes the cake. The cake is in the pan. The rat sees the cake, and he eats the cake. The cat sees the rat eat the cake. Go, rat, go. Run, run, run! The cat will get you rat. The cat runs fast. The rat runs fast, too. Will the cat get the rat?

- Bill had a ball and bat. He hits the ball into the van. Bang! The man sees the ball and is mad at Bill. The man gets the ball. The man lets Bill take the ball. Now Bill is happy.
- The rat sits in the sun. He sees the cat. The cat sees a big dog, so the cat runs and behind the red van. The dog looks for the cat but can not see him. The dog is mad at the cat. She barks, but he goes away. The rat sits still, and the cat does not see him.
- Pat had a cat and a red ball. The cat runs to the ball and sits on it. Pat can not see the red ball. She looks in the pan, but the red ball is not in the pan. She looks in the pit, but the ball is not down in the pit. Pat looks and looks but can not find the red ball. Then the cat jumps up, and Pat sees the ball. She says, "That is a funny trick to sit on the ball so I can not see it." She pats the cat, and the cat purrs.

PRINTING TEST

Sample Lesson

Purpose: To test printing ability.
Equipment: File folder with the child's name printed on it for each child; magic slate or chalkboard, several recent newspapers.
Seatwork: Printing Seatwork 1–3.
Procedure:

1. Print the date on the chalkboard.
2. Give each child a lined sheet of paper. Ask the children to print their names and copy the date at the top of the sheet without help.
3. Distribute Printing Seatwork 1, and tell the group that this year they are going to become good printers. Tell them that every two months they will complete some printing seatwork to keep in their folders as a record of how much they have improved.
4. Ask the children to copy Printing Sheet 2 onto their lined sheets of paper.
5. Give children their folders, and ask them to place their sheets inside.
6. Discuss the idea of progress through the year. Use as examples something in each child's printing that will be improved.
7. Ask how the children will know which printing sheet was placed first in the folder. (The date is on the paper.)
8. Give everyone a newspaper page from a different day, and ask each child to read the date on the newspaper. Help by telling them the word *September* (or appropriate month). Ask who has the oldest newspaper, and print that date on your magic slate. Ask who has the next most recent newspaper, and so on.

PRACTICE PRINTING

Sample Lesson One

Purpose: To give practice in printing.
Equipment: Teacher-made Printing Seatwork 5 (see p. 38) [print each child's name on each sheet], half-sheets of lined paper, chalkboard.
Seatwork: Printing Seatwork 4.
Procedure:

1. Begin at the chalkboard. Check to see that the children are holding the chalk like a pencil, then ask them to make circular movements on the board. Check that (a) they move their chalk counterclockwise, and (b) they do not lift the chalk off the chalkboard until they have made a number of circular movements.
2. Ask the children to make smaller circles, three or four inches in diameter.
3. Explain that you are going to review how to print letters and that probably a lot of children can already print letters properly.
4. Demonstrate an *a* and show the first movement.
5. Ask everyone to practice at the same time. Check that they start in the correct place and come back up the beginning point.
6. Demonstrate the complete letter *a*, mentioning that you don't take the chalk off the chalkboard until the letter is finished.
7. Ask the group to practice *a*'s and watch them closely to make sure the movements are correct.
8. Demonstrate the letter *d,* show the first movement, and ask everyone to practice.

9. Demonstrate the complete letter *d* again, mentioning that you do not take the chalk off the chalkboard until the letter is finished.
10. Ask the children to practice *d*'s, and watch closely.
11. Ask the children to return to the table, and distribute Printing Seatwork 4. Give individual help to make sure that each child prints each letter properly.
12. Distribute Printing Seatwork 5 as children are ready for it.
13. If any children quickly finish two satisfactory sheets, give them lined half-sheets and see if they can make ten perfect *a*'s and ten perfect *d*'s.

Sample Lesson Two

Purpose: To give practice in printing.
Equipment: Teacher-made Printing Seatwork 31 (see page p. 38), half-sheets of lined paper, chalkboard.
Procedure:

1. Begin at the chalkboard. Ask the group to print numbers 1 to 9 after you demonstrate. Watch carefully, and make a note of any numbers the group prints well. Ask everyone to practice numbers that are difficult for any child.
2. Ask the children to return to the table, and distribute Printing Seatwork 31. Ask what September is. Briefly explain that it is is the name of a month. Ask what happens in September. Ask the class to print it, filling up that part of the sheet.
3. Then ask what October is, and so on. Ask if the group knows what special day comes at the end of October. Have the class print in the October part of the sheet.
4. Use the same procedure for November and December.
5. Print the date on the board, and ask the group to copy it three times on the half-sheets of paper. Make certain to point out the uppercase letter and the comma after the date.
6. Ask what the date will be tomorrow. Print it on the board, and ask the group to copy it three times.

Sample Lesson Three

Purpose: To give practice printing and addressing envelopes.
Equipment: One stamp, and an inexpensive Christmas card and envelope for each child, paper bag, two dice, half-sheets of lined paper, chalkboard. (Teacher-made Printing Seatwork 56, page 38 can also be used as practice for addressing envelopes.)
Procedure:

1. Show the Christmas cards to the children and explain that they may each send one to someone in the class.
2. To see who has first choice, ask each child to roll the dice and say the number. (Write down the number on the chalkboard beside the child's name so there is no confusion.) The child with the highest total on one throw is first, and the child with the lowest total is last.
3. Place the address cards for the whole class in a paper bag. Each address card should have one child's name and address printed on it as for an envelope.
4. When the children have chosen their Christmas cards, shake the bag with the address cards in it, and ask each child to draw one card. If children pick their own cards they return them and take another turn.
5. Ask the children to practice printing the name and address once on the half-sheet.
6. Demonstrate how to rule three very light lines in the lower center of the envelope. Children should print the name and address on these lines, print their own names inside the Christmas card, put the card in the envelope, seal it, and put the stamp in the top right-hand corner.
7. Children should also rule three light lines and print their own names and addresses on the top left-hand corner. (Explain that if the letter is not delivered for some reason, it will come back to the sender *if* the sender's name and address are on the top left-hand corner.)
8. If there is a mailbox on the school grounds, send two children to post the letters, otherwise, mail them yourself.

Sample Lesson Four

Purpose: To give practice in printing.
Equipment: Teacher-made Printing Seatwork 33 and 34 (see p. 38), lined half-sheets.
Procedure:

1. At the chalkboard, demonstrate printing a

capital *A* in three strokes, and ask the children to copy each stroke. (Check to see that each child is holding the chalk like a pencil.)

2. Ask the group to practice *A*'s. Watch closely to make sure the movements are correct.
3. Demonstrate the capital letter *D* in two strokes, and ask the children to copy each stroke.
4. Ask them to practice the letter while you watch closely.
5. Ask the children to return to the table, and distribute Printing Seatwork 33.
6. Ask the children to print the date and their names neatly at the top right-hand corner. Give individual help to make sure that each child prints each letter properly.
7. Distribute Printing Seatwork 34 when the children are ready for it, and follow the procedure above. Stress neatness and well-made letters.
8. If there is time, ask the children to rule a margin on a half-sheet of paper, print the date and their names, and print five or more capital *A*'s, lowercase *a*'s, capital *D*'s, and lowercase *d*'s.

Sample Lesson Five

Purpose: To give practice in printing.
Equipment: Teacher-made Printing Seatwork 32 (see p. 38) half-sheets of lined paper, magic slate.
Procedure:

1. Discuss special days. Ask what special day was at the end of October (Halloween), the end of November (Thanksgiving) in December (Christmas), and in February (Valentine's Day).
2. Using the magic slate, print *Th*, and ask the children to sound it out. Print *anks*, and ask them to sound it out. Then print *Th* and *anks* close together, and ask them to blend the two sounds.
3. Follow the procedure above with *giv,* then *ing,* and then *giv-ing.* Then print *Thanksgiving,* and ask the children to say the whole word.
4. Print and ask them to say *Valentine's Day.* But for Christmas only tell them that the word says *Christmas*.
5. Ask the group to complete the sheet.

PRINTING SENTENCES

Sample Lesson

Purpose: To give practice in combining words to make sentences, completing sentences, and printing.
Equipment: Two sets of 1×2-inch word cards (made with thin cardboard and a black felt pen), magic slate (optional). Copy onto the cards any of the spelling words already taught as well as the following words:

bag	his	pet
beg	into	rat
big	is	red
bug	leg	run
cap	let	see
fan	like	tap
for	log	that
go	mat	wet
get	mop	win
gum	pad	
ham	pen	

Procedure: Making sentences.

1. Divide the group on either side of the table, and distribute to each side a set of cards to spread out in front of them.
2. Hold up one card at a time, and make certain that the children can read all the cards. If they can't, use the magic slate and review the word phonetically. If a child has difficulty with *cap*, print *ap*, and ask the child to sound it out; print *c*, and sound it out; then blend the sounds. Use several words ending in *ap*.
3. The children with one set of cards take turns setting out sentences, which all children copy; the children with the other set then take turns. Children put a checkmark beside their own sentences to read aloud later.

Additional Procedure: Completing sentences.

- Print the following sentences on the chalkboard where the whole group can easily see them:

  I see the ________.

  The cop put a ticket on the ________.

  Her cat is ________.

  I ________ for the bus. I was late.

  It was a red ________.

  It is ________ to play tag.

I live at ________.
My name is ________.

- Ask the children to copy the sentences and fill in the blanks.
- When the children have finished, ask one child to read the first sentence with the word he or she has put in. Ask anyone who has a different word to read the sentence. Follow this procedure for all the sentences. If any children have difficulty, let them copy another child's paper.

PRINTING STORIES

Sample Lesson

Purpose: To give practice in making up stories and in printing.
Equipment: Two large pieces of newsprint for the teacher.
Procedure:

1. Ask the children to make up stories about themselves.
2. Ask children to tell two or three things about themselves, such as "My name is ________. I am ________ years old. I go to ________ School. I am in ________ grade. I like to play ________."
3. As the first child has a turn, print the sentences on your paper.
4. As subsequent children make up their stories, add any different sentences to your paper so that you have an assortment of sentences that apply to the group.
5. Ask the children to select two sentences that you then print on another piece of newsprint.
6. With your sample clearly visible to the group, ask children to print stories about themselves using your sample.
7. Before the children start, introduce the idea and format of paragraphs. Explain that when the story is all about one thing, the first word is *indented*. Have the group put a light *x* where they will start. Use the word *paragraph* frequently in the lesson.
8. Ask each child to read his or her paragraph.
9. If there are errors or printing is untidy, have children copy them again after you have corrected the errors on the original.

Listening

The purpose of this section is to develop in the children a set to listen, that is, a readiness and ability to receive verbal input, to process it, and to retain it for a certain period. In addition, the child should develop an increasingly longer attention span.

The lessons increase in difficulty, beginning with very simple material. No seatwork is required with this section. Do not move on to the more difficult levels of one type of activity until the children can answer—without help—three-quarters of the questions in earlier activities.

It is essential in this program and in all other lessons that you do not repeat instructions or game content for a child who is not listening. Instead, give the next child the turn, award a token, if possible, and mention that a child who is a good listener will probably win more tokens. Avoid mouthing words of instructions in an exaggerated way in an effort to make what you are saying clearer to the children. Speak in a normal volume because this is the kind of speech that the children will hear in everyday activities, and because it is the manner of speaking they must be able to respond to proficiently.

It is important that listening skills be emphasized in all other lessons in the curriculum. Children should learn to be ready for their turns. For the first lessons say the children's names when they have a turn, starting with the child on your left. Always follow a clockwise direction when the activity calls for every child to have a turn in order. When the children are accustomed to the clockwise order (when they are ready for their turns just as you call their names), change to pointing at each child without saying the name. Continue the pointing procedure until some children know their turns, then stop pointing and look expectantly at children when they have a turn. Throughout these procedures reward with praise and stars any instances of progress in attentiveness. Occasionally conduct rounds in which you announce ahead of time that all who take their turns without prompting will receive a bonus star. At all times the good listener should be rewarded by bonus tokens, stars, praise, taking the first turn, and so forth.

FOLLOWING DIRECTIONS

Sample Lesson One

Purpose: To give practice in following directions.
Equipment: Familiar objects, teacher-made picture cards.
Procedure:

1. Spread out on the table six clearly different objects (for example, block, pencil, card, toy, crayon, and paper).
2. To the first child say, "Touch the pencil."
3. Award a token if the direction is followed.
4. To the next child say, "Give me the block," and so on for each child.
5. Vary the instructions so that no two consecutive children have the same task. For example:

   Touch the ________. Follow the ________. Give me the ________. Write with the ________. Put the ________ here. Pick up the ________. Take the ________. Roll the ________. Open the ________. Turn over the ________.

Additional Procedures:

1. Naming Picture Cards.
   - Spread out seven picture cards faceup.
   - Use teacher-made cards with simple drawings of familiar objects and animals.
   - Give instructions, such as:

     Give me a dog. Turn over the bear. Give (name of child) *the flower. Pick up the horse. Point to the fish.*
   - Add more cards, but keep the number under ten.
   - If the children have no difficulty naming the cards, set out fifteen or twenty cards faceup on the table.
   - Say to the first child, "Take away the train." (The child should pick up the train card and put it in front of him or her).
   - When everyone has had three turns, ask one child to put the three cards in the center of the table for everyone to see.
   - Ask the rest of the group to close their eyes while the child takes one card away.
   - Ask the children to open their eyes and to say which card is gone.
   - Ask a second child to set out his or her three cards, and follow the procedure that is outlined above.

2. Two-step directions.
   - If the children can follow one-step directions easily, give them simple two-step directions. Examples:

     Clap your hands, and touch your head. Stand up, and say your name. Walk around the table, and tap (name of child) *on the shoulder. Put your hand up, and touch your other arm.*
   - Spread out seven simple picture cards and vary the directions for consecutive children. Combine two steps for each child. Examples:

     Give me the card, and touch the tree. Take the wagon, and turn over the house.

Sample Lesson Two

Purpose: To give practice in following directions.
Equipment: Familiar objects, chalkboard.

Procedure: Play *Simon Says*.

1. Ask the children to stand side by side, facing you, about ten feet away.
2. Say, "Simon says reach up high," and the children stretch their hands above their heads.
3. If you say "Reach up high," but omit "Simon says," the children should not move.
4. To encourage listening, do not demonstrate the actions.
5. Pick actions that are simple for the children and not physically hazardous. Examples:

   Clap your hands. Hands on head. Hands on hips. Stand on one foot. Hands over face. Reach one hand up.
6. This game could also be played at the table, with the children sitting down. At the table, use actions such as:

   Close your eyes. Touch the table. Pick up a pencil.
7. If the child makes a move when he or she shouldn't, put a tally beside the name on the chalkboard but allow the child to play rather than drop out and wait.
8. The winner is the child with the fewest tallies.

Additional Procedure:

- Spread objects out on the table within reach of all players (for example, envelope, bank, penny, nickel, book, airplane, chair, cup, saucer, boy and girl pictures, pail, car, truck, clock, two blocks).
- The object of the game is to be able to remember a series of instructions and follow them in the correct order.
- Keep a tally beside the child's name on the chalkboard as each player makes a correct response.
- The winner is the child with the most tallies.
- Ask the children to identify each object, and tell them what an object is if no one knows.
- Begin with simple items and, as the players improve, combine two or three items. For example:

  Touch the bank and the airplane.
  Drive the truck around the pail.
  Put one block on top of the other block.
  Touch something that is red.

Make the airplane fly and land.
Give the girl the car and the truck.
Put the cup on the saucer.
Take the money out of the bank, and put it in the pail.
Touch something that is blue.
Put a penny in the bank.
Put a book on the chair.
Give the boy a penny.
Put the blocks on the truck.
Open the book, and tell what it is about.

Sample Lesson Three

Purpose: To give practice in following directions.
Equipment: Familiar objects, blocks, pennies, magic slate or chalkboard.
Procedure:

1. The object of this game is to listen to a series of instructions and to carry them out.
2. Use the materials, objects, and features of the room. Ask a player to bring you a book, a pencil, and a piece of paper.
3. Give similar directions to each player such as:

   Draw something on the paper. Put the paper over near the games. Bring your star card to me.
4. Award tokens for correct responses and a star to the child having the most tokens.
5. Keep the actions simple so that each turn is quite short in time (not necessarily in number of moves).
6. Begin with a single instruction, and increase the complexity gradually.

Additional Procedures:

1. Play *Jump and Stop*.
   - The children stand side by side, in a line, facing the teacher.
   - While the teacher says "Jump, jump, jump," the children move forward, feet together, in little jumps. (Demonstrate this, and have each child practice once.)
   - When the teacher says "stop," anyone who continues to jump must go back to the starting line and start over.
   - Try to trick the children so that they will have to listen carefully. For example, give a long series of jumps followed by a stop, then alternate jump and stop.
   - Watch carefully, and send back anyone who makes the wrong move.
2. Play *Giant, Child, Dwarf*.
   - Start with the children standing in a row, side by side, in front of you.
   - Explain that a giant is big and a dwarf is small.
   - When you say "Giant," the children must reach up as high as they can with both hands.
   - When you say "Child," they should stand the way a child stands, with hands at their sides.
   - When you say "Dwarf," they crouch down (stooping, not kneeling).
   - Write the children's names on the magic slate or chalkboard. Anyone who makes a false move receives a tally mark on the slate, and the winner is the child with the fewest tallies.
   - Keep the play brisk, and try to trick the players.
3. Following Two Directions.
   - Start at the table using blocks and pennies.
   - Give two instructions that require the child to leave the table.
   - Move on to three instructions, and if the children are proficient, increase to four.
   - Only one part of any series of instructions should involve bringing anything to the table.
   - The child should have to do something, such as make a mark on the chalkboard, open a door, move a chalkboard eraser, as part of each series. To make use of the route to an object, ask the child to go around or touch a chair, or sit on a chair, on the way.

Sample Lesson Four

Purpose: To give practice in following directions.
Equipment: Picture cards, blocks, paper cups, empty box, edible prizes.
Procedure:

1. Conduct a contest to test children's ability to listen and carry out directions.
2. Award edible prizes, and try to make the period a festive one.

3. Place cards out on the table facedown.
4. Each child tries to collect as many cards as possible of a specified number or picture.
5. When the teacher says a signal word, all children pick up cards together.
6. Encourage the children to return incorrect cards facedown to slow down opponents.
7. Explain the game once, and allow no questions.
8. Children can discard one of the blocks every time they find a block of a specific color. For example, one child might receive six red blocks, and he or she needs to discard the red blocks for yellow ones. (Assign each child a different pair of colors.)
9. The blocks on the table are hidden under paper cups, and often there are two different colors under one cup.
10. Children should take only what they need and leave other colors.
11. Provide a discard box; children must discard in pairs, one from their piles and one that they found.
12. If the children find the first game difficult, simplify the second game.

WORD SERIES RETENTION

Sample Lesson One

Purpose: To give practice in repeating one-syllable words.
Equipment: Tokens.
Procedure:

1. Place a pile of tokens in front of you.
2. Tell the group that children who say exactly what you say will get a token.
3. The child with the most tokens wins a star.
4. Choose common one-syllable words. Say the word clearly but with no undue emphasis; that is, say it in conversational tone.

One-Syllable Words

air	back	band
all	bag	bank
ant	bake	barn
arm	ball	bat

bath	curl	glove
beans	dance	glue
bear	dark	good
bed	day	grass
bee	deer	guess
beef	desk	gum
bell	dime	gun
bib	dish	ham
big	doll	hat
bird	door	head
boat	down	heat
book	dress	hen
box	drink	hill
bread	drop	hole
breeze	drum	home
bridge	duck	horse
broom	dust	hose
bug	ear	house
bunch	earth	hum
bus	egg	jam
bush	eye	joke
buy	face	key
cap	fall	kick
car	fan	king
cat	farm	knee
chair	fast	knock
chalk	fat	laugh
cheek	fence	leaf
cheer	fight	leg
cheese	fire	lid
chin	fish	light
clap	fist	luck
class	flag	lunch
clay	floor	man
clouds	food	milk
clown	fork	moon
club	fox	mouse
coat	friend	mouth
comb	frog	mud
corn	frown	nail
cough	fun	name
cow	game	neck
crack	gas	nest
cream	gate	night
crust	girl	noise
curb	glass	note

nurse
nuts
one
page
pail
paint
pan
pane
park
paste
path
pay
peach
pen
pet
pie
pig
pin
play
pool
pot
print
prize
purse
race
rag
rain
rake
ring
road
roar
rock
roof
room
rope
salt
saw
school
seat
shade
shape
sheep
shelf
shirt
shoe
shout
sing
sit
sleeve
smoke
snake
sneeze
soap
socks
song
sound
splash
spoon
spot
spring
square
stairs
star
strip
team
town
walk
wind
witch
word
work
yard
zoo

Sample Lesson Two

Purpose: To give practice in repeating one-, two-, and three-syllable words.
Equipment: Tokens.
Procedure: Play *Pass the Word Around.*

1. Give each child in the group five tokens.
2. The children's task is to earn ten tokens each before the end of the session. If they succeed, each child will get a star on his or her card.
3. Turn to the child on your left. Say one one-syllable word, making no attempt to keep the rest of the group from hearing.
4. The child must pass the word on to the next child and so on around the group back to you.
5. If the word reaches you in its correct form (for example, *dog,* not *dogs* or *doggie*), each child gets a token. If not, each child loses a token.
6. *If* the children can manage one-syllable words, go on to two syllables.
7. Use three-syllable words when two-syllable words have been mastered.

Two-Syllable Words

again
angry
answer
apple
apron
baby
bacon
balance
bandage
barber
baseball
basket
bigger
birthday
biscuit
blanket
bluejay
bookcase
bother
bottle
bottom
boxes
bracelet
breakfast
brother
bubble
building
bunny
busy
butter
button
cabbage
cabin
candle
candy
careful
carpet
carrot
cartoon
castle
catcher
ceiling
cement
center
cherry
chicken
children
circle
circus
city
coffee
collar
color
comics
contest
cookie
corner
costume
cousin
cover
cowboy
cracker
crayon
cupboard
curtain
cushion
daisy
dancer
danger
darkness
dentist
dessert
dial
dinner
dishes
distance
doctor
dollar
donkey
doughnut
dragon
elbow
engine
evening
farmer
father
feather
fender
finger
finish
flashlight
flower
follow
football
forehead
forest
fountain
gallop
garage
garbage
garden
giant
giraffe
grapefruit
guitar
hammer
happy
honey
hopping
inside
island
jacket
jelly
jungle
kitchen
kitten
ladder
laughter
lesson
letter
lion
lizard
magic
manners
measure
message
minute
mirror
mischief
mistake
money
monkey
morning
mother
motor

mountain	pilot	rubbers
movie	pizza	ruler
music	plumber	sailor
necklace	pocket	salad
needle	pony	sandwich
nickel	poodle	scissors
notice	popcorn	secret
number	postman	shadow
orange	practice	shoelace
orchard	present	shoulder
outside	princess	signal
oven	problem	siren
paper	promise	sister
partner	pumpkin	spider
party	puppy	squirrel
peanut	puzzle	teacher
pencil	question	turkey
people	rabbit	uncle
pepper	reason	wagon
person	recess	waitress
picnic	reindeer	window
picture	ribbon	winter
pillow	robin	zigzag

Three-Syllable Words

accident	envelope	messenger
acrobat	example	newspaper
animal	excitement	pajamas
attention	exercise	passenger
avenue	family	patio
banana	furniture	photograph
barbecue	hamburger	pineapple
bicycle	handkerchief	policeman
bumblebee	happiness	potato
butterfly	holiday	prettiest
calendar	hospital	property
cereal	idea	radio
company	Indian	raspberry
customer	janitor	restaurant
daffodil	ladybug	strawberry
direction	lemonade	somersault
eleven	library	tricycle
enemy	magazine	umbrella
elephant	medicine	visitor

Sample Lesson Three

Purpose: To give practice in following a series of color signals.
Equipment: Teacher-made color cards, pennies.
Procedure: Play *Signals Game.*

1. Make twelve cards, four each with red, blue, and yellow dots on them.
2. Place cards faceup in the center of the table.
3. Give each child in the group five pennies.

   The teacher says,

   Let's play a signals game. Signals tell you what to do. What does this signal tell you to do? [Put finger over mouth for quiet.] *What does this signal tell you to do?* [Stretch out arm, and point finger.] *I'll say some color signals, like "blue, red, red." You listen and pick up the right colors and put them in the right order, like this.* [Pick up a blue card and two red cards, and put them in order in front of the first child.] *If you follow the signal correctly, you earn a penny. If you don't follow the signal correctly, you give me a penny. Whoever has the most pennies wins.*

Additional Procedures: Whenever this game is played, play only one or two of the variations. For the more able children, use a longer series.

1. Signals Race. Put out more cards, and have a race with all children picking out cards at the same time.
2. Child-Directed Series.
   - Ask Child A to say the series for Child B, then B for C, and so on.
   - If Child B can't arrange the series, Child A should arrange it and receive a penny if it is correct.
   - Each child should be able to produce the instruction for the next child and to remember what the instructions were.
3. Finding Colors.
   - Place three of each color (nine cards) facedown in a block in the center of the table.
   - Announce the color that the children must find.
   - Give each child a turn to pick up one card, show it to the group, and replace it if it is wrong or keep it if it is the right color.
   - The winner is the child who has the most

correct cards. Encourage children to remember the cards that others have picked up and replaced.

4. Finding the Color. Use only one card of one color and all the rest in the remaining colors. Proceed as in the procedure above.
5. Second Signals Game.
   - Give one child four yellow cards and one blue card; another child four red cards and one blue card; another four blue cards and one yellow card.
   - Children place their cards faceup in front of them.
   - The teacher says, "red, red, blue," and anyone with one or more of these colors puts them one at a time in the center of the table until the sequence is complete.
   - The child with four red cards and one blue may be very quick to put a red, a red, and a blue in the center, one at a time. But any child may add one or more cards to the series at any time.
   - The winner is the first child to have placed all his or her cards in the center of the table.
6. Color Series.
   - Give children six cards: two red, two blue, and two yellow.
   - Ask them to place their cards in a row six inches from the edge of the table.
   - Say the colors, for example, "blue, red, yellow."
   - The winner is the first child to pick up the right cards and place them in the correct order.

Sample Lesson Four

Purpose: To give practice in following a series of color signals.
Equipment: Teacher-made color cards.
Procedure: Play *Color Game.*

1. Spread cards with several colors faceup in a block on the table within reach of all players.
2. Point to the colors, and make certain all players know the colors. Take out any color that causes difficulty.
3. Name two, three, four, or five colors, depending on the players' ability.
4. Ask all players to pick up the named cards, place them facedown, and raise their hands.
5. The winner is the child with the correct cards in the correct order who raised his or her hand first.

Additional Procedures:

1. Say a sentence with one or two card colors in it. Children all play at the same time. The winner is the one who says the color name and picks out the color card first.
2. Use the same procedure as above except leave out the color word. For example, "I ate a ________ apple." The winner is the child who says "Red" (or "Green") and picks out the red (or green) card first.
3. Say a sentence with one or more color words in it. Players take turns one at a time. The player repeats the sentence and, if correct, picks up and keeps the color card. The winner is the one with the most cards.

Sample Lesson Five

Purpose: To give practice in remembering months and days of the week.
Equipment: Cards listing days of the week.
Procedure:

1. Ask the first child to give the name of the first month of the year (January), the next child the next month, and so on until someone is unable to answer.
2. Supply the answer and ask the child to say it.
3. Then the group begins again with January to see if they can get past the month that stopped them on the first round.
4. Repeat this several times, starting with different children but always going around in a clockwise direction.

Additional Procedure: Days of the Week.

- Starting with Sunday, teach the days of the week by asking each child to say one day.
- Go around the group several times so that each child has to say a different day on each turn.
- Give each child a card with the days on them.
- Read the days, pointing to each one as you do so.

- Giving each child one turn, ask the following questions:

  What day is it today?

  What day will it be tomorrow?

  How many days is it until Saturday?

  What is another name for Saturday and Sunday?

  Two days ago I went to the library. What day was that?

  In three days it will be ________.

  In two days it will be ________.

  What day comes after Saturday?

  What day is tomorrow?

  What day comes before Saturday?

Sample Lesson Six

Purpose: To give practice in remembering a list of objects.
Procedure: Play *Shopping.*

1. Talk about going to the store and remembering what to buy.
2. Ask the children how they remember when they don't have a list (define *list*).
3. Tell the children that you are going to send each of them to the store and that they will each get something nice (a small, wrapped edible) when they come back if they remember what it was they were to get.
4. Send them off one at a time to some designated place in the room.
5. Use common words, and assign three purchases to each child, such as, *soap, spinach, milk; apples, oranges, cookies; bread, beans, meat;* and *jam, jelly, cereal.*
6. Tell one child a list and send him or her off, then tell the next one.
7. When each child returns, ask him or her to repeat the three purchases.
8. Award the small, wrapped treat.

NUMBER SERIES RETENTION

Sample Lesson One

Purpose: To give practice in listening for and identifying numbers.
Equipment: Pennies.
Procedure:

1. Say to the children,

   Often people have to remember numbers. You have to remember your telephone number. What other numbers do you have to remember? We're going to play a number game. I'll say some sentences with numbers in them, and when it's your turn, you say the numbers. For example, "It is nine o'clock." What is the number in that sentence? Nine. If you can say the number correctly, you get a penny. Whoever gets the most pennies wins.

2. Use these sentences:

   Tom is eight years old.

   Betty lives at twenty-four Oak Drive.

   Jack's big brother is seventeen.

   There were thirty-one birds in the garden.

   Mary's mother said she needed six eggs so that she could bake a cake.

   There were ten candles on the cake.

   The bell rang three times.

   Bill has two dogs.

   Ninety-eight children were in the park.

   The temperature was only ten degrees.

   Tom saved thirty-four cents.

   Jane needed two new tires for her bicycle.

Sample Lesson Two

Purpose: To give practice in remembering number series.
Equipment: Teacher-made number cards (1–5), checkers.
Procedure: Play *Number Game.*

1. Give each player two sets of teacher-made number cards 1 to 5. Ask each player to place them on the table, faceup, in a row and to identify each number.
2. If the players know all or almost all of the numbers, leave all of them on the table.
3. If a player knows very few numbers, leave the known numbers on the table, and add one number that he or she does not know.
4. Ask each child to take a turn for several rounds.
5. Call out one, two, or three numbers (depending on the child's skill).

6. Players pick up the numbers called and place them in the correct order in front of them on the edge of the table.
7. Children must wait until you have finished calling the numbers before they start to pick them up.
8. As soon as they are finished, they put their hands on their knees.
9. When the children understand this routine, play the game as a race. The winner is the first one who has picked out the correct cards, put them in the correct order, and placed hands on knees.
10. The winner of each round receives a checker, and the player with the most checkers receives a star.

Additional Procedures:

1. Play *Lucky Numbers.*
   - Place all the number cards faceup in the center of the table.
   - Tell the group that *2* will be the lucky number. When they hear a *2,* they pick up a card with a *2* on it.
   - For those having difficulty, begin with a two-number series (such as, 2,4; 1,3; 5,2).
   - If children pick a card when they have not heard the lucky number, they lose one of the cards they already have.
   - The winner is the player with the most cards.
   - Change the lucky number frequently.
2. Play *Listening for the Numbers Words.*
   - Use each child's address as one of the sentences.
   - Include it among the following:

     I catch the school bus at eight o'clock. Bob's bicycle went twenty miles an hour down the steep hill. Mary was fifteen minutes late. On Saturday, Bill is going to a parade at nine o'clock. Bob only needed twenty cents more to buy the bell for his bicycle. At least one hundred people came to watch the circus parade. Betty could jump rope eight times without stepping on the rope. The movie started at seven thirty.

Sample Lesson Three

Purpose: To give practice in remembering number series.
Equipment: Teacher-made number cards and cardboard phone dials.
Procedure: Play *Cue Word.*

1. Give each child number cards 1 to 5.
2. Say the sentence, "I have five new books."
3. *All* the children pick up the number, say it, receive tokens, and then put the number down.
4. Sample sentences:

   My puppy is three months old. For lunch I have one apple and two cookies. He lives at 124 Green Street. At three o'clock I'm going out to play. She picked four flowers, and gave one to Betty. That program is on TV at two o'clock. One dog had two bones. We counted one, two, three. Bob clapped three times.

Additional Procedure: Play *Phone Dialing.*

- Give each child a teacher-made cardboard phone dial and a card with his or her telephone number printed on it.
- If children have no phone, give them a card with a friend's phone number (someone whom they might like to phone).
- Explain that everyone should know how to telephone and that later you will have a telephone for them to practice on.
- Ask the first child to read the first three numbers from the card.
- Demonstrate the correct dialing procedure; then ask the child to practice dialing on the phone dial.
- Watch children carefully to make certain they copy your finger movements exactly.
- Give each child a turn, making certain that the correct dialing procedure is followed, including lifting the finger off the dial before putting it onto the next number.

SENTENCE RETENTION

Sample Lesson One

Purpose: To give practice in repeating sentences.
Equipment: Teacher-made picture cards.
Procedure:

1. Provide tokens.
2. Set out six teacher-made picture cards faceup,

each showing one simple object (for example, car, apple, flower, boy, girl, dog, cat, house, wagon, and ball).

3. Place one card in front of the child whose turn it is, and say, "See the car."
4. Ask the child to repeat the sentence after you to receive one token.
5. Return the card to the center of the table.
6. Choose a different card, set it in front of the next child, and say, "See the dog."
7. Continue until everyone has had two turns.

Sample Lesson Two

Purpose: To give practice in remembering phrases and sentences.
Equipment: Tally sheet and pencil.
Procedure:

1. Keep a tally beside each child's name on a piece of paper.
2. Say a sentence. If children can repeat it exactly, place a tally mark beside their names.
3. For those having difficulty, begin with two words and build up to a complete sentence over a number of sessions. For example:

brown dog	play games
big house	go home
blue sky	I see Tom.
three bicycles	Mary likes ice cream.
lunch time	Bob likes swimming.
recess	It is raining.

4. For those having no difficulty, warm up with a round of two words, then move on to sentences about the class and school.

   This is __________ School.
   My room is number __________.
   We go swimming after school.
   In the morning we play games.

Additional Procedure: Play *Send a Message.*

- Practice whispering first.
- Explain that you are going to whisper something to the first player, who will then whisper the same thing to the next player, and so on back to you.
- If the message gets back to you correctly, each player wins a token.
- When the children understand, let one of them be the first one to send a message. Sometimes use an instruction as the message (for example, "Go to the window").
- If the last child can follow the instruction correctly, each child receives a token.

Sample Lesson Three

Purpose: To give practice in remembering addresses.
Equipment: Tokens.
Procedure:

1. Say to the children, "Everyone has an address. An address tells where you live. An address tells the number and street your house is on. Do you know your address?"
2. Wait very briefly for answers, then say, "We are going to learn our addresses." Give the first child's address.
3. Ask the child to repeat it once; then go on to the next child.
4. Play two rounds where you say the house number and street and the child repeats it.
5. Say, "Let's play a game. I'll say somebody's address, and whoever lives there says, 'I live at [number, street],' then receives a token. Whoever gets the most tokens wins."
6. Give one child's address as an example, and ask the child to make the correct response before the game begins.
7. Play several rounds.

Additional Procedure: Play *Gossip.*

- Talk about the importance of being able to repeat verbal comments and messages accurately.
- To demonstrate how a message gets changed as it is passed from one person to another, ask the children to pass a whispered message from one to another.
- The teacher may start the message by whispering to the child on the left.
- The last child tells the group what he or she hears, and the teacher repeats the original message, which is usually quite different.
- After you have played, discuss people who mix up messages because they are excited at times of crisis, such as a fire. Point out the importance of accuracy at such a time.

SELECTING AND SUPPLYING WORDS

Sample Lesson One

Purpose: To give practice in supplying words.
Equipment: Familiar objects.
Procedure: Play *Missing Words.*

1. Place on the table six small objects (for example, toy car, bank, doll, box, airplane, and crayon).
2. Tell the group that you are going to pick up something, and you want the child whose turn it is to tell you what you have.
3. Pick up the crayon, and say, "I have a __________" (the child fills in the blank).
4. Replace the crayon, and pick up another object. Say, "I have a __________" (the next child fills in the blank).

Additional Procedure: Play *Help Me Tell a Story.*

- Tell a short, simple story and interrupt the story by asking questions that the group must answer before the story can go on.
- The questions must be very simple.
- When you get to a question, point to a child.
- Give help in answering if necessary. Example:

  Farmer Brown was going to market in his truck. There was a lot of noise in the truck. A farmer in another truck behind him asked, "What kind of animal is that in your truck?" Farmer Brown laughed and said, "That is a __________." [Point to a child and ask, "What kind of animal shall we have it be?" The child names a farm animal, such as a pig.]

  "What is his name?" asked the other farmer. "His name is __________ [point for his name]," said Farmer Brown.

  "Why is he making all that noise?"

  "He doesn't want to go to market to be sold to someone else."

  Just then the [name of animal] kicked his way out of the truck, ran into the field, and hid behind a __________. [Point.]

  Along came a police officer who said, "What is that [name of animal] doing hiding behind that __________?" [Point and ask what Farmer Brown should tell the police officer.]

End the story with the pig, or other farm animal, coming out only if the farmer promises to let him stay instead of going to market.

Sample Lesson Two

Purpose: To give practice in supplying words.
Equipment: Tokens.
Procedure: Play *Guess What I Saw?*

1. Turn to the child on your left, and ask, "Guess what I saw at the zoo?"
2. Accept and praise whatever animal the child names.
3. Say, "Yes, I saw a bear at the zoo." If the next child names a lion, say, "Yes I saw a lion and a bear at the zoo."
4. Repeat with the third child, and add the animal to your sentence.
5. When each child has had a turn, say to the group, "What did I see at the zoo?"
6. Children receive as many tokens as animals they name. If the children name four animals, give each child four tokens.
7. Occasionally pretend that you have forgotten one of the animals, and ask the children to help you remember.

Additional procedure: Play *Missing Words.*

- Make up simple sentences about things, people, or activities in the classroom or school.
- Say the sentence, leaving a blank.
- As children take turns, give tokens if they can fill in the blank correctly.
- Examples:

  We are sitting at the __________. *We sit on* __________. *There are* __________ *chairs.* [If possible, ask one child to count and point while counting. Otherwise count out loud, and point as you do. Then say the sentence again so the child whose turn it is can fill in the number you have counted.] *I see* __________ [point to a child]. *We go out to play at* __________ *(recess or lunch). The teacher's name is* __________. (Name of child) *is wearing a* __________. *I can see out the* __________. *The name of our school is* __________. *Our room number is* __________. (Name of child) *can catch a* __________. *The sky is* __________.

Sample Lesson Three

Purpose: To give practice in supplying words.
Equipment: Tokens, tally sheet, pencil.
Procedure: Play *Guess What I Found?*

1. Use tokens; the game ends when the children have ten tokens. Say to the children, "Last night before I went to bed I heard a noise at the door. I went to the door and opened it, and guess what I found?"
2. Ask the children to guess.
3. Arbitrarily select one simple answer as the correct answer, for example, two dollars.
4. Say to the children, "Let's pass it around and see it if will come back to me."
5. Lean over to the child on your left and say, "I found two dollars. Pass it around."
6. Help if necessary to pass it on. If it gets back to you intact, give each child two tokens.
7. Once the children see that an answer including two of something leads to two tokens, they will give answers that include numbers of objects.
8. Award tokens only for responses up to *three.*
9. Keep this game fast and funny.
10. If children are capable of starting (that is, "Guess what I found?"), let them. (The answer must get back to the starter.)

Additional Procedure: Play *Fill in the Blank.*

- The children will listen to a sentence with one or more words omitted and fill in each blank with an appropriate word.
- Tell the children to listen to the whole sentence before giving the missing word.
- Keep a tally beside each child's name on a piece of paper. Ask the first child for the missing word, and award a tally mark for a correct answer.
- If Child A cannot answer but Child B can, then Child B should receive two tally marks.
- Vary the game by allowing children who know the answer to raise their hands.

Mary went to a birthday __________.

The party was lots of fun, and there was a birthday __________ with candles on it.

The children waited on the corner for the school __________ to come to take them to school.

The boys were riding their __________.

They were going to the park to fly their __________.

Tom's mother made him a peanut butter and __________ sandwich.

Bob had a piece of chocolate __________ for dessert.

One day when Jan was going to the store, she saw a car crash into another ______.

There was a loud __________, and both cars stopped.

Sample Lesson Four

Purpose: To give practice in selecting words.
Equipment: Colored cups, pennies.
Procedure: Play *Listening for a Cue Word.*

1. Ask the children to listen for the color word in each sentence.
2. Sample sentences:

   John wore a new red sweater. Jan got mud on her brown shoes. The house was painted white. The red fire engine went racing by. Bill's kite was a beautiful blue. Mary hit her head on the door and got a black eye. John had a yellow banana for lunch. The flowers in the garden were pink. Jane's shirt was yellow. Jack had on a brown cowboy hat.

3. Listen for the food word:

   Bob had a piece of birthday cake in his lunch. Ann had cookies after school. There were three apples on the tree. At the movie Jean ate popcorn. Bob went to the store to buy some bread for his mother. Betty likes to drink milk. Jill dropped the eggs, and they all broke. Tom bought some carrots for his rabbit. Mr. Brown left the butter in the sun, and it melted. Jean said, "I'd like chocolate ice cream, please."

Additional Procedures:

1. Play *Lucky Colors.*
   - Explain that in this game the colors *blue* and *green* will be the lucky colors. (In later games, vary the colors.)
   - Place some cups of four different colors on the table with a penny under each of the blue and green cups.
   - Say to the first child, "Pink, yellow, blue."
   - After hearing *blue,* the child picks up one blue cup and receives the penny. (The cup is then put to one side.)

- If the blue cup isn't picked up, the next player may pick it up if he or she remembers the color series without having it repeated.
- Sometimes omit the lucky colors; a player who then picks up a cup loses a penny.
- Keep play brisk. Move on to the next child if some children aren't listening when it is their turn.
- The winner is the one with the most pennies.
- For those having difficulty, begin with one lucky color and a simple series.

2. Fill in the Blanks.
   - In the following sentences there are many acceptable answers.
   - Ask the children to fill in the blanks.

   We read about a circus. There were pictures of elephants, ________, and ________. There was a clown who rode a ________ and had a funny face and a funny ________ on his head. There were red balloons, ________ balloons, and ________ balloons. We had ________ and ________ to eat, and then we had some ________ to drink.

   Bob saved up twenty-five ________ to buy a present for his brother's ________. His brother was going to be eight ________ old. He was going to have a ________ and invite eight ________ to it.

   We go to ________ School. We are in the ________ grade. There are ________ children in our class. There are ________ boys and ________ girls.

Sample Lesson Five

Purpose: To give practice in selecting words.
Equipment: Pennies, tokens.
Procedure: Play *Listening for a Day of the Week.*

1. Children must repeat the day mentioned.
2. Use pennies as tokens for correct answers.
3. Sample sentences:

   Bob went to bed very late on Tuesday night. Mary did not go to school on Monday because she had a bad cold. Friday Fun and Games is lots of fun. Tom gets his allowance every Saturday. Next Friday Jan is going to be in a bicycle race, and she thinks she can win it. Anne's birthday is next Thursday, and she is having a cowboy party. Last Saturday we took the train into the city and we went to the zoo.

Additional Procedure: Play *Listen for This Word.*

- Say a word, and use the word in a sentence or word series.
- The children must signify with a token when they hear the word again.
- Begin with sentences because it is often easier to pick out a word from a meaningful word string than it is from a word series.
- Say, "The word is *yellow.* Listen and see if you hear *yellow* in what I say next. [Pause.] I live in a green house. [Pause.] Did you hear the word that you were listening for?"
- As soon as the children understand the procedure, eliminate as much of the preliminary instructions as possible. Say only, "The word is *rich.*"
- Pause for two seconds, then say, "The king was very rich."
- Then wait two seconds. If no one raises a hand, tell them to listen again.
- Repeat the entire set of instructions, starting with "The word is *rich.*"

Sample Lesson Six

Purpose: To give practice in selecting and supplying words.
Equipment: Stopwatch.
Procedure: Play *Listening for the Cue Word.*

1. Begin with several quick rounds in which the children listen for a *color* word.
2. Sample sentences:

   The big old house was painted brown. Jean's brown pants were too short. The garden looked pretty because the yellow roses were in flower. The black and white puppy was four months old. Mary has dark brown hair and brown eyes. The green leaves were beginning to grow in the garden. Pat had new white sneakers. Mike saw red, orange, and yellow in the rainbow. Tom could easily jump over the white fence.

3. Tell the group to listen for words that mean something that someone *rides* on:

   The truck went speeding down the street. The police officer hopped on his motorcycle and rode away. An airplane landed at the airport. Anne's new bicycle is a beautiful shade of blue. [Point out to the group that one color has many different shades. If possible, use as an example the children's clothes or some other things easily seen in the room. Try to get across the idea that the shades are all called by one color name, for example, blue.] *The helicopter made a lot of noise. Sally's little sister was asleep in her stroller. The car stopped at the corner. Mike fell off his skateboard, but he didn't hurt himself.* [Make certain everyone recognizes a skateboard.] *The people waited in the station for the train to come. The bus was late, and everyone was angry.*

4. Ask the children to think of all the things to ride on that they can.

Elicit the things in the sentences above as well as new suggestions.

Additional Procedure: Play *Sounds of People.*

- The teacher uses terms associated with some profession, occupation, or activity. The group's task is to identify the profession, for example, as quickly as possible.
- Keep a record of the times required for accurate identification, and encourage the children to try to beat their own record.
- Some items can be very easy, such as, "Come right in and sit here. Open your mouth. [Note that this could be a doctor or a dentist.] Which tooth is it?"
- Others might be more difficult, such as, "All right, you can bring him in now. Put him on the table where I can see him. Where is the cut? Maybe it needs stitches. Too bad—it's her front *paw.*"
- Encourage the children to listen for definite clues.

STORY COMPREHENSION

Sample Lesson One

Purpose: To give practice in sentence comprehension.
Equipment: Tokens.
Procedure:

1. Say a sentence, and ask the child whose turn it is the question.
2. For a one-word answer, the child wins a token.
3. The child with the most tokens wins a star.

Betty's new party dress is pink. What color is her dress?
Tom is six years old. How old is Tom?
We ate chocolate cake. What did we eat?
Bob has a new bicycle. What does Bob have?
We saw a fire. What did we see?
I like doughnuts. What do I like?
Bill watched TV. What did Bill watch?
Mary can swim. What can Mary do?
Jean likes flowers. What does Jean like?
The girls shouted. What did the girls do?
We had a picnic. What did we have?
I lost my sweater. What did I lose?
Bob ate a cookie. What did Bob eat?
Mary has one brother. What does Mary have?
Joan spent ten cents. How much did Joan spend?

4. Begin to use single sentences that form a cluster, that is, that are about one topic:

We had a picnic. What did we have?
We ate hamburgers. What did we eat?
Tom ate a hot dog. What did Tom eat?
We went swimming. What did we do?
Ann was the best swimmer. Who was the best swimmer?
Tom and Jean had a race. What did Tom and Jean do?
Jean won the race. Who won the race?
Mary spilled her pop. What did Mary spill?
Jim found some flowers. What did Jim find?
We sang songs. What did we sing?

Additional Procedure:

- When children readily answer single questions about single topics, combine two sentences, and ask one question about one part of the sentence.
- Example: We had a picnic, and we ate hamburgers. What did we eat?
- Combine sentences from the previous procedure (sentences about a picnic).

We went to the grocery store and bought some milk. What did we buy?
Tom had saved ten cents, so he bought some penny candy. What did Tom buy?
Mary wanted to buy a balloon, but she didn't have any money. What did Mary want to buy?

Bob found a nickel on the floor. What did Bob find?

He decided to save it instead of buying something. What did Bob do with his nickel?

Ann is saving for a bicycle. What is Ann saving for?

When the children got home, their father gave them each a cookie. What did their father give them?

- If the children find a two-part sentence too difficult, return to a simple one-part sentence for every question by breaking up each of the following sentences into two sentences.

Bob was very excited because he was going to visit his aunt. Why was Bob excited?

She lived far away, and Bob was going on the train. What was Bob going on?

He was going by himself; his mother and father stayed home because they had to work. Why did his mother and father have to stay home?

His mother and father went to the station to see him off. Where did they all go?

Bob had his train ticket and a small suitcase. What did Bob have?

He had his pajamas, toothbrush, and play clothes in his suitcase. Can you tell me something that he had in his suitcase?

Sample Lesson Two

Purpose: To give practice in story comprehension.
Equipment: Tally sheet, pencil.
Procedure:

1. Keep a tally beside each child's name on a piece of paper.
2. Read the story below as though you are telling it.
3. Ask the first child the question, and award a tally mark for a correct answer.
4. If Child A cannot answer, but Child B can, then Child B should receive two tally marks.
5. You probably will be able to play several rounds by making up additional simple sentence stories. But stop before the children lose interest, particularly if they also find the task a little difficult.
6. Say something like this:

Put your hands on your knees like this and listen. We're going to play a story game. I'll read a story and ask you a question about it. If you can answer the question, you receive a tally mark. If you can't answer the question, maybe (next child) *can. If* (next child) *is right,* (next child) *receives two tally marks. Whoever has the most tally marks when the game is finished wins a star.* (Name of child) *can have the first turn,* (next child) *will be next, and then* (next child) [point and name each child, and make a circular movement with your arm].

Tom has a new red bicycle. What does Tom have?

Betty is going to the circus. Where is Betty going?

Jack likes playing after school. Who likes playing after school.

Next Sunday we are going on a picnic. Where are we going next Sunday?

My dog is brown and white, and her name is Tiger. What is my dog's name?

I like playing on the swings in the park. What do I like to do in the park?

We ate candy and popcorn at the movie. What did we eat at the movie?

John saw a parade with his mom and dad and little sister. What did John see?

Bob is saving up to buy a bicycle and he has $8.00 so far. How much has Bob saved?

Yesterday, Mary and Betty saw the fire engine go by. What did Mary and Betty see?

Sample Lesson Three

Purpose: To give practice in story comprehension.
Procedure: Read the stories below and follow with questions indicated.

Tom wanted a train for his birthday. He was a very good boy and his dad and mom gave him one. His sister gave him a flashlight that flashed a red or blue or green light.

1. Ask:

Whose birthday was it? What did mom and dad give Tom for his birthday? What was the flashlight like?

Mary was saving up to buy a new baseball glove. She saved and saved and finally had enough money to buy the glove. When she played baseball, she was very good at catching, and her team won a lot of games.

2. Ask:

   What skill did Mary have? What did she save for?

   Dave's bicycle was very muddy. He said, "I think I'll get a rag and some soap and the hose, and wash my bicycle." He put soap on his bicycle with the rag, and then he hosed it off. When he was finished, his bicycle looked like a new one. His mother said, "What a good bicycle washer you are."

3. Ask:

   Why did Dave wash his bicycle? What did he use to wash it? How did the bicycle look when he was finished?

   One rainy day Pat and Joy put on their rubber boots and raincoats and went out to play. They each had a small boat made of little pieces of wood. The rainwater was running down the side of the street (the gutter). Pat and Joy decided to race their boats in the gutter. Pat put one stone in the gutter to mark the starting point and a second stone farther along the street to mark the finish line. Then the girls put their boats in the water. Joy's boat won the first race.

4. Ask:

   What kind of day was it? What did the girls wear? What did they have to play with? Where did they race their boats? Who won the first race?

Sample Lesson Four

Purpose: To give practice in story comprehension.
Procedure: Four Children. Read the description below of each child's behavior. Then ask the questions, and ask the children to support their answers with a reason.

A girl walking along dropped three dimes but did not notice that she had dropped them. Tom saw her drop them but ran right by because he was late. Bill saw her drop them and picked up the dimes and kept them. Jack saw her and told the girl she had dropped her money. Mary saw her and picked them up because she needed three more dimes to buy the kite she wanted.

1. Ask:

   Which child was honest? Why? What are some other things to do that are honest? Which children were not honest? We call them dishonest. Dishonest is the opposite of honest.

   Some little boys were playing in the park while Mary and her friends were playing ball. One of the little boys fell off the swing and hurt himself and started to cry. Pat went on playing ball. Sandra yelled at the boy to stop making so much noise. Betty said, "Babies shouldn't be on the swings." Mary went over and helped the little boy.

2. Ask:

   Which child was kind? Why? What are some other things to do that are kind?

Sample Lesson Five

Purpose: To give practice in story comprehension.
Procedure: Read the story and ask the questions that follow.

Bill's big brother Jack was very good at playing games and could do a lot of things that Bill couldn't do yet. One day their uncle brought them each a bicycle. Bill got on his bicycle, rode a very short way, and fell off. He got on and fell off again.

Jack laughed and laughed and said, "Anyone can ride a bicycle. All you have to do is sit on it and pedal."

Then Jack got on his bicycle, but he didn't even get as far as Bill did before he fell off. Jack tried again and fell off again.

Then Bill said to Jack, "You hold the back of my bicycle while I ride it and see if I can keep my balance. Then I'll hold your bicycle for you." Bill's idea was a good one, because the boys learned to ride their bicycles and didn't fall off anymore.

Even boys who are very good at playing games fall a few times when they first start learning to ride a bicycle.

1. Ask:

   What were the boys' names? Which boy was particularly good at games? What did their uncle bring them? Could Bill ride right away? What did Jack do when Bill kept falling off? Then what happened to Jack when he tried to ride his bicycle? What was Bill's idea? Did Bill's idea work? Can anyone here ride a bicycle? How did you first learn?

Sample Lesson Six

Purpose: To give practice in story comprehension.
Procedure: Read the story, and then ask why the story character couldn't do what she wanted to do.

> Ann wanted to burn all the old paper in her backyard, but her mother wouldn't let her. She said, "It's too dangerous. You might set the house on fire. Wait until later; then we can burn the paper together."

Make up stories using the following situations: (a) Bobby wanted to catch up to his friend, but the safety patrol wouldn't let him cross the street because the light was red; (b) Joanie wanted to go out in a T-shirt and shorts, but her mother said that it was too cold; (c) Billy wanted to give all his friends Christmas presents, but he didn't have enough money; (d) Barbara wanted to go swimming, but her father said it was too soon after lunch.

RHYMING

Sample Lesson One

Purpose: To give practice in identifying rhymes.
Procedure:

1. You may want to refer to Rhyming, p. 15.
2. Ask the children to listen for and say the words that rhyme in these sentences:

   I see the bee. The mouse is in the little house. Airplanes fly up in the sky. Betty has one blue shoe. Tom took the book home. For twenty-five cents we can buy three red tents. Bob ate a chocolate bar in the car. Joan sat on the chair and brushed her hair. Mary will make a chocolate cake. The dogs jumped right over the logs. That is the same game we played yesterday. Rats do not like cats.

Sample Lesson Two

Purpose: To give practice in rhyming.
Equipment: Pennies.
Procedure:

1. Teach words that sound alike.
2. Say,

   I am going to say a word, and I want you to say a word that sounds like it. Every time you say a word that sounds like the one I say, you get a penny. If you can't think of a word, you have to give a penny to the next player. Whoever gets the most pennies wins.

3. Allow sounds that rhyme to count as correct, even if they are not words.
4. Use the words *cat, tree, one, wet, pan, bite, red, fall, sit, play, look, hen, car, same, fish, hay, fix, ghost, dark,* and *wet.*

Sample Lesson Three

Purpose: To give practice in rhyming.
Procedure:

1. Say three words, two that sound the same and one that does not.
2. The player must identify the one that does not sound like the other two.
3. Use these combinations:

rat	cat	milk
run	find	one
two	you	me
show	pop	candy
sky	cloud	why
red	fed	door
down	bridge	brown
silk	milk	green
road	toad	book
street	milk	meat
paper	look	book
three	in	tin
hate	plate	fire
cut	candy	handy
out	spout	run
square	dare	tree
light	dark	night
who	you	puppy
green	seen	school
bird	nest	rest
hope	soap	water

4. Ask the players to tell you the two cards that do sound the same.

Additional Procedure:

- Say the word in the first column, and ask the child to give any rhyming word or nonsense syllable sound.
- Play three rounds briskly.
- Tell children that you are going to say three words and that they must tell you which two rhyme.

fat	tree	cat
in	win	flower
door	store	blue
cake	pet	bake
sit	pit	hat
run	house	fun
cow	chair	how
far	car	boot
sky	rain	fly
red	bed	dog
rose	nose	dress
bad	hot	sad
tree	free	sun
pan	can	eye
book	took	see

Sample Lesson Four

Purpose: To give practice in rhyming.
Procedure: Give practice in rhyming using names of animals.

(1) Billy sat down on a log. *Tell me the name of an animal that rhymes with* log *(dog). (2) We are building a new* house *(mouse). (3) Guess what I found under the* mat *(cat, rat). (4) This cloth is thick and* coarse *(horse). (5) The cat gave a big* meow *(cow). (6) I don't think this is* funny *(bunny). (7) We drank apple* cider *(spider). (8) What is in this pretty* box *(fox)? (9) You told a* lie *(fly). (10) The water here is* deep *(sheep).*

Additional Procedures:

1. Toy Rhymes. Give practice in rhyming using names of toys.

   (1) My dress and your dress are the same. *Tell me something you play that rhymes with* same *(game). (2) Be careful that you don't break the* plates *(skates). (3) The room is at the end of the* hall *(ball). (4) Can you hear the bell* ring *(swing)? (5) Look, here comes my* cat *(bat). (6) Let's all go and* hide *(slide). (7) There is a surprise in this* box *(blocks). (8) Parties are a lot of* fun *(gun). (9) Don't go too* far *(car).*

2. Body Parts Rhymes. Give practice in rhyming using names of body parts.

   (1) My mother makes good apple pie *(eye). (2) My favorite flower is a red* rose *(nose). (3) The house was as neat as a* pin *(chin). (4) There was a bad storm and a* shipwreck *(neck). (5) Christmas comes near the end of the* year *(ear). (6) My sister's name is Anabel* Ruth *(tooth). (7) In the summer we go on a lot of* trips *(lips). (8) Our dog knows how to sit up and* beg *(leg). (9) We played Hide and Go Seek, and I got home* free *(knee). (10) For a garden, you need a small piece of* land *(hand).*

3. Food Rhymes. Give practice in rhyming words using edibles.

   (1) It is time for bed. *Tell me the name of something we make sandwiches with that rhymes with* bed *(bread). (2) The dress is made of* silk *(milk). (3) My sweater is* yellow *(marshmallow). (4) The store next door is really* handy *(candy). (5) There is water in the* gutter *(butter). (6) Chickens live in a* coop *(soup). (7) We have a lot of door* keys *(cheese). (8) We put things that break out of the baby's* reach *(peach). (9) A big tree has a big* root *(fruit). (10) The picnic was lots of* fun *(bun).*

Sample Lesson Five

Purpose: To give practice in rhyming.
Equipment: Pennies.
Procedure: Play *Five or More.*

1. Each child has ten pennies; the teacher has thirty.
2. The teacher says a familiar one-syllable word.
3. Together the children try to think of more than five rhyming words.
4. If the group thinks of more than five, the teacher must give each child a penny for each word in excess of five.
5. If the group fails to reach five, each child must give the teacher a penny for each word short of five.

Additional Procedures:

1. Play *Rhyme Riddle.*
   - Use a three-sentence riddle ending in a question, as follows:

     I rhyme with *toy,*
     I am not a girl,
     Who am I?

   - Use the same format with *mouse-house, curl-girl, blue-glue,* and *sing-king.* Encourage the children to make up their own riddles.
2. Play *Rhyme Lines.*
   - The teacher says a line, and the children see how many lines they can add, each line ending with a rhyming word (such as words ending in *an, at, en, ig,* and *ip*).
   - The teacher might say "I petted the pig."
   - The first child could say, "He was very big."

CONVERSATION

Sample Lesson One

Purpose: To give practice in conversation.
Procedure:

1. The children should be able to sit and talk about topics within their own experience.
2. General rules of standard social conversation would apply here and should be taught over a period of time: (a) Everyone listens when one person is talking and may ask questions if they want to; (b) No one talks all the time; (c) No one interrupts while someone is talking; and (d) If it is necessary to stop someone, say, "I'm sorry to interrupt you, but. . . ."
3. One topic may be sustained for the rest of the period or several topics may be discussed.
4. Try to get the children to go beyond the questions, that is, to answer a question and then add to it.
5. Topics might include bicycles, the last prize the child won, something the children did the day before, their pets, their brothers and sisters, where and when they do their homework, what they like to do at recess, how they help around the house, what they like (or have) for lunch, holidays and other seasonal topics, clothes, and the park.
6. Continue the conversation only as long as the children are talking easily. Try to stop before the conversation drags.
7. Be on the alert for possible topics as things occur in the classroom or on the playground. The conversation will go best if you use topics familiar to the children.

Additional Procedure:

- Talk about where the school is.
- Ask the children to say where they live. (Some may not live in the same city as the school.)
- Explain that there are many streets in a city.
- Ask what else is in this city.
- Talk about other schools the children know about, parks, stores, churches, cars, buses, and people who work for the city (for example, fire fighters and police officers).

Sample Lesson Two

Purpose: To give practice interrupting politely.
Procedure:

1. Ask the group is anyone knows what *interrupting* means. (It means starting to talk when another person is still talking.)
2. Explain that if two teachers are talking on the playground when a boy falls down and hurts himself, then some other child should interrupt the teachers to tell them about it.
3. Say: "When you have to interrupt someone, you say, 'I'm sorry to interrupt you, but. . . .' "
4. Ask children to practice saying this by themselves.
5. Ask the children to think of situations in which interrupting would be justified.

CLASSIFICATION

Sample Lesson One

Purpose: To give practice in classifying.
Procedure: Play *I'm Thinking Of.*

1. Define words in terms of class or function so that the children become familiar with categorizing words.

2. Ask the children to name objects with these characteristics:

   I'm thinking of an animal that has a long trunk. An animal that can purr and meow. A place where airplanes land and take off. Something that has four legs and is flat on top. Something that is round, and you can catch it and hit it. Something that is a lot of different colors, and you see it in the sky when it is raining and the sun is out. A person who wears a helmet and rides on the big red truck with ladders. An animal that can fly, sing songs, and build nests.

3. If possible, conduct a few rounds with the children making up similar items.

Additional Procedure: Play *Word Classes.*

- Give the first child the first sentence: "A dog is an ________."
- Ask each of the other children to say a different animal: "A ________ is an animal."
- Give a different child the next sentence, and repeat the procedure.
- If the children need help say, "What other animals can you think of?"
- They should answer in this way: "A ________ is an animal."
- Examples:

  A dog is an ________. A cabbage is a ________. A coat is a piece of ________ (clothing or something you wear). Thanksgiving and Christmas are ________. Spring and summer are ________. A chocolate cake is a kind of ________ (dessert or food). A horse is an ________. A table and chairs are ________. A hammer is a ________.

Sample Lesson Two

Purpose: To give practice in classifying.
Procedure: Play *One of These Words Doesn't Belong.*

1. Use sets of four words, one of which differs markedly in sound.
2. Say a set of words, such as *snake, star, mother, school,* and then say that one word doesn't belong because it doesn't begin with an *s.*
3. The children should be able to remember the words and give you the answer. If not, repeat the series but encourage them to try to remember the next series.
4. With this game you can use beginning or ending sounds; or categories such as names of fruit, names of people, and plurals; or any other variation. For example, all the words but one could be Halloween words.

SOUND IDENTIFICATION

Reviewing Listening

Purpose: To practice listening to familiar sounds.

Procedure:

1. Talk about what you listen with, what you do when there is a very loud noise and you don't want to hear it, and what people do when they can't hear well.
2. Tell the children to listen to the sounds in the room.
3. Ask them to close their eyes and raise their hands if there is a sound they can identify.
4. Discuss the sounds you hear in a classroom, on the playground, and in stores.
5. Talk about animal sounds, and ask the children to imitate them.
6. Discuss listening as a *distance sense,* that is, you can hear something even though it's too far away for you to see it.
7. Use as an example the siren on a police car to alert you to get out of the way long before you see the police car.
8. Note that smell and hearing are distance senses while touch and taste are clearly *close senses.*

Sound Identification Routine

Purpose: To give practice in identifying sounds.
Equipment: Tape recorder, paper bags, miscellaneous objects and instruments.
Procedure:

1. Use the following procedure in activities and lessons that call for identification of common sounds.
2. Record a series of eight sounds that occur frequently in the child's environment.

3. Examples of familiar sounds are sharpening a pencil, cutting paper, tearing paper, blowing up a balloon, stapling paper together, counting money, using a hand eggbeater, dialing a telephone, pouring a glass of water, opening a can, turning the pages of a book, filing fingernails, hammering, sawing, zipping up a zipper, knocking at a door, and cutting food on a dinner plate.
4. Note that all of these can be demonstrated in the classroom if a tape recorder is not available. You can put paper bags with ear holes over the children's heads or place a barrier between you and the children.
5. If you record, it is not necessary to eliminate background sounds unless they are confusing.
6. For additional practice in identification of common sounds, ask the children to close their eyes and to listen to the sounds in the classroom and identify them.

Additional Procedures:

1. Play *The Name of That Sound.*
   - Ask the children to place paper bags over their heads and to identify sounds that you make with coins, staples, scissors, chalk, brushes, nail files, and musical instruments.
   - Also use sounds that are occurring naturally in the room in other groups.
2. Play *Near or Far.*
   - The task is to discriminate between sounds inside or outside the school that are near or far away.
   - The teacher should be alert at all times for sounds such as sirens to call attention to the way sounds change as they come near and then fade away.
   - During the listening lessons this phenomenon may be heard with trucks and planes and to a lesser extent with cars, voices, and classes walking by in the hall.
3. Play *Whose Voice Is This?*
   - Early in the year you should tape the children's voices as they read.
   - Make certain that no names are used.
   - You could tape during the individual testing periods in reading.
   - Play the tapes and ask the children to identify their classmates' voices as well as the voices of familiar people in the school, such as the principal.

SEQUENCE SPECIFICATION

Sample Lesson One

Purpose: To give practice in identifying sequences.
Procedure: Play *Sequences.* Read a short story; then ask questions.

> Sandra opened her piggy bank, put all her money in her purse, took her fourteen friends to the store, and bought them each an ice cream cone.

1. Ask:

   What did Sandra do first? What did she do next? And after that?

   Billy climbed up the tree, pulled all the leaves around him so no one could see him from the ground, and didn't answer his father when his father called him.

2. Ask:

   What did Billy do first? What did he do next? And after that?

   Barbara climbed on her pony, rode to school, tied the pony to the fence, went into the school, and told the teacher her name. Peter made sandwiches, wrapped them up in paper, put them in his lunch box, and put his school books beside the lunch box.

3. If the children can't tell you the sequence, read the story again.

Additional Procedure:

- Give practice in listening for the sequence of events:

  On the night before Christmas, Stewart hung up his stocking, got into bed, went to sleep, woke up very early, tiptoed into the living room, and opened his biggest present.

  Paula put on her coat, walked to the library, asked the librarian to help her find a good dog story, checked out *Harry the Dirty Dog,* and went home.

  Peggy opened her piggy bank, took out the money, went to the store, and bought a Mother's Day card.

  John took off his shoes and socks, got into his boat, put up the sail, and went for a boat ride.

  Sally tiptoed upstairs, went into her room, hid in the closet, and pretended she didn't hear when her father called her.

- Repeat the story two times or more if necessary, but remind children to pay attention and remember the sequence correctly.

Sample Lesson Two

Purpose: To give practice in identifying sequences.
Procedure:

1. Tell the story below once, and ask what happened first, what happened next, and so on.
2. Ask if any child can tell you the complete sequence of events.
3. Note that no pictures should be used.

The Fox and the Crow

A crow looked in the open window of a little red house and saw some good things to eat. There was no one around. The crow flew in and quickly took some food. He flew with the food in his mouth to the top of an old tree in the woods.

A hungry fox saw the crow fly to the old tree. The fox wanted the food. The fox went over to the tree, looked up, and said, "Good morning, Mr. Crow, you are a very fine looking crow."

The crow was pleased to hear this.

"I would like you to sing something for me," said the fox. "I am sure that you know some beautiful songs."

The crow was very pleased. He opened his mouth to sing and down fell the food!

The hungry fox quickly ate the food. Then she said, "You silly old squawky bird! After this, think before you open your mouth!"

Sample Lesson Three

Purpose: To give practice in identifying sequences.
Procedure: Ask about the sequence of events with the following fables of Aesop.

1. *The Shepherd Boy and the Wolf:*

   In this fable a shepherd boy decides to play a trick on the villagers. He calls "Wolf!" and they all come running to help him only to find that there is no wolf. He does this several times, and each time it works. One day a wolf does come along, but when the boy calls for help, no one comes because they assume he is playing another trick on them. The wolf catches two sheep before the boy finally receives help.

2. *The Town Mouse and the Country Mouse:*

   A country mouse goes to visit his town cousin who lives in comfort. The only problem is that the town is dangerous. The country mouse returns thankfully to his poor, but fear-free, way of living.

3. *The Wolf in Sheep's Clothing:*

   A wolf disguises himself as a sheep in order to prey on the flock. He completely fools the shepherd, who locks him up that night with the sheep. The shepherd was still fooled by the wolf's disguise, and when the shepherd needed meat for the next day, he killed the wolf by mistake.

Seatwork

Reading

SEATWORK 1: Letter Recognition

NAME ____________________

- Trace the letters and print the missing letters.

Reading

SEATWORK 2: Letter Recognition

NAME ______________________________

- Trace the letters and print the missing letters.

Reading

SEATWORK 3: Letter Recognition

NAME ______________________

a b c d e f g h i

j k l m n o p q r

s t u v w x y z

a b d e g i

j l m o p q r

t v x y z

a b c d e f g h i

j k l m n o p q r

s t u v w x y z

- Trace the letters and print the missing letters.

Reading

SEATWORK 4: Letter Recognition

NAME ______________________________

• Trace the letters and print the missing letters.

Reading

SEATWORK 5: Plurals

NAME ______________________

I fan, 2 ______	I cat, 2 ______
I fin, 2 ______	I hat, 2 ______
I kit, 2 ______	I mat, 2 ______
I fig, 2 ______	I tap, 2 ______
I sip, 2 ______	I hog, 2 ______
I bed, 2 ______	I van, 2 ______
I lid, 2 ______	I dog, 2 ______
	I log, 2 ______

- Write the plural of each word.

Reading

SEATWORK 6: Verbs Ending in *S*

NAME ______________________

I sit. He ______________. I jump. She______________.

I run. She______________. I smile. He ______________.

I hop. He ______________. I talk. She ______________.

I eat. She______________. I turn. He ______________.

I skip. He ______________. I throw. She ______________.

I play. She ______________. I sing. He______________.

I stand. He ______________. I dance. She______________.

- Change the ending for each verb.

Reading

SEATWORK 7: Sentences

NAME ______________________

dog I the see ⟶ I see the dog.

bat see the I ______________________

has ants Jill ______________________

run hill I up the ______________________

wet Sam's is hat ______________________

away dog runs the ______________________

red the is van ______________________

big is cat that ______________________

is wet not ball the ______________________

fills he can tin the ______________________

- Change the order of the words and print the sentence.

Reading

SEATWORK 8: Sentences

NAME ______________________________

can see	→	I see the can.

tin fill ______________________________

met dog ______________________________

she mad ______________________________

ball hit ______________________________

hat see ______________________________

cat dog ______________________________

man van ______________________________

red hat ______________________________

- Make up and print a sentence including the given words.

Reading

SEATWORK 9: Reading Improvement

NAME ______________________________

I see a cat. I see 2 cats.

The 2 cats see a rat. The

rat is a fat rat. The rat is

on the mat. The rat sees the

cats. Go, rat, go. Go, cats,

go. The cats <u>catch</u> the rat.

- Learn to read the page smoothly.

Reading

SEATWORK 10: Reading Improvement

NAME ______________________

The man has a hat. His hat is on the mat. The cat is in the hat. The man pats the cat. The man has a can. The cat sees the can. The cat sits on the can on the mat. The cat bit the mat. No, cat, no.

- Learn to read the page smoothly.

Reading

SEATWORK 11: Reading Improvement

NAME ______________________________

Dan ran in a <u>race</u>. Can Dan win the <u>race</u>? Go, Dan, go. See Dan win the race. Dan wins a pin and a fan. Dan has the pin on his hat. Dan has ten pins and 3 fans. The man has 1 pen, 2 hats, 3 cats, 4 mats, and 5 cans.

- Learn to read the page smoothly.

Reading

SEATWORK 12: Reading Improvement

NAME ____________________

Can the cat go in the race? No, cat, no. Dan is in the race. Dan got a pin and a hat. Dan sat on the mat. He is hot. He has a fan. The man fans Dan. Dan has a tan. He sees a fat rat in the can. The cat sees the rat. The rat ran. The cat ran. Go, cat, go. The cat bit the rat.

• Learn to read the page smoothly.

Reading

SEATWORK 13: Reading Improvement

NAME ______________________________

This is Dan, and this is Ben. Dan and Ben race to the tree. See them run. Go, Dan, go! Dan runs as fast as he can. Dan wins the race. Dan is hot and so is Ben. Ben gets fans. He fans Dan, and Dan fans Ben.

- Learn to read the page smoothly.

Reading

SEATWORK 14: Reading Improvement

NAME ______________________

This is Bellboy. Bellboy is Jan's cat. He sits on the mat in the sun. Now Bellboy sees a big dog. Will the dog get Bellboy? No. Bellboy goes ssssss, and the big dog runs as fast as he can. Run, big dog, run, or Bellboy will get you.

- Learn to read the page smoothly.

Reading

SEATWORK 15: Reading Improvement

NAME ______________________________

Pat has a dog. Her name is Bingo. Bingo got wet, and then she got a bad cold. Bingo has to go to the vet to get a shot. The vet tells Pat that Bingo will soon be well. The vet says that Bingo is a good dog. Bingo wags her tail.

- Learn to read the page smoothly.

Reading

SEATWORK 16: Reading Improvement

NAME ______________________________

Jan and Ted and Pat play Hide and Seek. Jan is it, so Ted and Pat run and hide. Ted hides in the den. Pat hides in the hall. Jan calls, "Here I come." Jan sees Ted, but she cannot see Pat. Pat runs and gets in free.

- Learn to read the page smoothly.

Reading

SEATWORK 17: Reading Improvement

NAME ____________________

This is Nell. Nell is in bed. She fell and got a cut on her leg. Will Nell get well? Yes, she will get well, and then she will get up. Nell sits up in bed and eats hot buns. Nell likes hot buns. Pat comes to see Nell, and Nell gives Pat a hot bun.

- Learn to read the page smoothly.

Reading

SEATWORK 18: Reading Improvement

NAME ______________________________

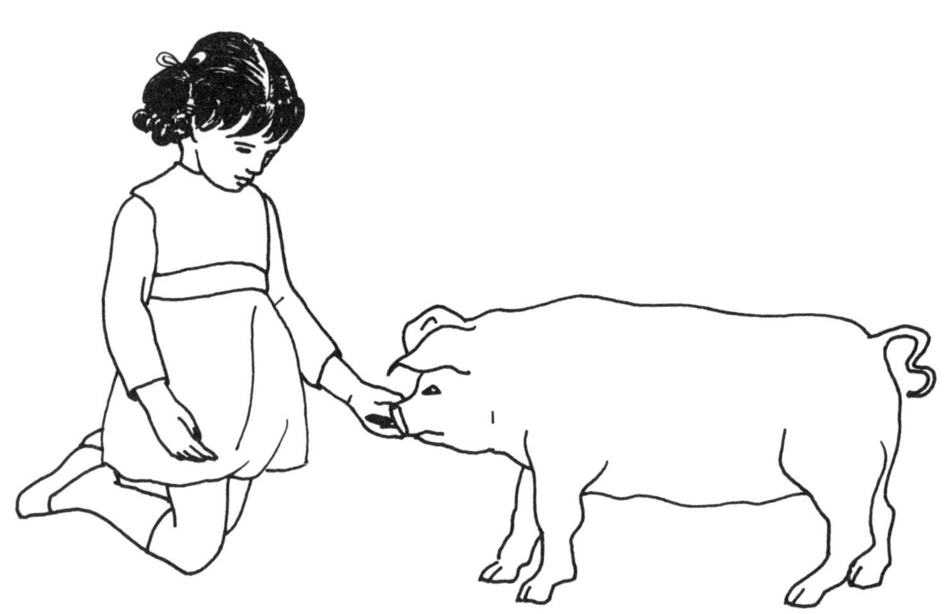

Jan has a can of figs. She has ten figs in the can. The pig likes figs, so Jan gives the pig a fig. The pig eats the fig. She goes, "Oink, oink." Jan sees the dog. Do dogs like to eat figs? No. Dogs like to eat meat. Jan sees Ben. Ben likes figs. Jan gives Ben a fig.

- Learn to read the page smoothly.

Reading

SEATWORK 19: Reading Improvement

NAME ______________________________

Jack and Jill run to the well. Jill falls down the hill.

Jack cannot see Jill. "Where are you, Jill?" he yells.

Jill gets up. "I fell down, but I am not hurt," she says.

Jill and Jack walk to the well and get a drink.

• Learn to read the page smoothly.

Reading

SEATWORK 20: Reading Improvement

NAME ______________________________

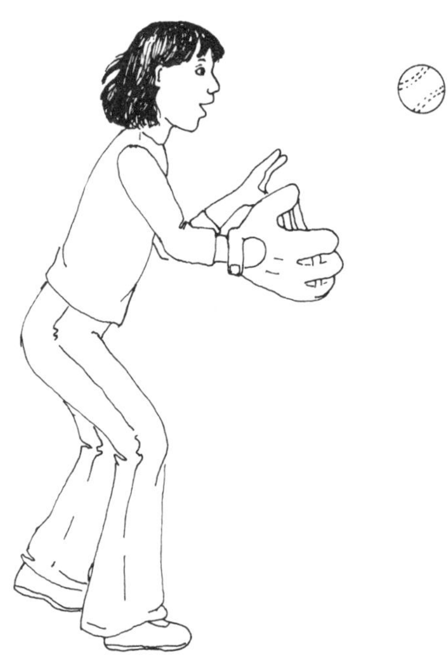

Bill has a bat and a ball. He hits the ball to Jan. Will Jan get the ball? Yes, Jan runs fast and gets the ball. Now Jan hits the ball, and it goes up in a tree. Bill goes up the tree and gets the ball. Now Jan hits the ball, and the dog sees it. The dog runs and gets the ball. Bill and Jan play with the dog.

- Learn to read the page smoothly.

Reading

SEATWORK 21: Reading Improvement

NAME ______________________

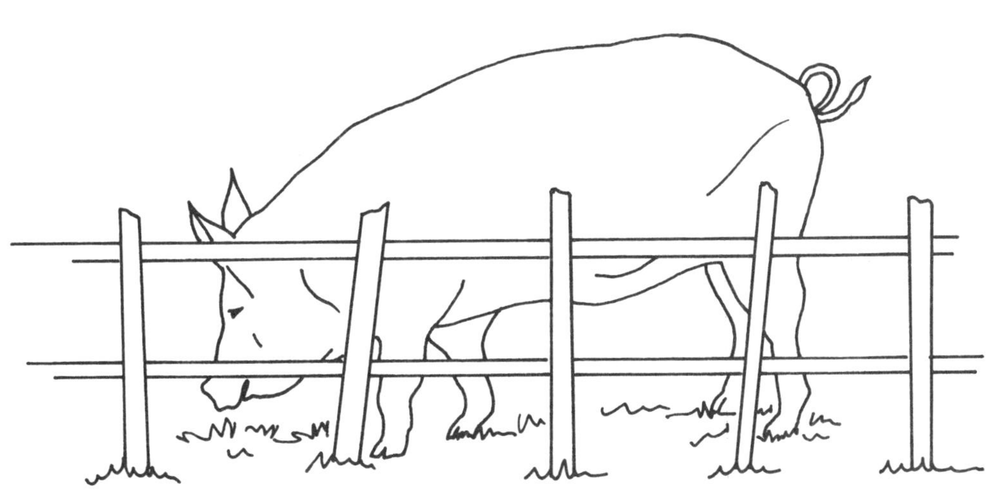

Jill and Dan go to the farm. At the farm they see a lot of hens, a dog, a cat, and a pig. The pig is in a big pen. Dan pats the pig, and the pig goes, "Oink, oink." The cat goes, "Meow, meow," and Jill pats it. Does the dog go, "Oink, oink"? No. Does he go, "Meow, meow"? No. How does the dog go?

- Learn to read the page smoothly.

Reading

SEATWORK 22: Reading Improvement

NAME ______________________________

This is Hilltop City. This is Redmill School. It is a big school. Many girls and boys go to Redmill School. All the boys and girls run and play till the bell rings. Now the bell rings, and they all go in. See Jill. Jill is late for school. Run, Jill, run. Jill runs to school.

- Learn to read the page smoothly.

Reading

SEATWORK 23: Reading Improvement

NAME ______________________________

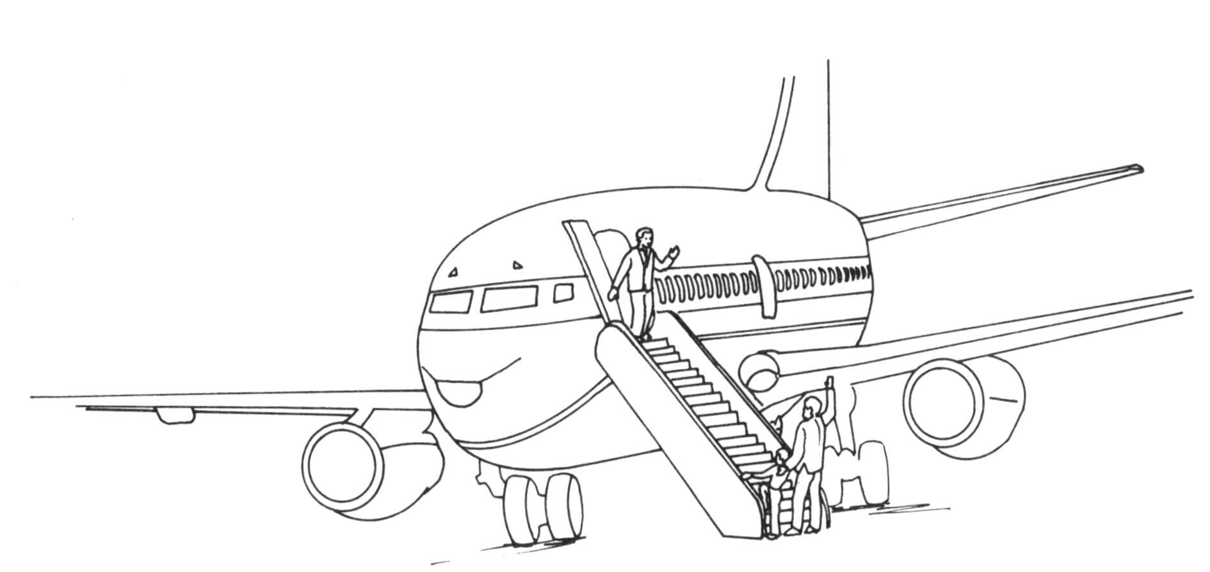

Ken and his father go to Hilltop City to see Mr. Bell. Mr. Bell is on a jet.

"Oh, Dad," Ken says, "see the big jet! It is a **707**."

Ken's father says, "Get in the jet, Ken. We will see Mr. Bell on the jet. We will go for a ride with Mr. Bell."

Ken goes for a ride with his father and Mr. Bell. The jet goes up, up, up. Ken can see all of Hilltop City.

- Learn to read the page smoothly.

Reading

SEATWORK 24: Reading Improvement

NAME ______________________________

One morning Ann and her mother go to get Ann a puppy. Ann sees a puppy, and the puppy wags his tail.

Ann says, "Hi, puppy, will you be my puppy?" The puppy wags his tail a lot.

Ann says, "Mother, can I get this puppy?"

"Yes," says Mother. Ann calls her puppy Billyboy. Ann and her mother go to Dr. Penman. He is the vet. Billyboy has to get a shot. Billyboy is a good puppy.

• Learn to read the page smoothly.

Reading

SEATWORK 25: Reading Improvement

NAME ______________________

Ann and Pat play jump rope. Jump! Jump! One, two, three.

"Oh, oh," says Ann, "here comes my dog, Billyboy." Billyboy gets the rope. Ann and Pat cannot play jump rope now.

Ann says, "Let's run and hide from Billyboy. Then we can play jump rope." They run in the house and hide, but Billyboy finds them. So Ann gets the ball, and they play ball with Billyboy.

"Get the ball, Billyboy," says Pat. Billyboy gets the ball.

"Good dog," says Ann.

- Learn to read the page smoothly.

Reading

SEATWORK 26: Reading Improvement

NAME ____________________

See Mr. Pike. He is the milkman. He goes all around Hilltop City in his red milk truck. He brings milk and ice cream for lunch to Redmill School. He brings milk and ice cream for Bill and Pat and Ted and Jan.

Ann goes home for lunch. Ann lives at 23 Canpan Way in Hilltop City. Mr. Pike brings milk to Ann's house. He brings milk to many houses in Hilltop City.

- Learn to read the page smoothly.

Reading

SEATWORK 27: Reading Improvement

NAME ______________________________

One night it rained and rained in Hilltop City. Pat looked out the window at the rain. Then Pat looked at Ann's house.

"Oh, mother," said Pat, "look, look! Ann's house is on fire. Oh, mother, can we go and help Ann?"

Mother said, "Here come the fire trucks. The firemen and the rain will put out the fire. Then we will go and help Ann."

The firemen worked hard, and soon the fire at Ann's house was out. Ann said that Billyboy had smelled smoke, and he had barked and barked. Then her father had smelled smoke, too. He had called the fire trucks. Billyboy was a good dog.

- Learn to read the page smoothly.

Reading Test

SEATWORK 28

NAME ______________________

1. pat pip pup	2. fill fell fed	3. fig fit fin	4. sell sin sill	5. sat sit set
6. till Ted ten	7. pup pun up	8. hub hut hip	9. cat can cap	10. Len let leg
11. ban fan tan	12. mop map man	13. wit win wet	14. din pin tin	15. go on no
16. rub rib rut	17. and as has	18. ball bill bell	19. vet fat van	20. is if it
21. hen the ten	22. as a is	23. lid did rid	24. and an as	25. run rut ran

- Use for reading test.

Reading Test

SEATWORK 29

NAME ______________________________

1.	2.	3.	4.	5.
tip	sun	cap	will	tub
top	sin	cat	wall	Ted
tap	sad	can	well	tan

6.	7.	8.	9.	10.
kit	Ned	the	bit	Dad
lit	Nan	a	bin	Dan
hit	Nell	then	pin	den

11.	12.	13.	14.	15.
men	till	pit	pop	nut
met	tell	pip	pup	nip
net	tall	pin	pip	net

16.	17.	18.	19.	20.
fun	mad	cut	mill	cad
gun	fad	cup	man	can
bun	sad	cop	men	cap

21.	22.	23.	24.	25.
lip	bib	wig	had	rub
lap	bid	win	hip	run
lid	bed	wit	hop	rut

- Use for reading test.

Reading Test

SEATWORK 30

NAME ____________________

1.	2.	3.	4.	5.
tin tan ten	out at it	book look hook	dub Dad Dan	pig pin pit

6.	7.	8.	9.	10.
rig rip wig	pop pup pun	kill hill Jill	rub tub rib	pad pan pat

11.	12.	13.	14.	15.
yet yell vet	sun sat sin	jig jab Jan	Ned Nan Jan	dip din den

16.	17.	18.	19.	20.
cut can cub	fin fan fun	be we see	led bed fed	bid bit bin

21.	22.	23.	24.	25.
sip sit sin	pad pan pat	on no of	is if it	wed wan wet

- Use for reading test.

Reading Test

SEATWORK 31

NAME ________________

1. mat man met	2. Dan Ben Ken	3. so as is	4. this that then	5. bid bad bed
6. if on of	7. pop top cop	8. hid hill hop	9. Jill Bill fill	10. it at an
11. I he me	12. see set sup	13. bell pill dill	14. Dan Nan Jan	15. up on in
16. rat pan win	17. Ben den pen	18. Len Ken Ben	19. he hat has	20. well yell will
21. bat cat fat	22. red ran wed	23. me we he	24. big pig dig	25. see be bin

- Use for reading test.

Reading Test

SEATWORK 32

NAME ____________________

1.	2.	3.	4.	5.
bay	the	pail	big	cub
day	this	bail	but	cut
pay	that	tail	bun	cup

6.	7.	8.	9.	10.
dog	mother	book	come	pill
bog	morning	hook	some	fill
hog	many	look	same	dill

11.	12.	13.	14.	15.
may	mail	hub	fine	bull
ray	nail	pub	pine	full
say	Nell	rub	line	pull

16.	17.	18.	19.	20.
good	call	boy	man	light
Gail	city	girl	many	fight
game	caps	bay	men	might

21.	22.	23.	24.	25.
father	fell	dip	fit	bog
mother	fall	din	fin	dog
school	fill	den	fed	log

- Use for reading test.

Reading Test

SEATWORK 33

NAME ____________________

1.	2.	3.	4.	5.
hits	man	hug	hut	back
this	many	hot	cut	pack
tell	men	hog	huts	lack

6.	7.	8.	9.	10.
she	pip	tall	bet	sub
he	pit	till	get	cub
me	pin	tell	jet	rub

11.	12.	13.	14.	15.
fig	big	out	hit	cad
fit	dig	on	hot	can
fin	pig	of	hut	cog

16.	17.	18.	19.	20.
city	wig	down	sip	jet
call	we	gown	sap	jig
cats	wit	town	sup	Jan

21.	22.	23.	24.	25.
they	one	stop	people	street
the	two	store	pen	city
then	ten	school	pats	many

• Use for reading test.

Reading Test

SEATWORK 34

NAME ______________________

1. kit cat can	2. jet jig Jen	3. an at as	4. pail tail fail	5. she her hot
6. fine fan fits	7. like bike back	8. yes no go	9. side hide tide	10. stop pop top
11. Dan Jan Ann	12. go no so	13. good bad ban	14. he she they	15. lunch bunch hunch
16. bird bad beds	17. truck tall tells	18. dogs digs dug	19. ray way may	20. on of no
21. fit lit kit	22. cop cot cod	23. calls city come	24. bad pad lad	25. father fills morning

- Use for reading test.

Reading Test

SEATWORK 35

NAME ______________________

1. slow sill sits	2. bump dump jump	3. like look lack	4. town down gown	5. sees sits sets
6. sight might right	7. bibs Bob's Ben's	8. some come room	9. mother might morning	10. full pull doll
11. toy boy Roy	12. house mouse louse	13. dog bog log	14. mail man main	15. school sill sell
16. no go so	17. fire tire hire	18. good bad sad	19. on an at	20. book look took
21. main mine man's	22. hi he ho	23. on one of	24. out in on	25. fill till fall

- Use for reading test.

Reading Test

SEATWORK 36

NAME ______________________

1. pull people pills	2. TV ten OK	3. turn ten tins	4. boy bay day	5. Mike mail main
6. last lame lent	7. look light line	8. pun pumps pulls	9. sex set sent	10. hen pen ten
11. who wet win	12. sing ring wing	13. high hide hike	14. cooks pack pick	15. hug hut hog
16. hail hill hall	17. people pulls pumps	18. frog from Fran	19. little bottle settle	20. line fine dine
21. about around again	22. fly fan fall	23. cool call cell	24. with wits wins	25. my me am

• Use for reading test.

Reading Test

SEATWORK 37

NAME ______________________________

1.	2.	3.	4.	5.
yes	fire	fins	cow	box
yet	fine	fans	pow	backs
yaps	fight	fill	how	fox

6.	7.	8.	9.	10.
went	wigs	ill	came	drip
wit	wins	it	game	drop
will	wits	in	comes	drat

11.	12.	13.	14.	15.
an	beg	her	stop	turn
all	bet	his	sits	tire
as	Ben	who	sill	till

16.	17.	18.	19.	20.
bar	man	here	side	boy
far	men	hen	tide	bay
car	mine	hall	hide	bag

21.	22.	23.	24.	25.
wash	tin	tack	let	out
who	tan	tail	lit	about
wall	town	tame	lot	house

- Use for reading test.

Reading Test

SEATWORK 38

NAME ______________________________

1.
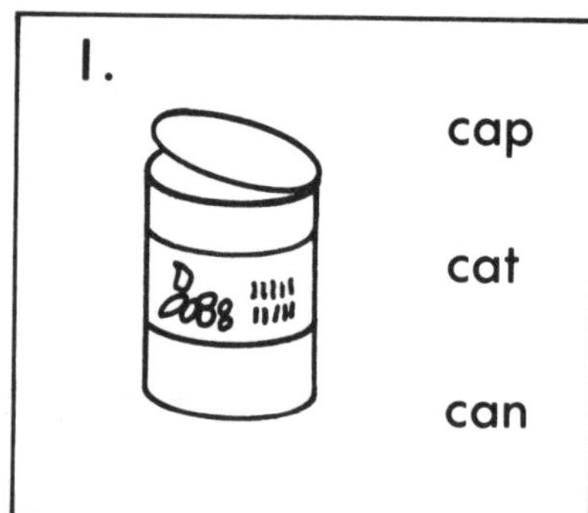
cap
cat
can

2.
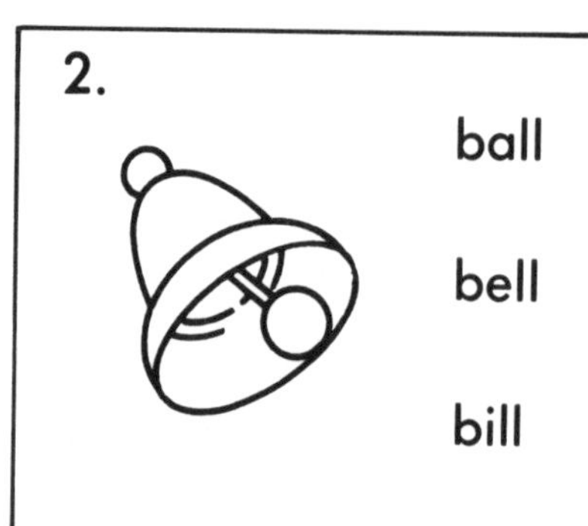
ball
bell
bill

3.
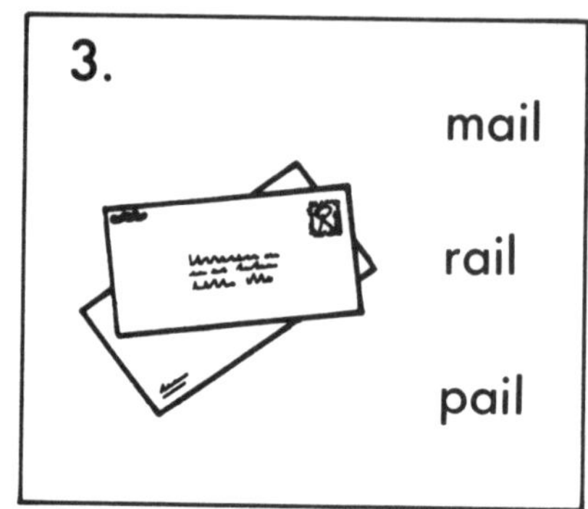
mail
rail
pail

4.
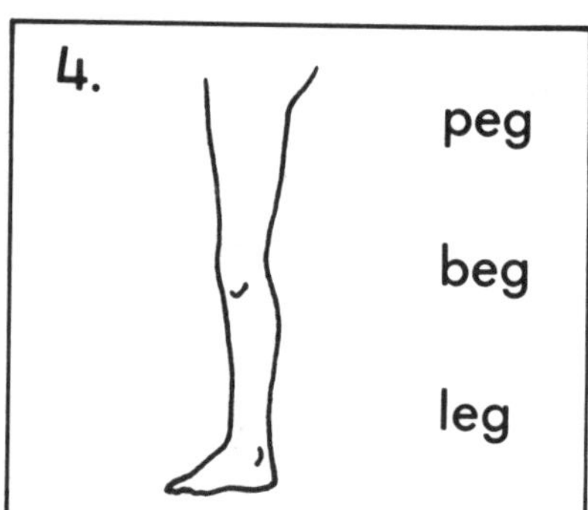
peg
beg
leg

5.
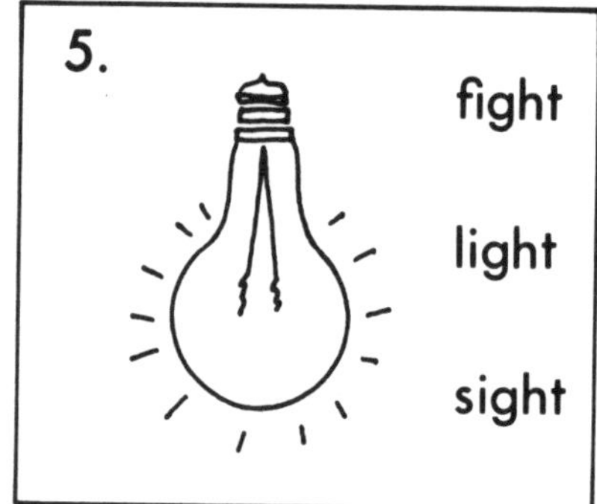
fight
light
sight

6.

look
took
book

7.
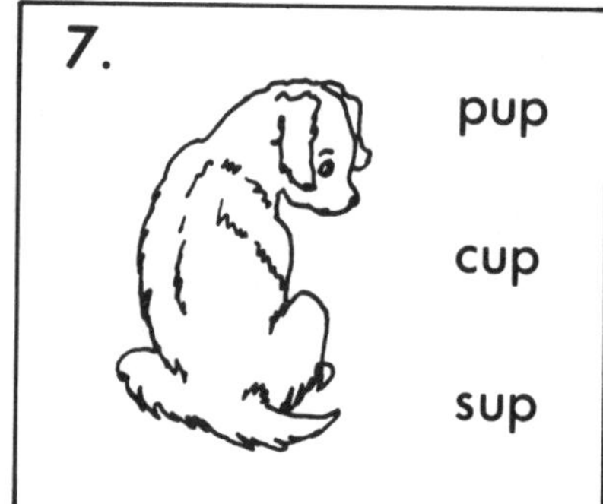
pup
cup
sup

8.

doll
roll
toll

9.

hike
bike
like

10.
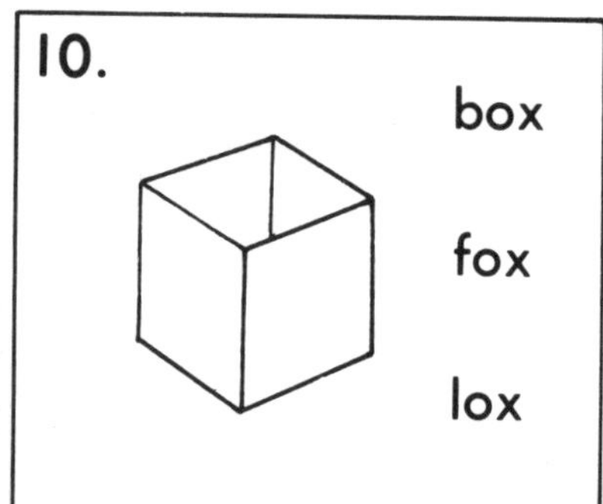
box
fox
lox

11.
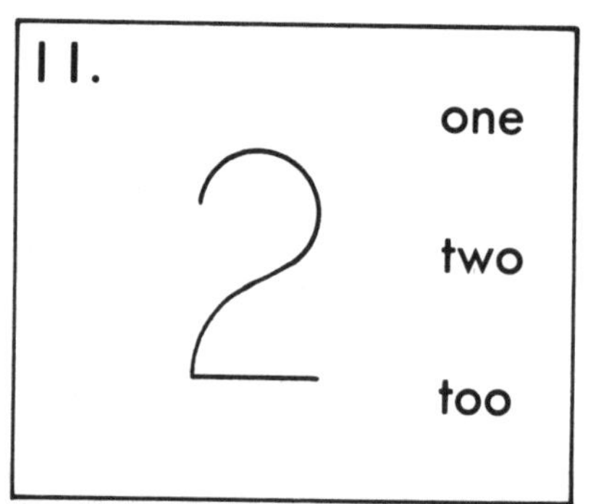
one
two
too

12.
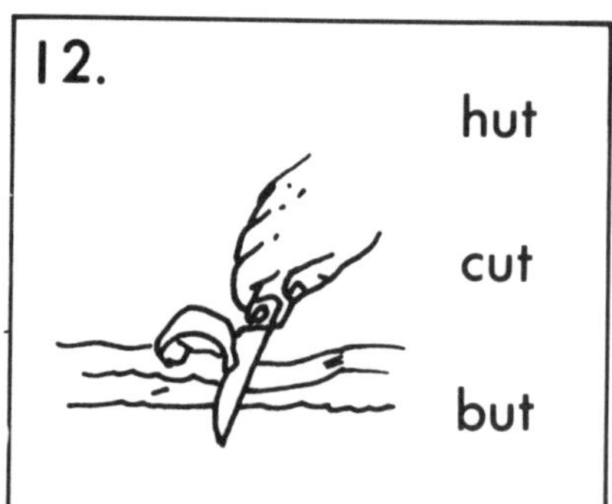
hut
cut
but

- Underline the word that matches the picture.

Reading Test

SEATWORK 39

NAME ____________________

1\.
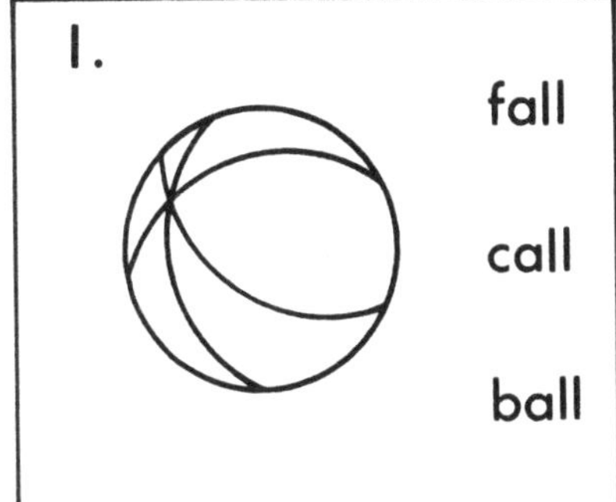
fall
call
ball

2\.
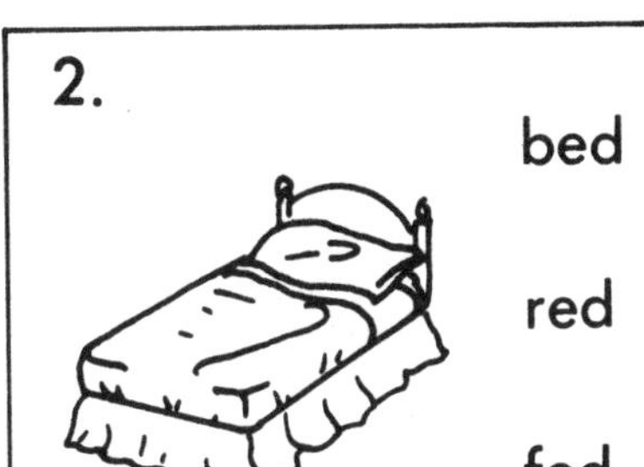
bed
red
fed

3\.
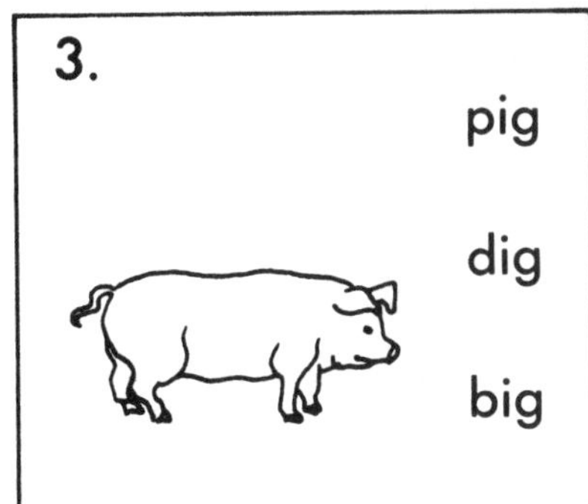
pig
dig
big

4\.
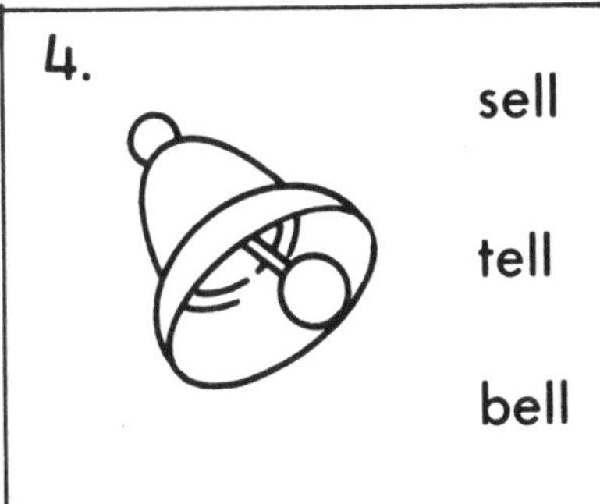
sell
tell
bell

5\.
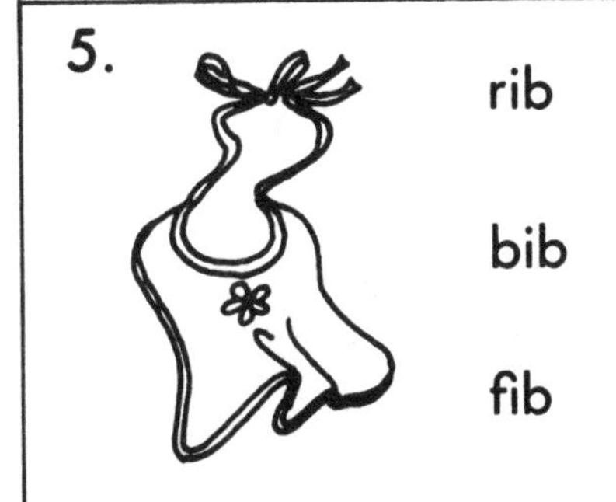
rib
bib
fib

6\.

gun
pun
bun

7\.
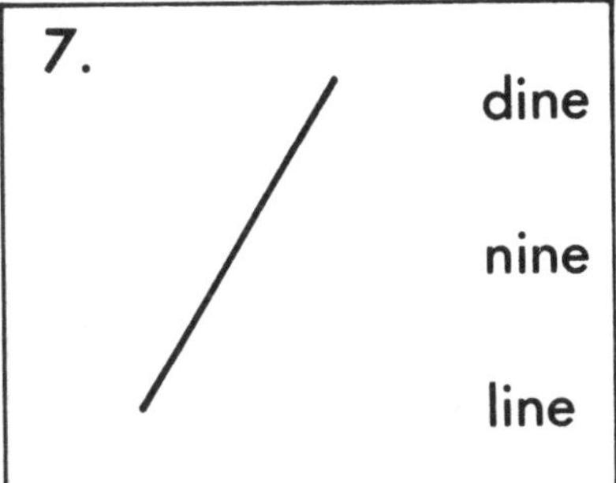
dine
nine
line

8\.
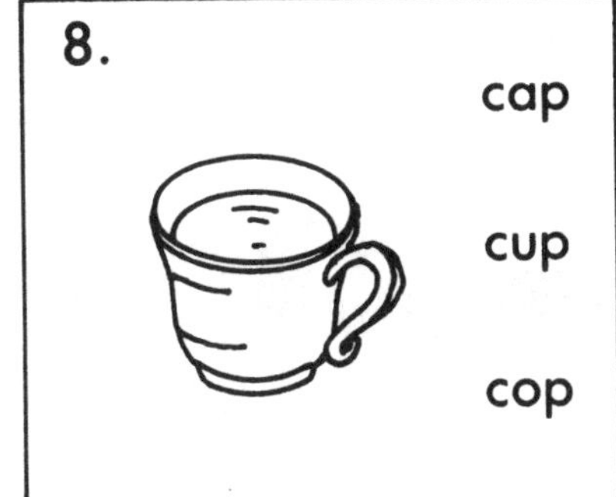
cap
cup
cop

9\.

hall
hull
hill

10\.

boy
toy
soy

11\.
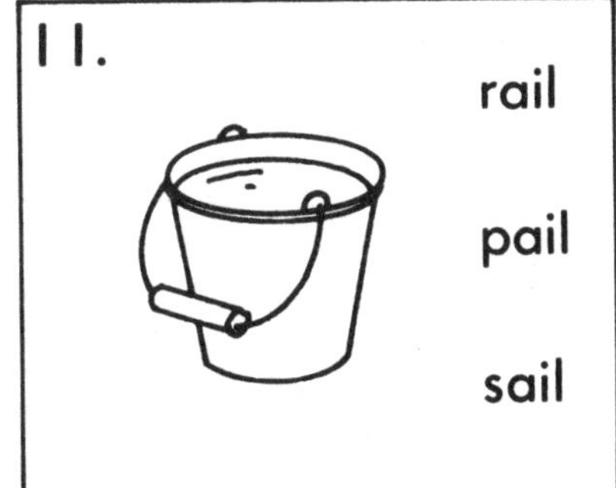
rail
pail
sail

12\.
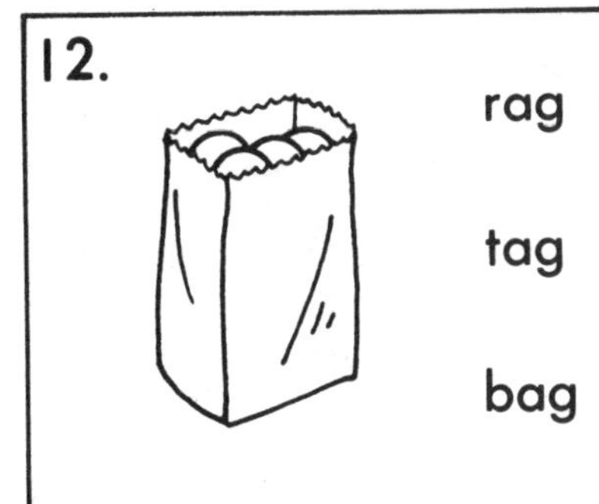
rag
tag
bag

- Underline the word that matches the picture.

Reading Test

SEATWORK 40

NAME ______________________________

1.
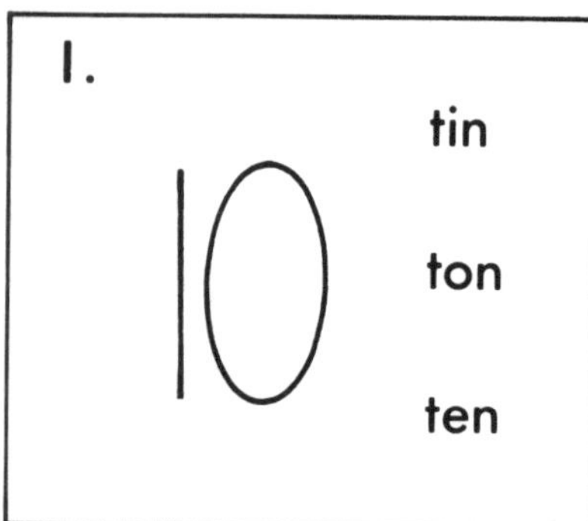
tin
ton
ten

2.
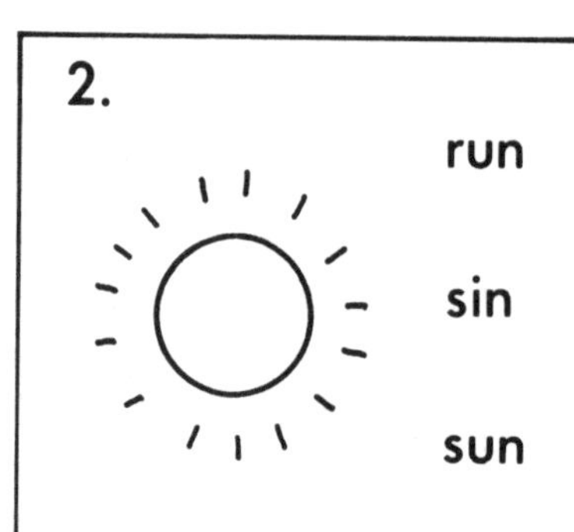
run
sin
sun

3.
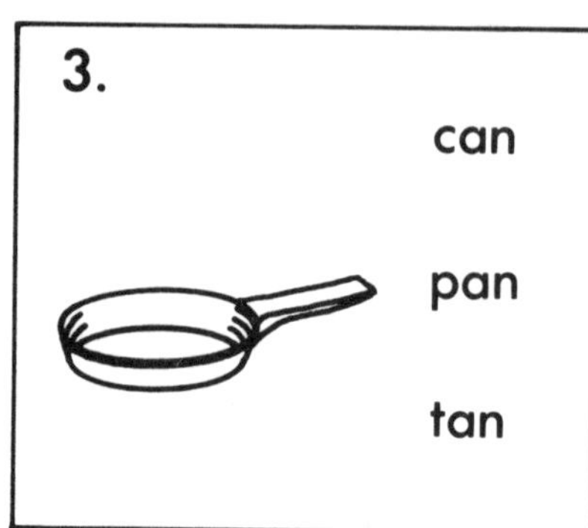
can
pan
tan

4.
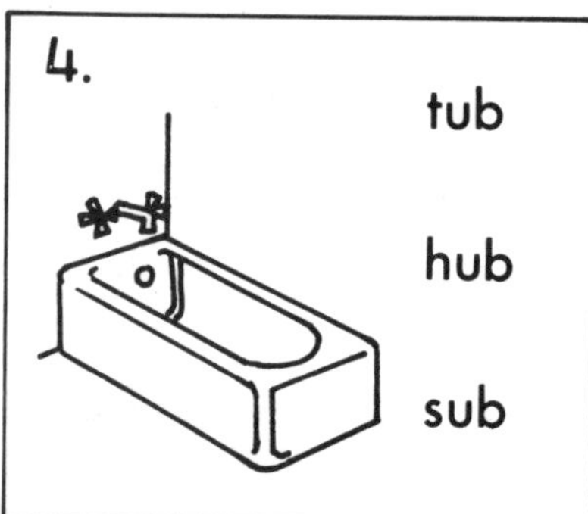
tub
hub
sub

5.

bunch
lunch
punch

6.
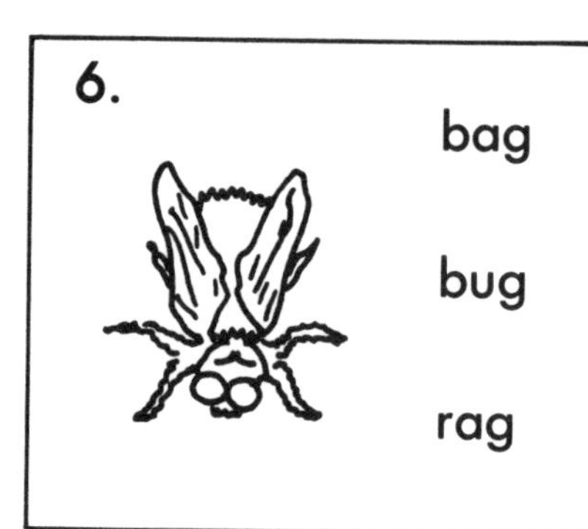
bag
bug
rag

7.
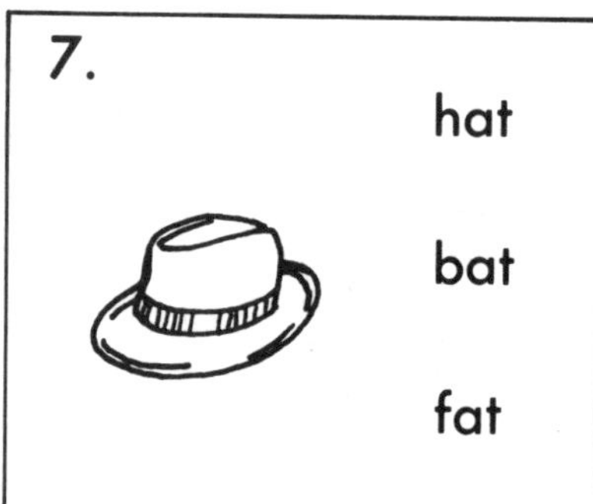
hat
bat
fat

8.
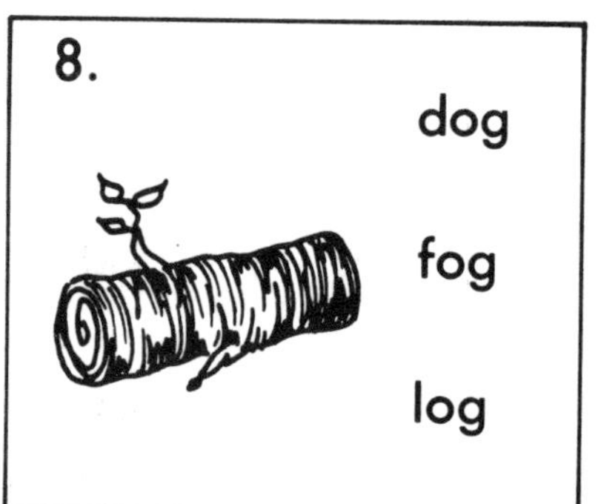
dog
fog
log

9.
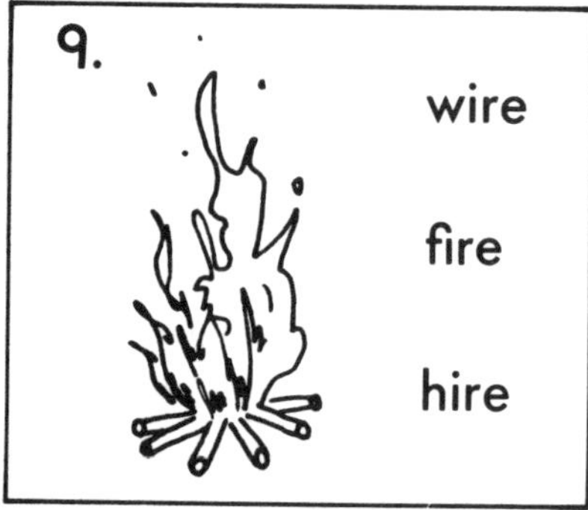
wire
fire
hire

10.
bat
but
bit

11.

fun
gun
bun

12.
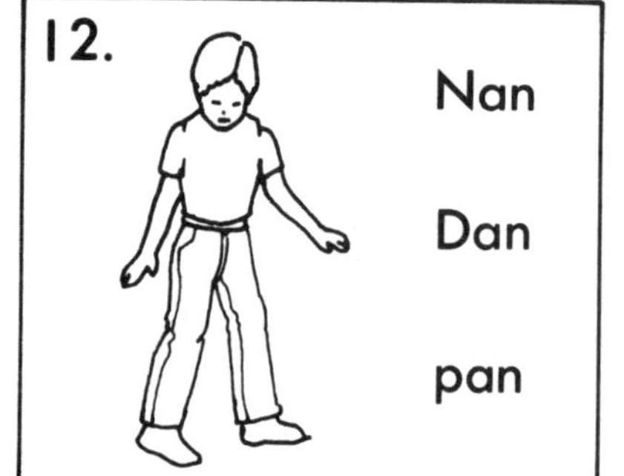
Nan
Dan
pan

- Underline the word that matches the picture.

Reading Test

SEATWORK 41

NAME ____________________

1.

hook

book

look

2.

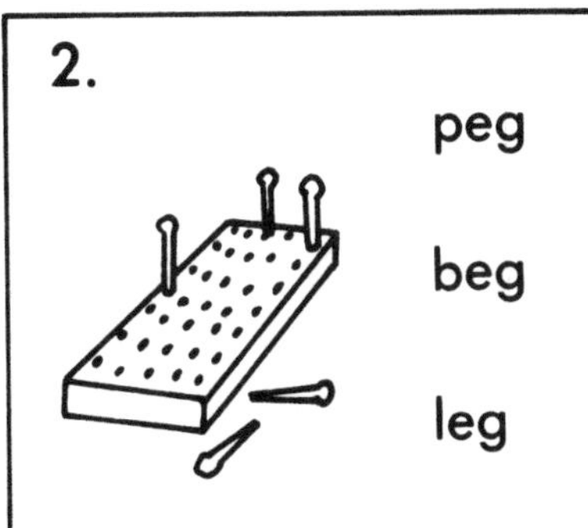

peg

beg

leg

3.

mail

rail

pail

4.

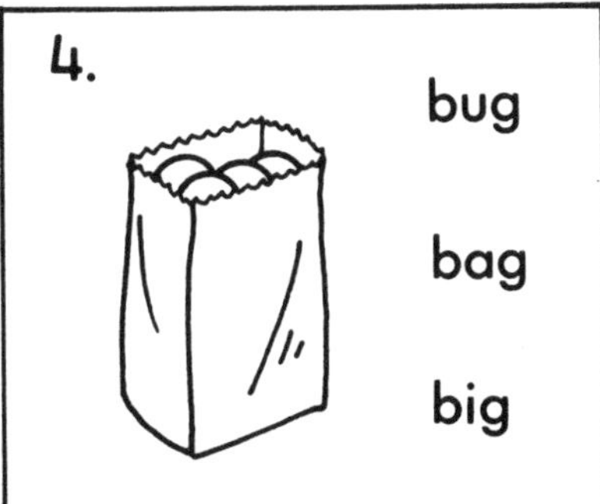

bug

bag

big

5.

house

hill

hats

6.

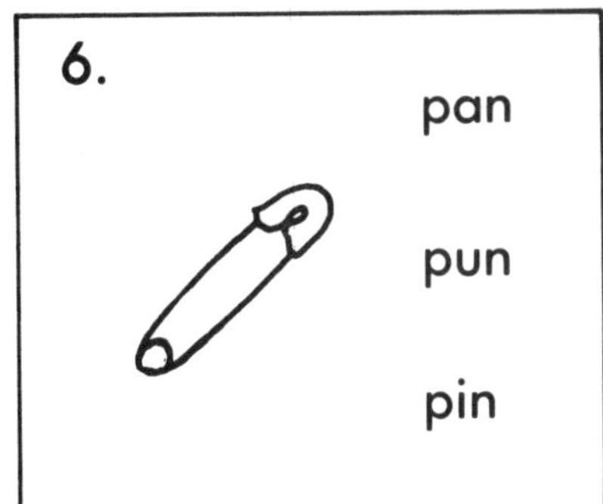

pan

pun

pin

7.

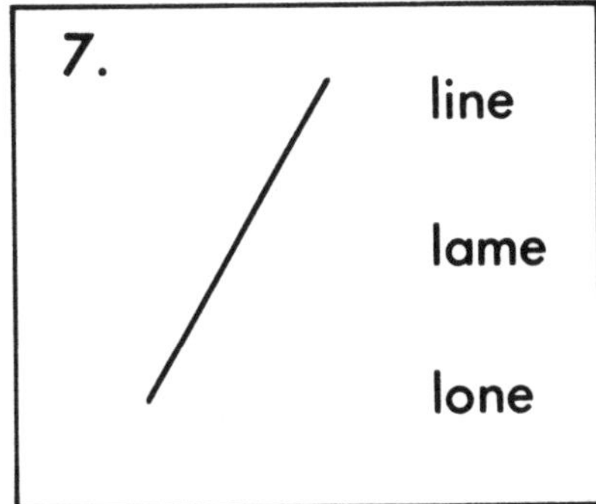

line

lame

lone

8.

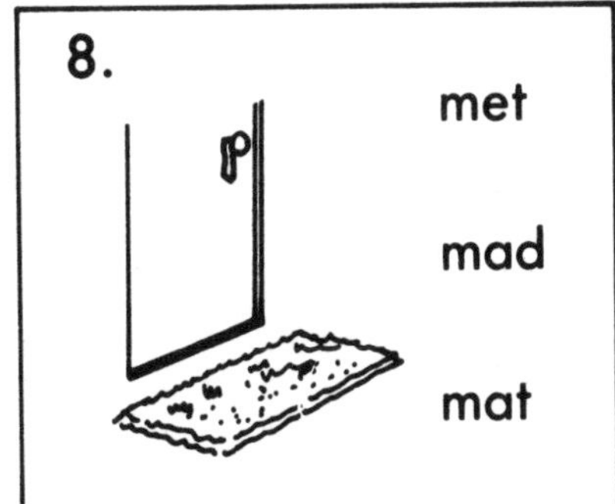

met

mad

mat

9.

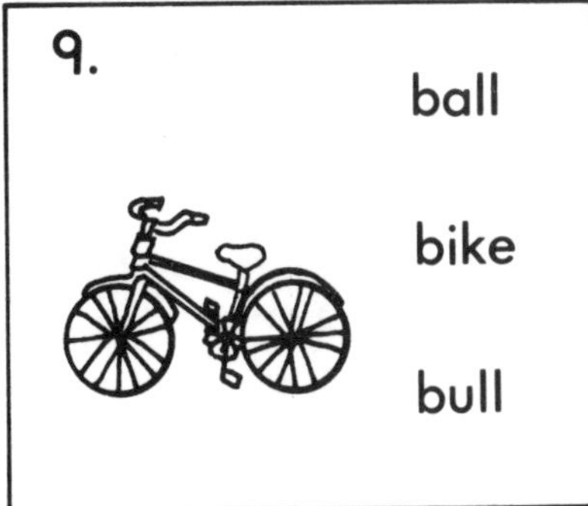

ball

bike

bull

10.

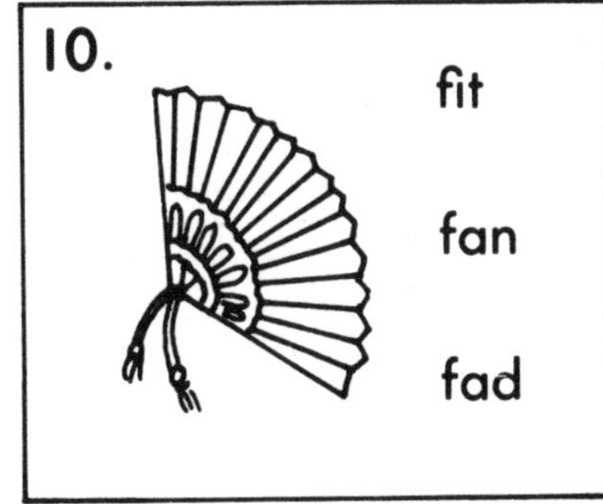

fit

fan

fad

11.

pool

fool

school

12.

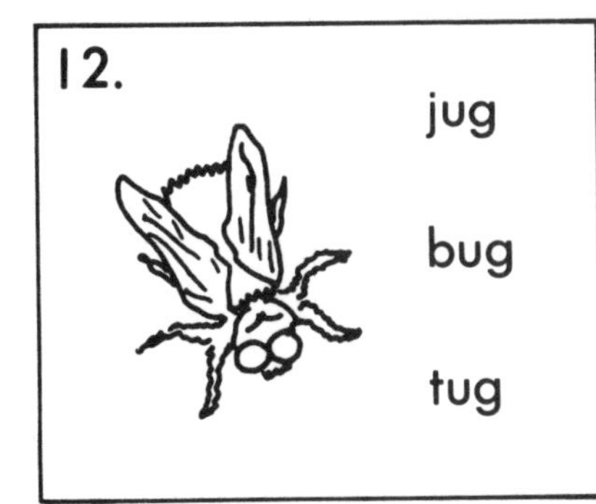

jug

bug

tug

- Underline the word that matches the picture.

Reading Test

SEATWORK 42

NAME ______________________________

1.
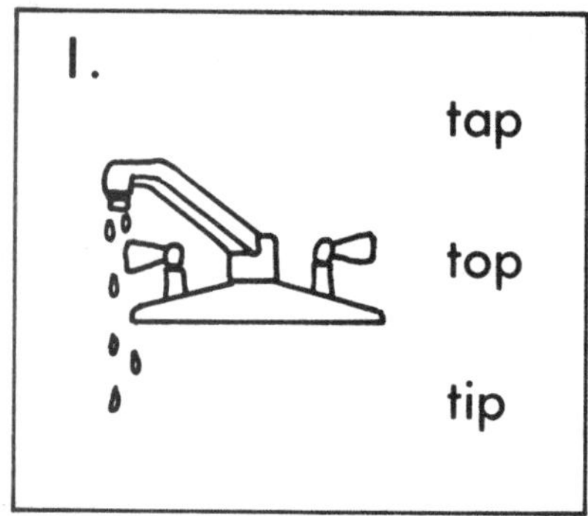
tap
top
tip

2.
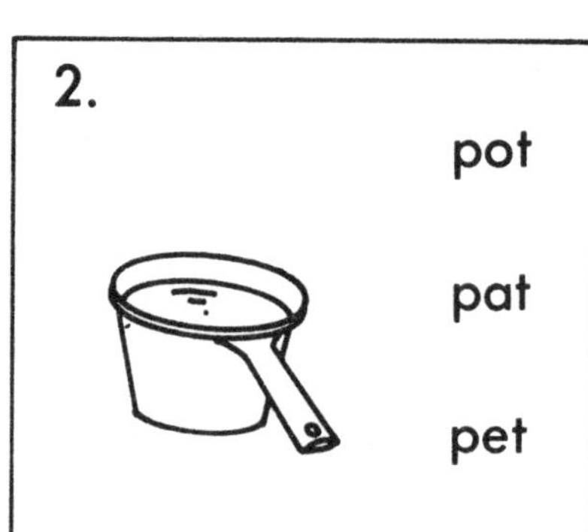
pot
pat
pet

3.
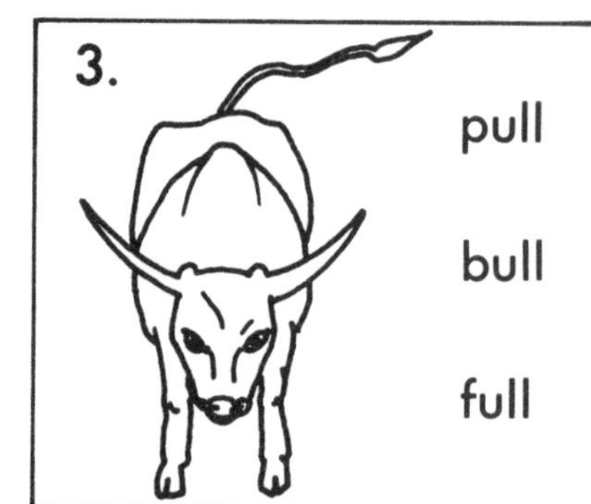
pull
bull
full

4.
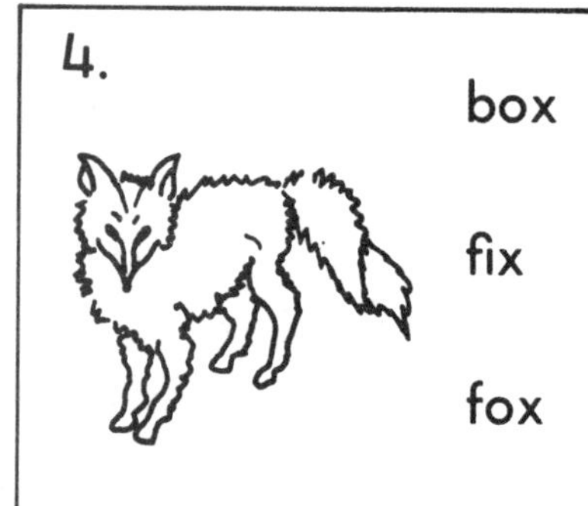
box
fix
fox

5.

mail
milk
mill

6.

bird
bike
girl

7.
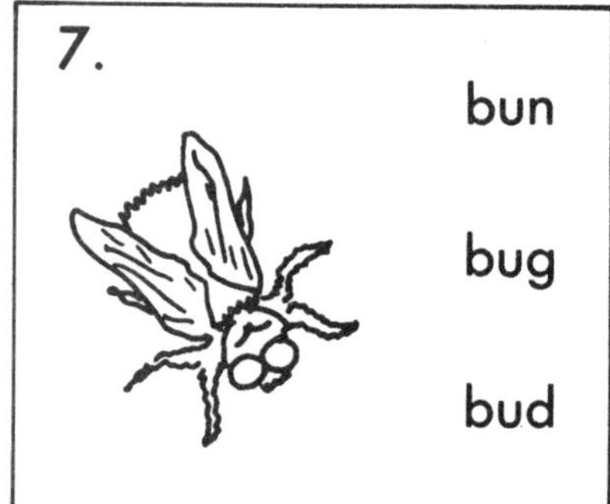
bun
bug
bud

8.
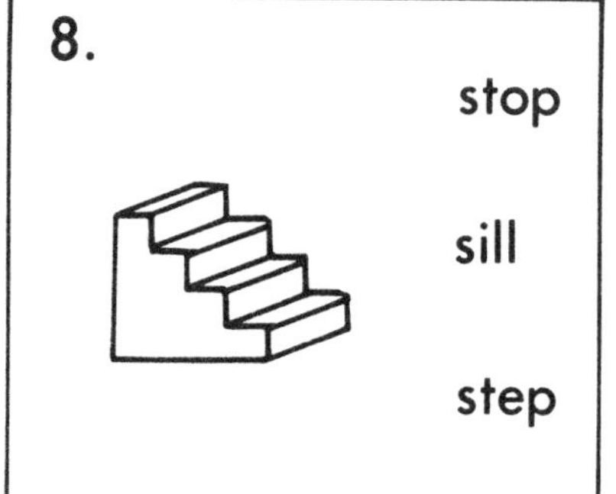
stop
sill
step

9.

ban
bat
bad

10.
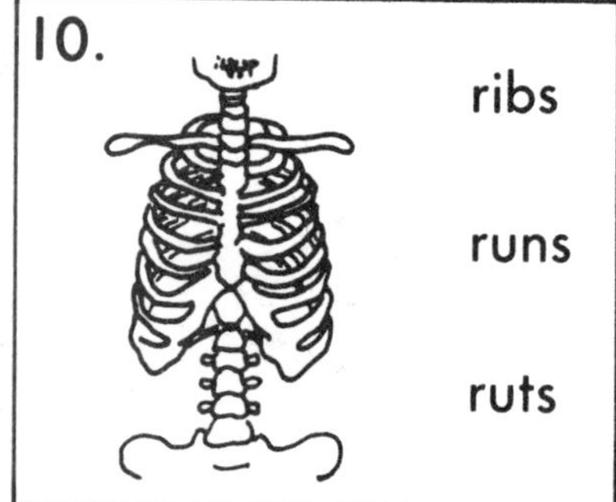
ribs
runs
ruts

11.
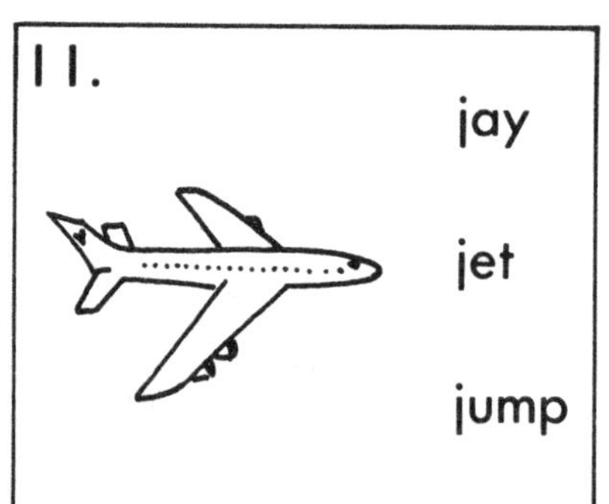
jay
jet
jump

12.
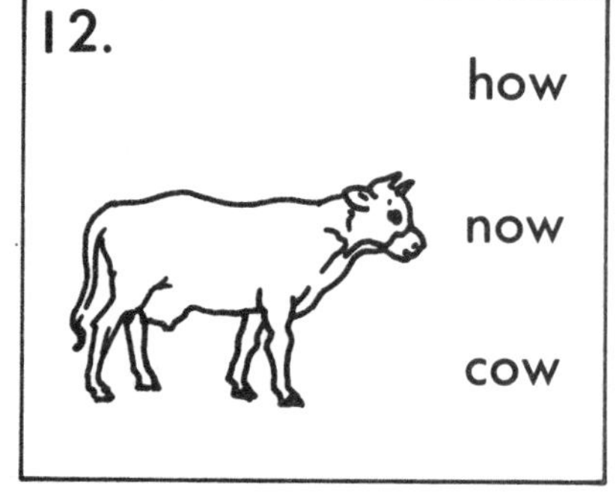
how
now
cow

- Underline the word that matches the picture.

Reading Test

SEATWORK 43

NAME ______________________________

1.

pin
pig
pit

2.
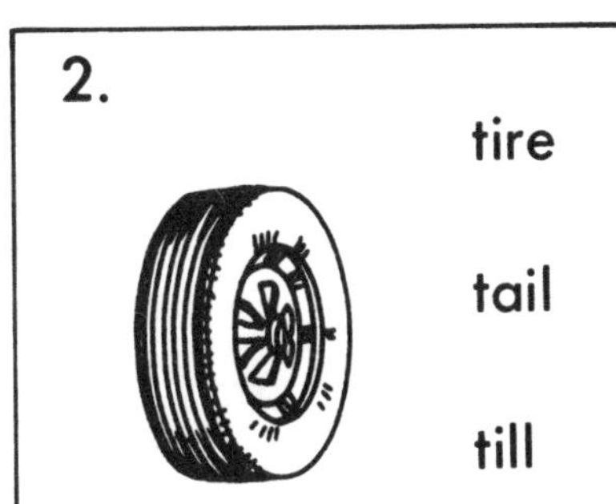
tire
tail
till

3.
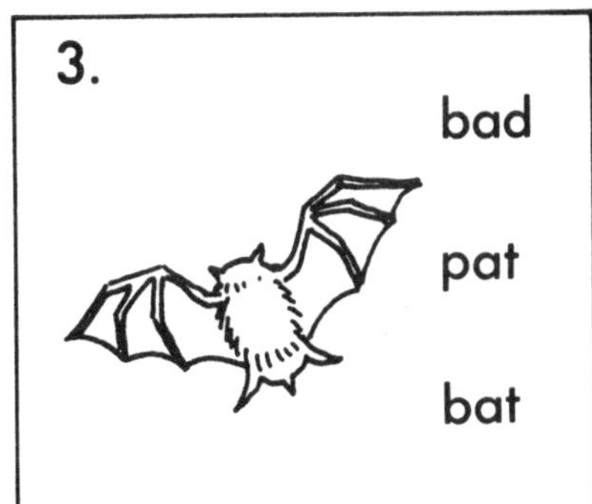
bad
pat
bat

4.
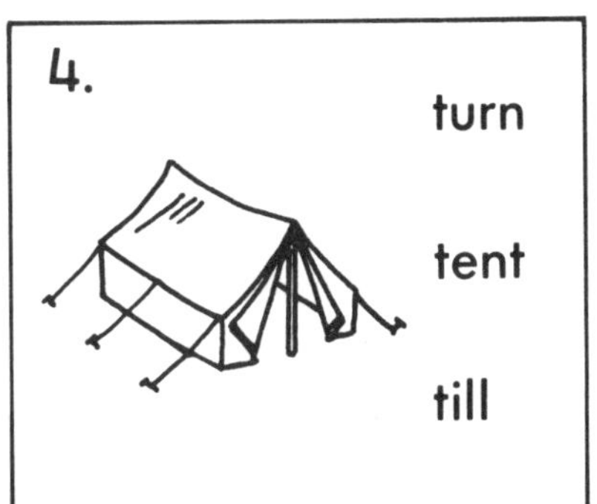
turn
tent
till

5.
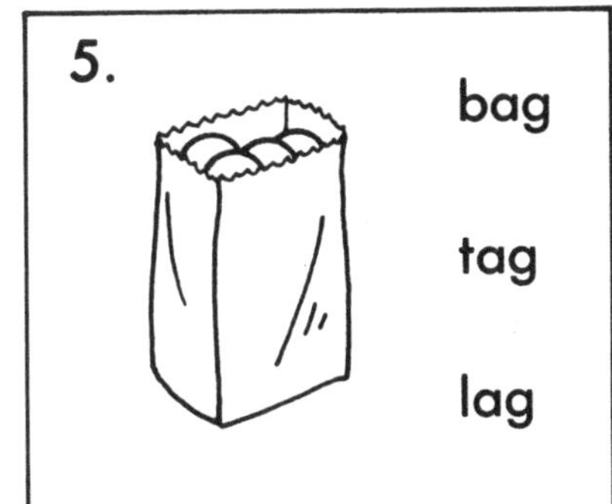
bag
tag
lag

6.
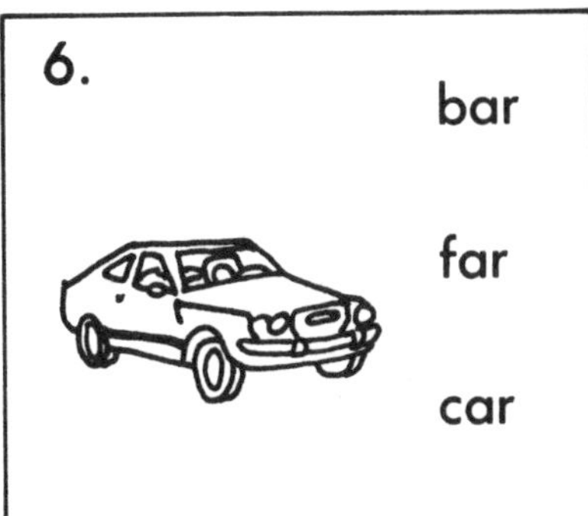
bar
far
car

7.
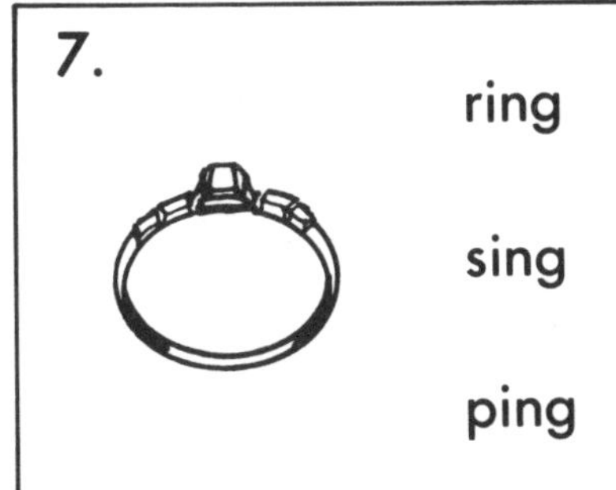
ring
sing
ping

8.

hike
hall
hill

9.
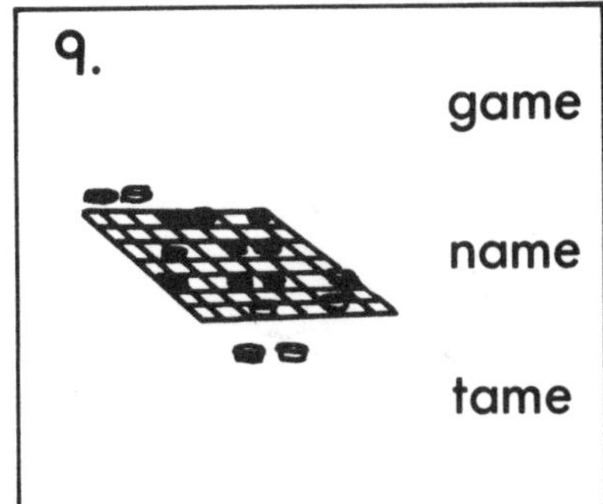
game
name
tame

10.

sun
nun
run

11.
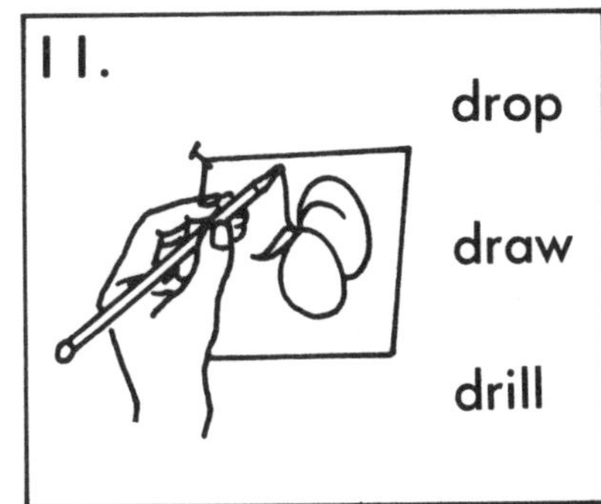
drop
draw
drill

12.
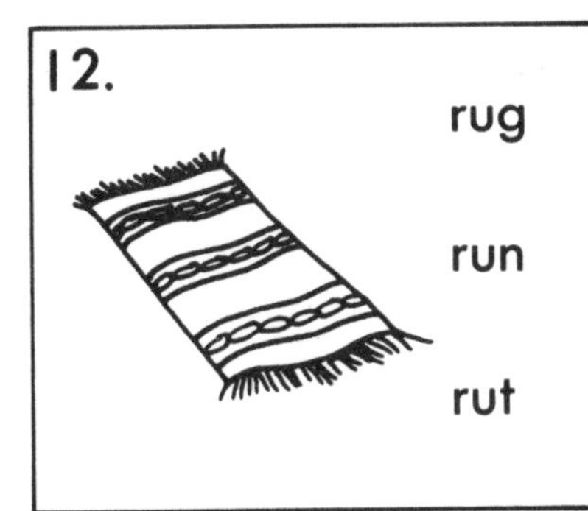
rug
run
rut

• Underline the word that matches the picture.

Reading Test

SEATWORK 44

NAME ______________________________

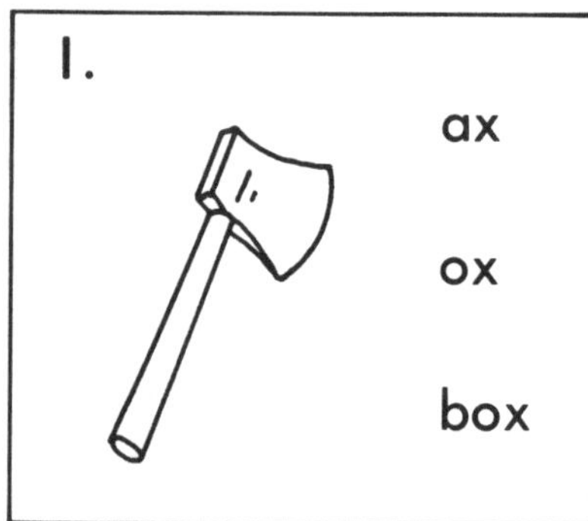
1.
ax
ox
box

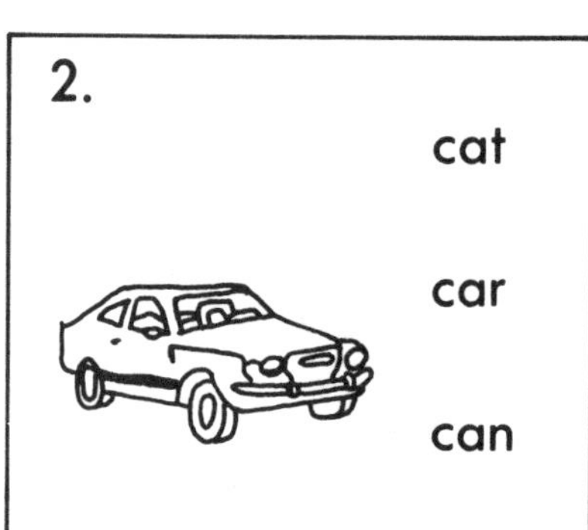
2.
cat
car
can

3.
cluck
clock
click

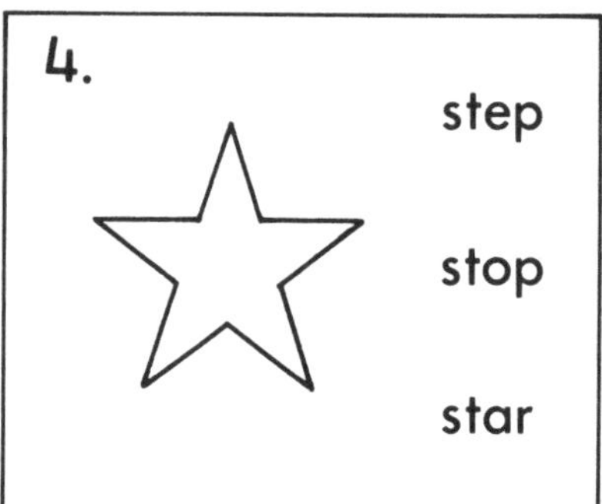
4.
step
stop
star

5.
dill
doll
ball

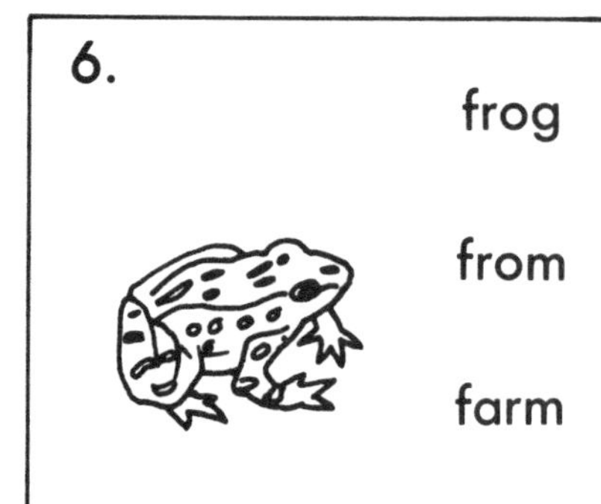
6.
frog
from
farm

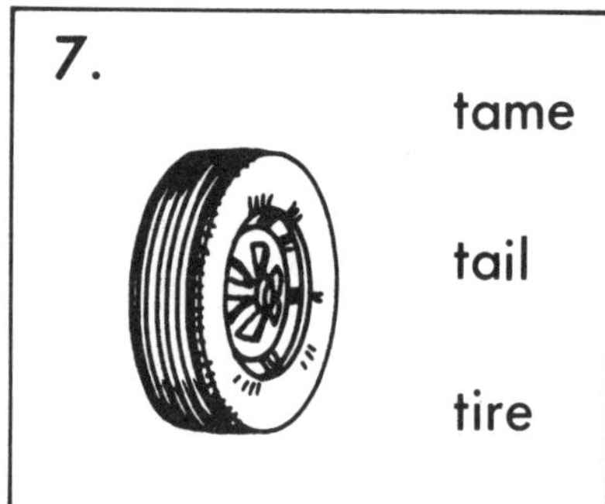
7.
tame
tail
tire

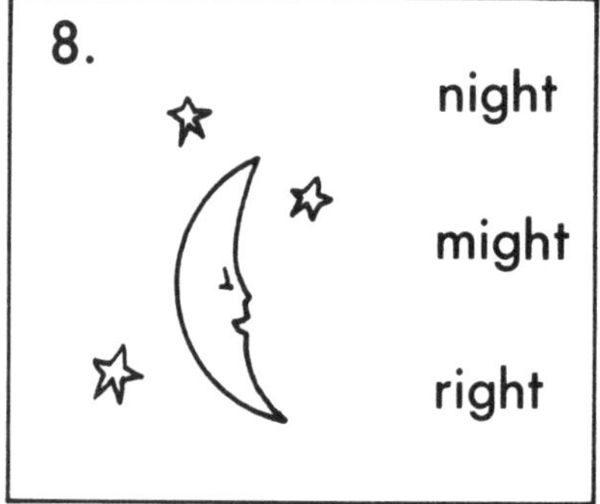
8.
night
might
right

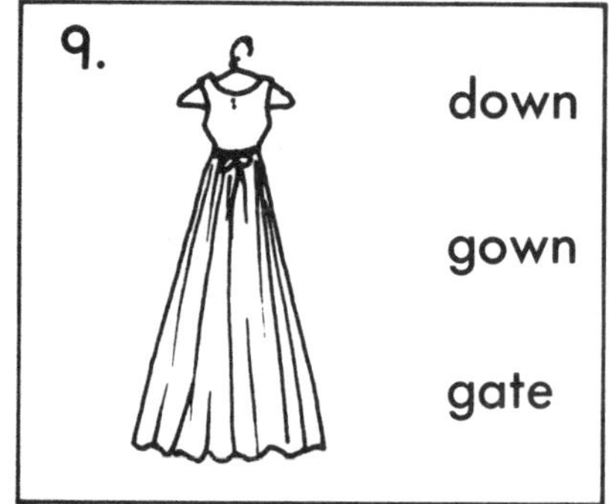
9.
down
gown
gate

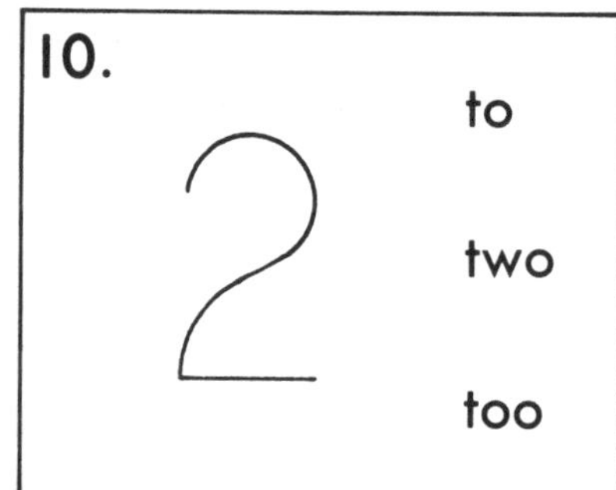
10.
to
two
too

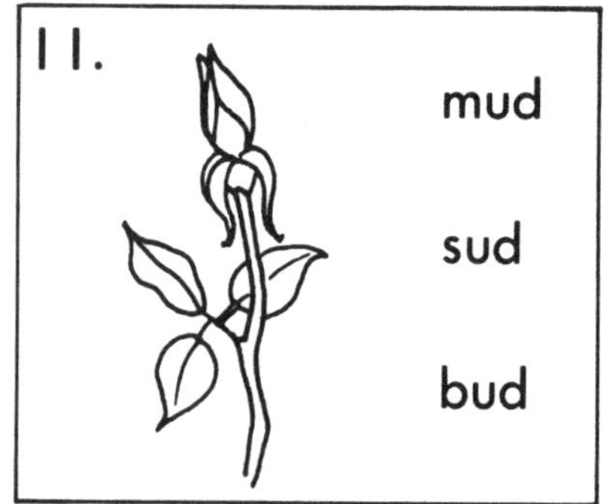
11.
mud
sud
bud

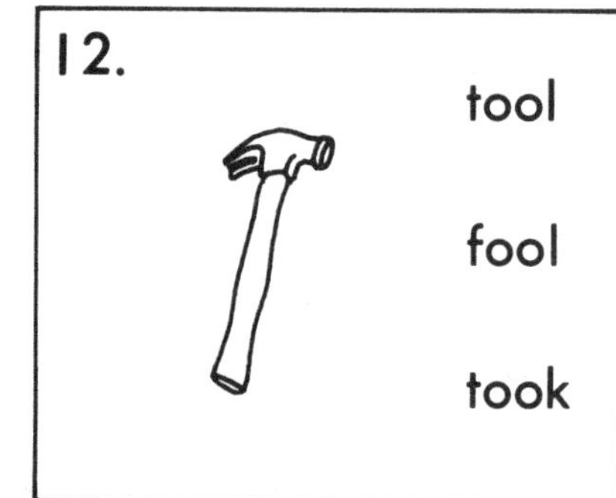
12.
tool
fool
took

- Underline the word that matches the picture.

Spelling

SEATWORK 1

NAME ______________________

I ______ ______ ______ ______

the ______ ______ ______ ______

and ______ ______ ______ ______

to ______ ______ ______ ______

a ______ ______ ______ ______

I see the cat and the dog.

____

The dog ran to the boy.

____

- Copy the words and sentences using the learning-to-spell routine.

Spelling

SEATWORK 2

NAME ____________________

cat ________ ________ ________ ________

cot ________ ________ ________ ________

cup ________ ________ ________ ________

can ________ ________ ________ ________

cop ________ ________ ________ ________

cat pat rat mat sat bat

cat

can ran man pan Dan

can

- Copy the words using the learning-to-spell routine.

Spelling

SEATWORK 3

NAME ______________________

big ________ ________ ________ ________

but ________ ________ ________ ________

bet ________ ________ ________ ________

Bob ________ ________ ________ ________

bad ________ ________ ________ ________

bet pet let met set net

bet

bad mad sad lad pad dad

b

- Copy the words using the learning-to-spell routine.

Spelling

SEATWORK 4

NAME ______________________

you of in we for

The cop saw Bob and the dog.

The

He likes the dog. He pats him.

He

The cop likes Bob and the dog.

The

• Copy the words and sentences using the learning-to-spell routine.

Spelling

SEATWORK 5

NAME ______________________

mat pet lot sit cut

lot pot got not hot dot

lot

sit pit hit bit fit lit

sit

cut nut hut but rut

cut

- Copy the words using the learning-to-spell routine.

Spelling

SEATWORK 6

NAME ______________________

can ________ ________ ________ ________

hen ________ ________ ________ ________

pin ________ ________ ________ ________

fun ________ ________ ________ ________

Don ________ ________ ________ ________

Don and Bob had lots of fun.

Don

Don bet he could hit the ball.

Don

He won the bet. He

- Copy the words and sentences using the learning-to-spell routine.

Spelling

SEATWORK 7

NAME ______________________

it	that	is	your	have

The dog has a bad cut.

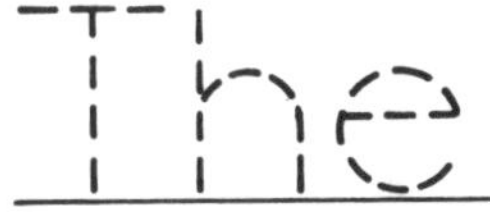

He will go to the vet.

The vet will fix the cut.

- Copy the words and sentences using the learning-to-spell routine.

Spelling

SEATWORK 8

NAME ______________________

bet	get	jet	let
bet			

net	pet	set	vet
net			

• Copy the words using the test-study routine (for words with a vowel-consonant common ending).

Spelling

SEATWORK 9

NAME ____________________

will ________ ________ ________ ________

be ________ ________ ________ ________

are ________ ________ ________ ________

not ________ ________ ________ ________

as ________ ________ ________ ________

will bill hill fill kill pill sill

will

be he we me he we me

be

We will not be late today.

We

- Copy the words and the sentences using the learning-to-spell and the test-study routines (where appropriate).

Spelling

SEATWORK 10

NAME ______________________________

ban	can	fan	man	pan
______	______	______	______	______
______	______	______	______	______
______	______	______	______	______
______	______	______	______	______
ran	**tan**	**van**	**Jan**	**Dan**
______	______	______	______	______
______	______	______	______	______
______	______	______	______	______
______	______	______	______	______

- Copy the words using the test-study routine.

Spelling

SEATWORK 11

NAME ______________________

bag	________	________	sag	________	________
tag	________	________	wag	________	________
beg	________	________	leg	________	________
peg	________	________	dig	________	________
fig	________	________	pig	________	________
wig	________	________	dog	________	________
fog	________	________	hog	________	________
jog	________	________	log	________	________
dug	________	________	hug	________	________
jug	________	________	mug	________	________
rug	________	________	tug	________	________

- Copy the words using the learning-to-spell routine.

Spelling

SEATWORK 12

NAME ______________________________

at this with but on

The pig and dog play in the mud.

The

They dig up a big bag.

They tug at it and get it out.

• Copy the words and sentences using the learning-to-spell routine.

Spelling

SEATWORK 13

NAME ____________________

bad	______	______	Dad	______	______
had	______	______	mad	______	______
sad	______	______	bed	______	______
fed	______	______	led	______	______
red	______	______	Ted	______	______
bid	______	______	hid	______	______
lid	______	______	rid	______	______
cod	______	______	mod	______	______
nod	______	______	pod	______	______
sod	______	______	bud	______	______
dud	______	______	mud	______	______
sud	______	______	did	______	______

- Copy the words using the test-study routine.

Spelling

SEATWORK 14

NAME ____________________

at ___

at ______	no ______	sit ______
a ______	and ______	see ______
I ______	fun ______	an ______
an ______	bit ______	has ______
fat ______	pen ______	run ______
in ______	rat ______	me ______
sat ______	as ______	go ______
pin ______	gun ______	the ______

- Copy each word once using the learning-to-spell routine.

Spelling

SEATWORK 15

NAME ______________________

bin ________ ________ ________

the ________ ________ ________

as ________ ________ ________

mat ________ ________ ________

can ________ ________ ________

if ________ ________ ________

it ________ ________ ________

is ________ ________ ________

see ________ ________ ________

has ________ ________ ________

I ________ ________ ________

- Copy each word three times using the learning-to-spell routine.

Spelling

SEATWORK 16

NAME ______________________

yet ________ ________ ________

I ________ ________ ________

see ________ ________ ________

vet ________ ________ ________

wit ________ ________ ________

kit ________ ________ ________

on ________ ________ ________

jet ________ ________ ________

the ________ ________ ________

is ________ ________ ________

go ________ ________ ________

- Copy each word three times using the learning-to-spell routine.

Spelling

SEATWORK 17

NAME ______________________________

big ________________	dip ________________
dig ________________	hip ________________
fig ________________	lip ________________
jig ________________	nip ________________
pig ________________	pip ________________
rig ________________	rip ________________
wig ________________	sip ________________
	tip ________________

- Copy each word once using the test-study routine.

Spelling

SEATWORK 18

NAME ______________________

ad

ad	in	o	at
an	et	am	it
up	ed	en	ee

- Make up words using these endings.

Spelling

SEATWORK 19

NAME ______________________

am

am	et	at	it	an
ad	in	o	ip	ap

- Make up words using these endings.

Spelling

SEATWORK 20

NAME ______________________

pan

cat	pin	bet	tan	bad
sit	bed	Sam	sap	Bob
wig	gun	will	dot	sand

• Print other words with the same ending.

Spelling

SEATWORK 21

NAME ______________________

look ______ ______	look ______ ______

see ______ ______

ring ______ ______

cook ______ ______

sing ______ ______

do ______ ______

bark ______ ______

end ______ ______

turn ______ ______

• Copy the word once, then again, adding *ing*.

Spelling

SEATWORK 22

NAME ____________________

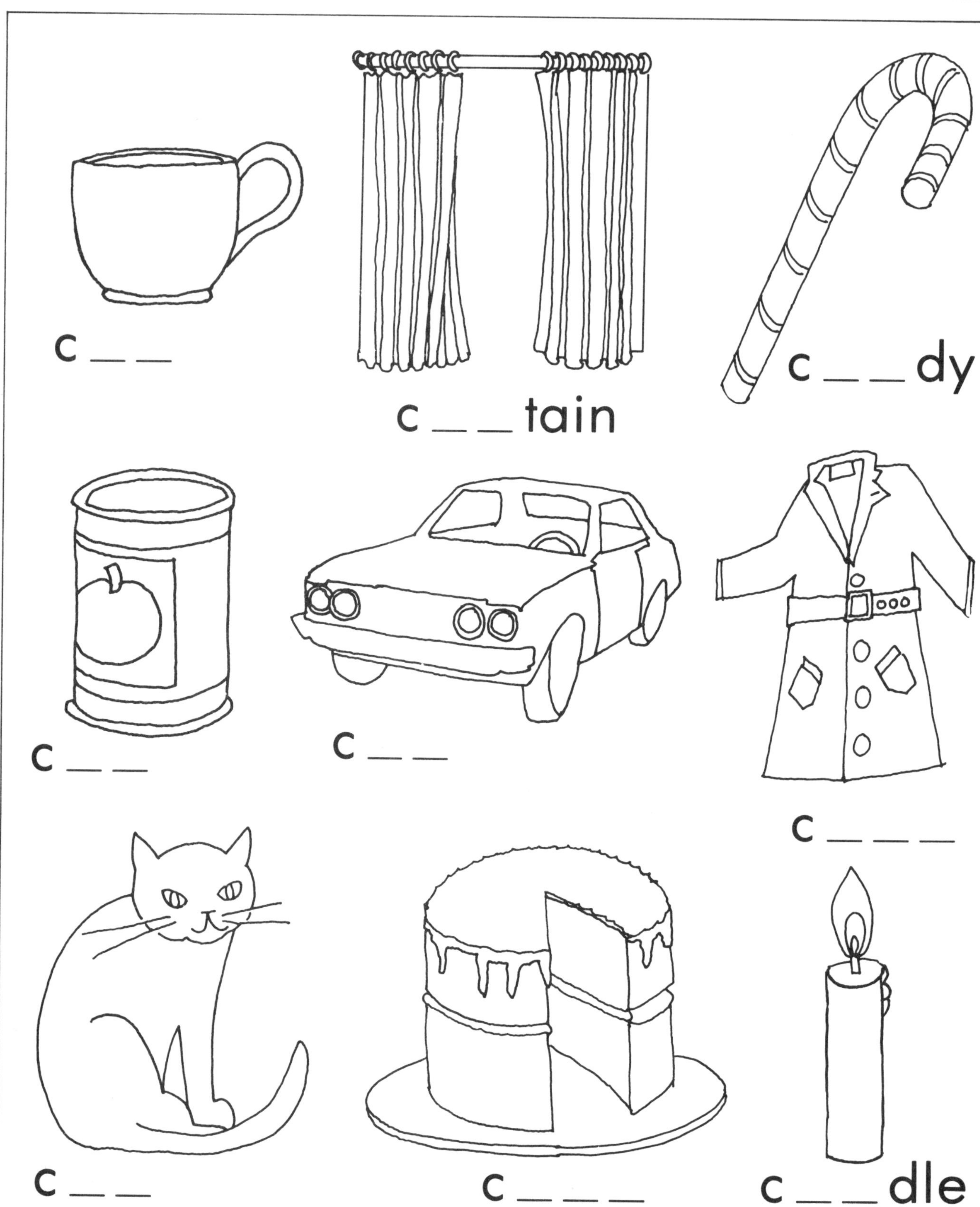

• Complete each word.

Spelling

SEATWORK 23

NAME ______________________

- Complete each word.

Spelling

SEATWORK 24

NAME ______________________

• Complete each word.

Spelling

SEATWORK 25

NAME ____________________

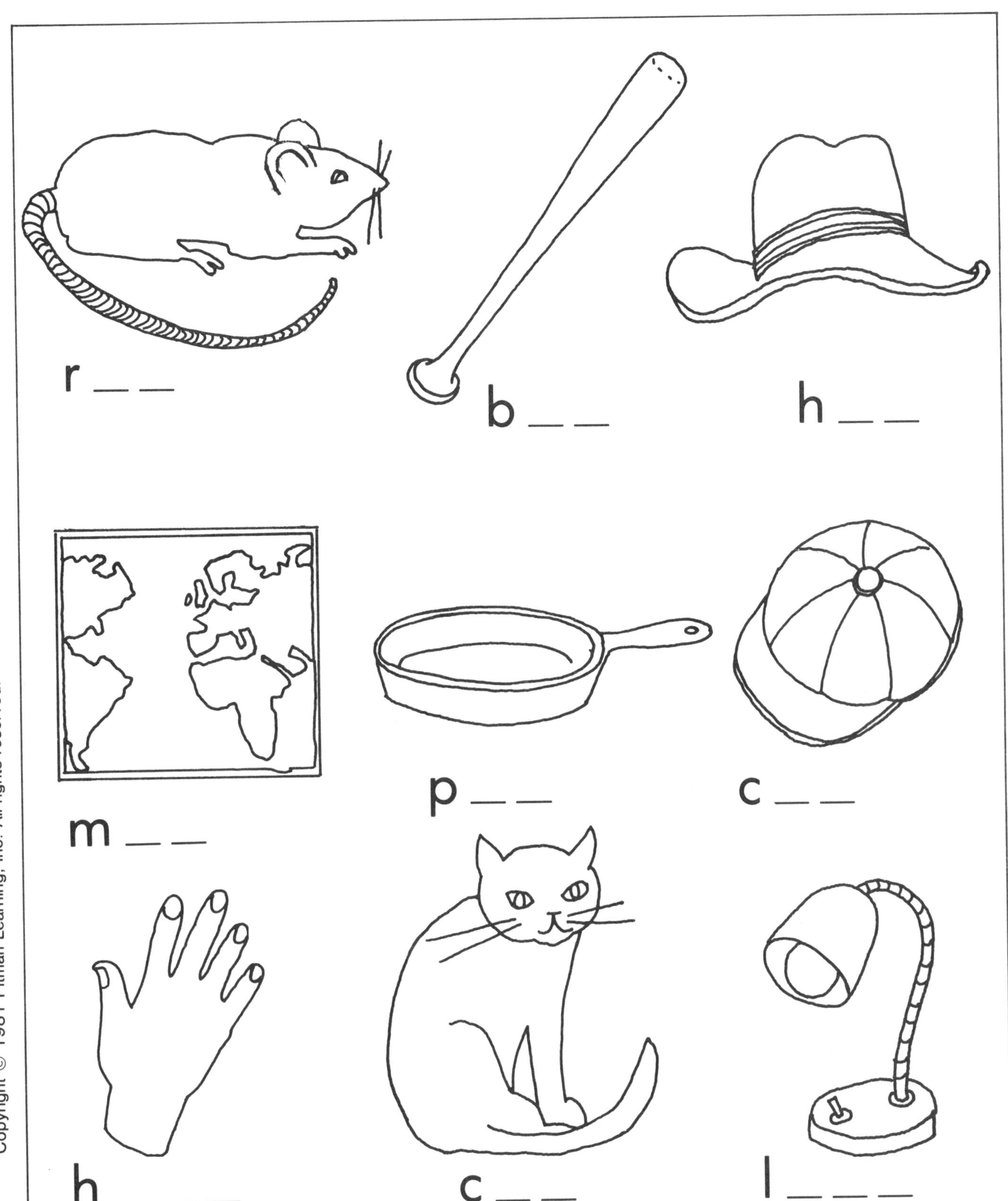

• Complete each word.

Spelling

SEATWORK 26

NAME ______________________________

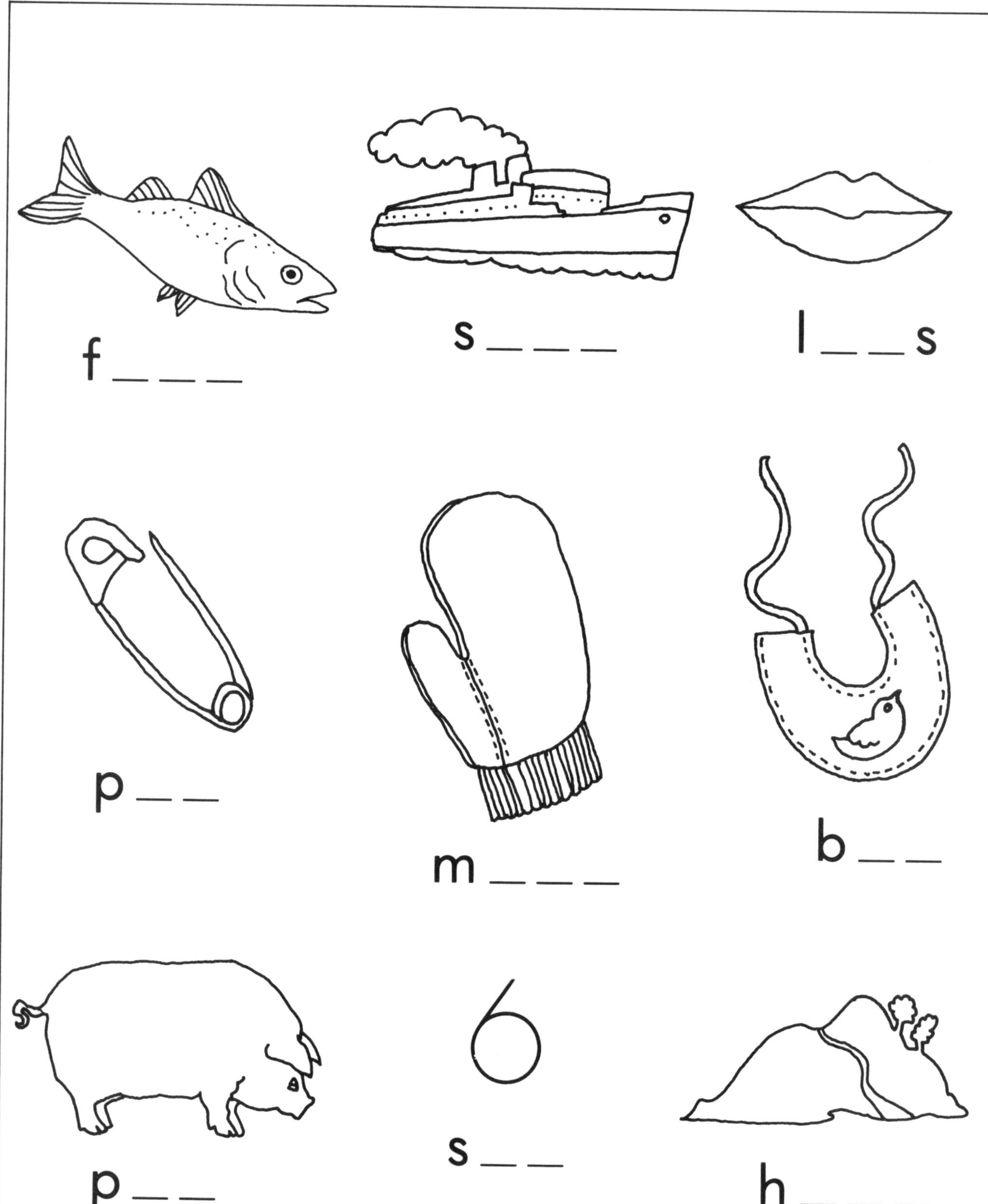

- Complete each word.

Spelling

SEATWORK 27

NAME ______________________

- Complete each word.

Spelling

SEATWORK 28

NAME ______________________________

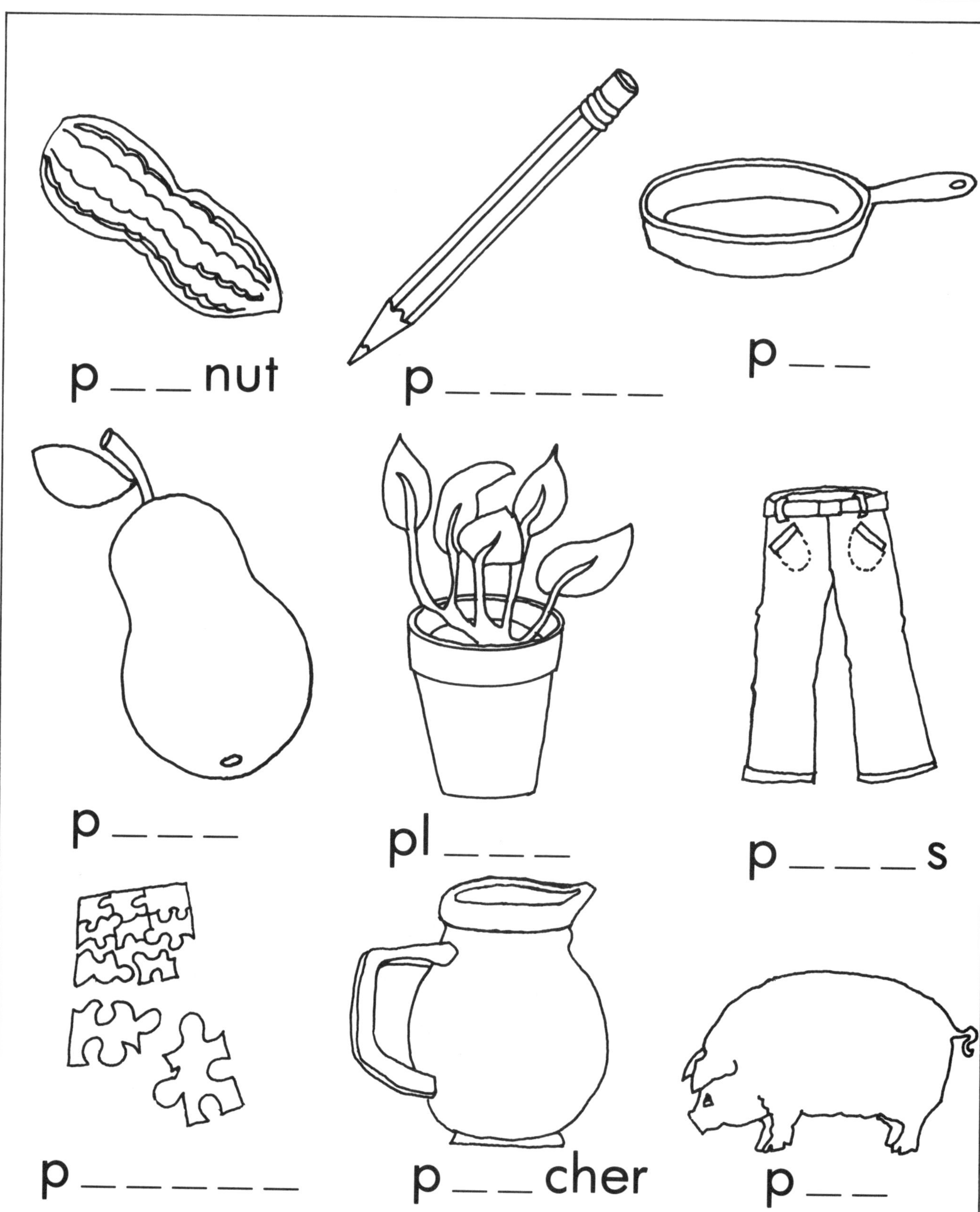

- Complete each word.

Spelling

SEATWORK 29

NAME ______________________________

- Complete each word.

Spelling

SEATWORK 30

NAME ______________________________

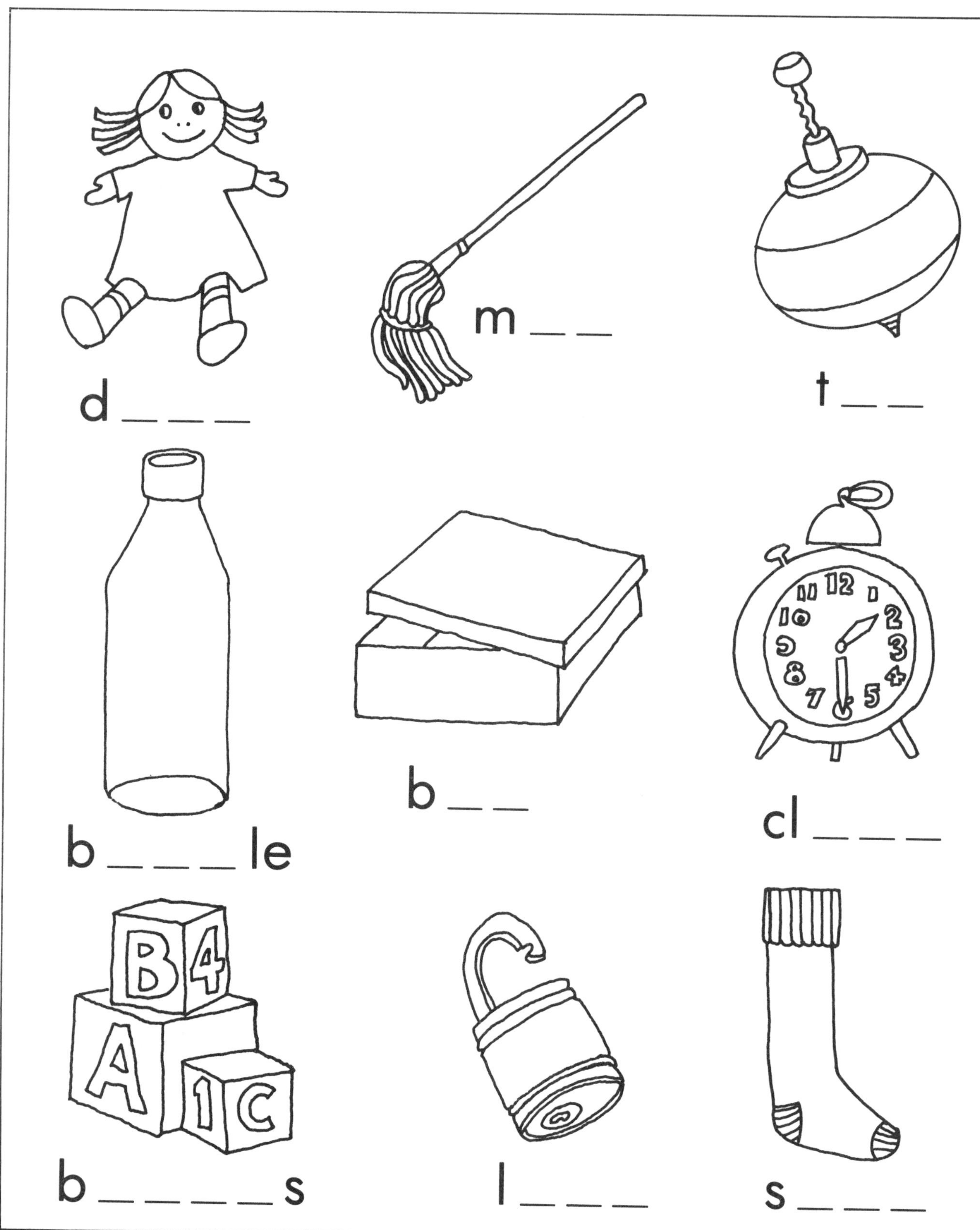

- Complete each word.

Spelling

SEATWORK 31

NAME ______________________________

- Complete each word.

Spelling

SEATWORK 32

NAME ______________________

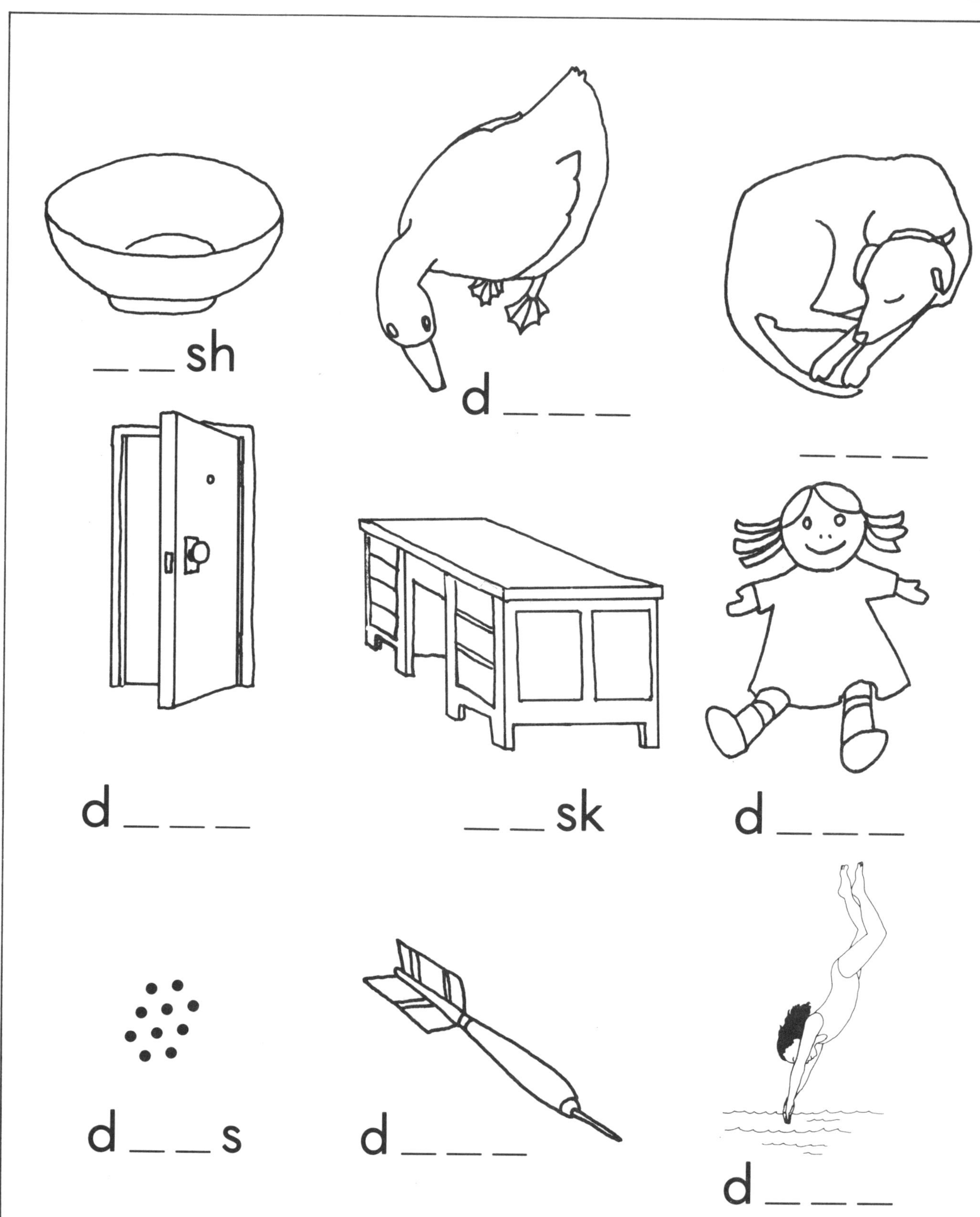

- Complete each word.

Spelling

SEATWORK 33

NAME ______________________

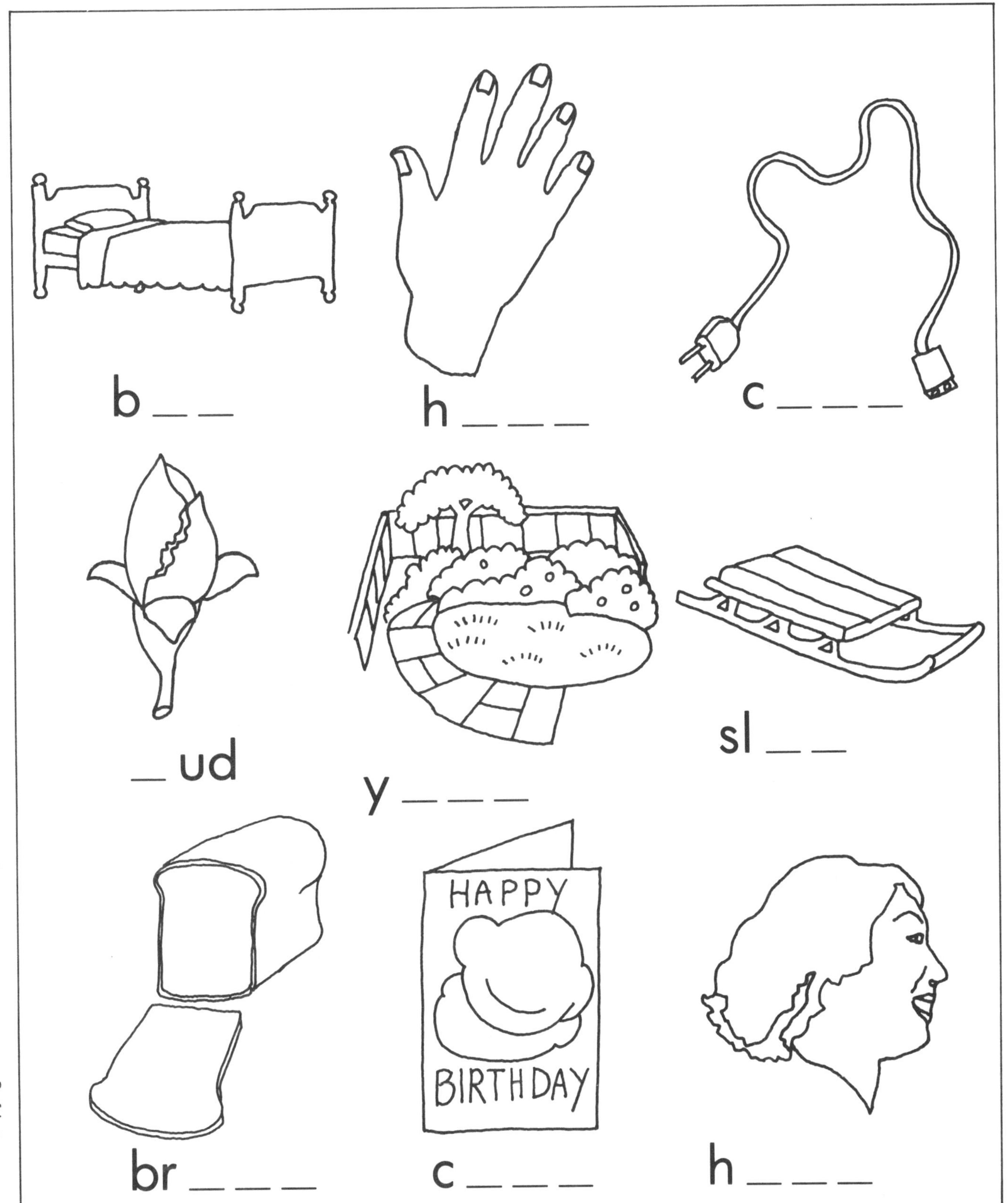

• Complete each word.

Spelling

SEATWORK 34

NAME ____________________

_ _ _ _ _ s

fl _ _ _ _ s

_ _ _ s

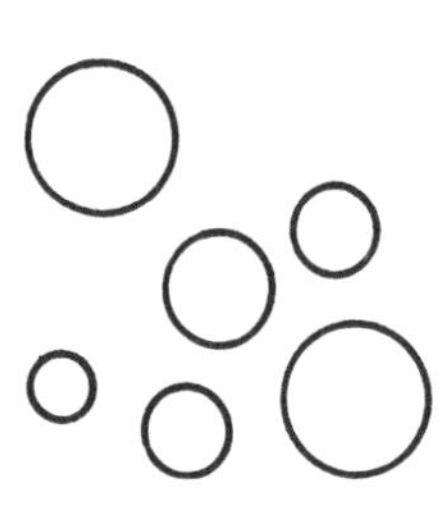

bu _ _ les

c _ _ _ s

_ _ _ s

s _ _ _ s

umbrella _

_ _ _ s

• Complete each word.

Spelling

SEATWORK 35

NAME ________________________

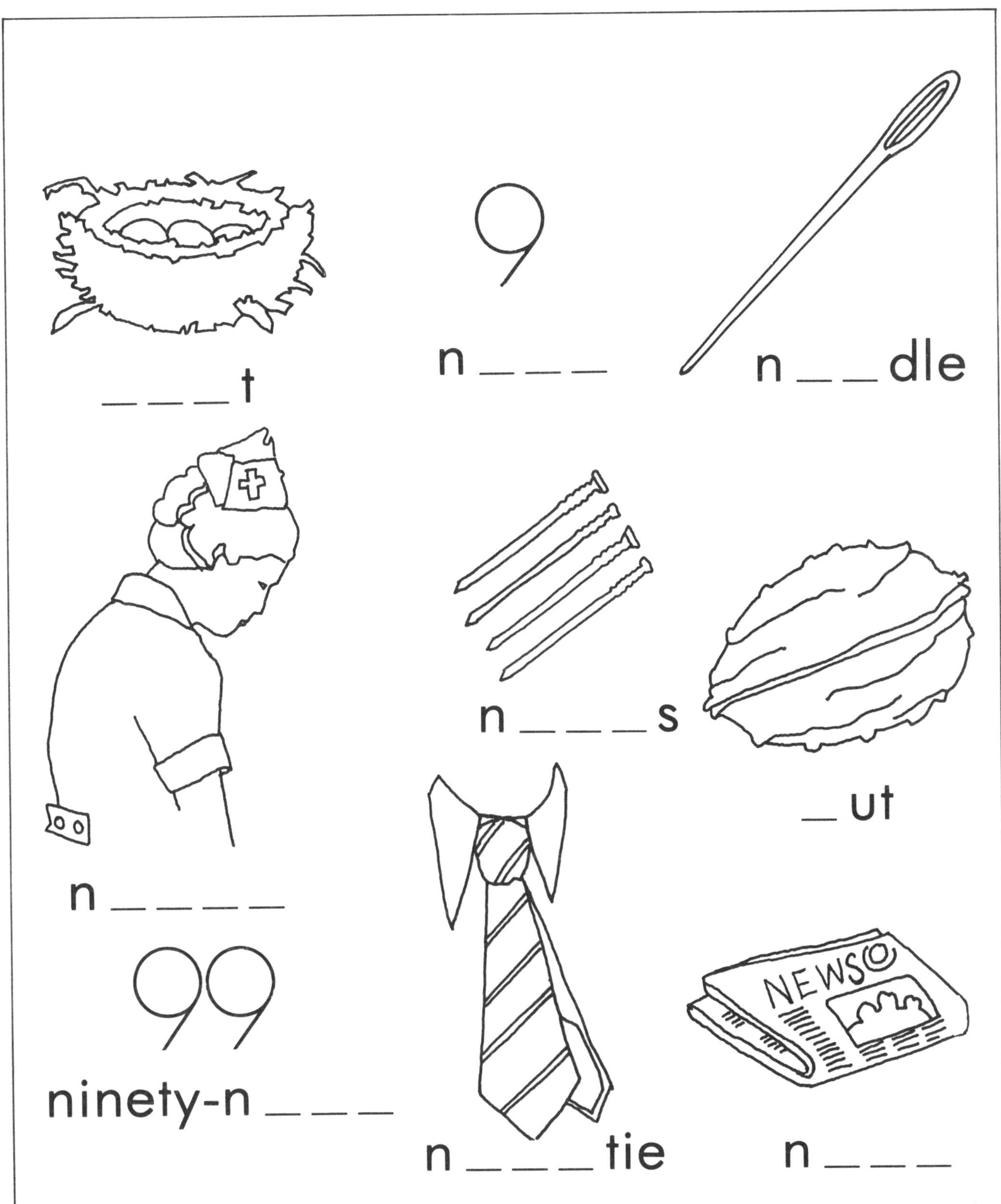

- Complete each word.

Spelling

SEATWORK 36

NAME ________________

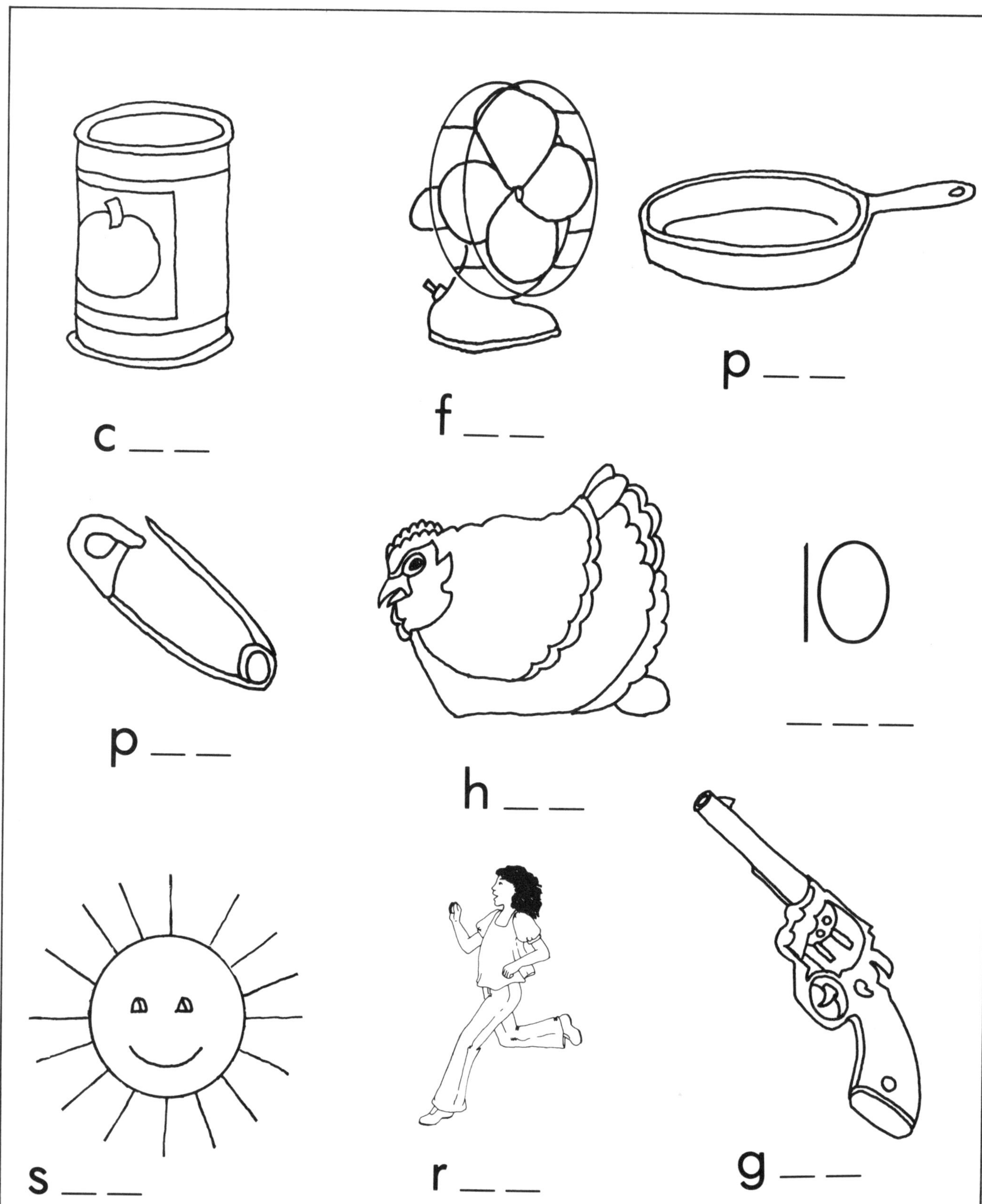

• Complete each word.

Spelling

SEATWORK 37

NAME ______________________________

___ ___ ___

7

s ___ ___ ___ ___

p ___ ___ cil

s ___ ___ ___

b ___ ___ ___

b ___ ___ ch

10

___ ___ ___

t ___ ___ t

b ___ ___ ___

- Complete each word.

Spelling

SEATWORK 38

NAME ______________________

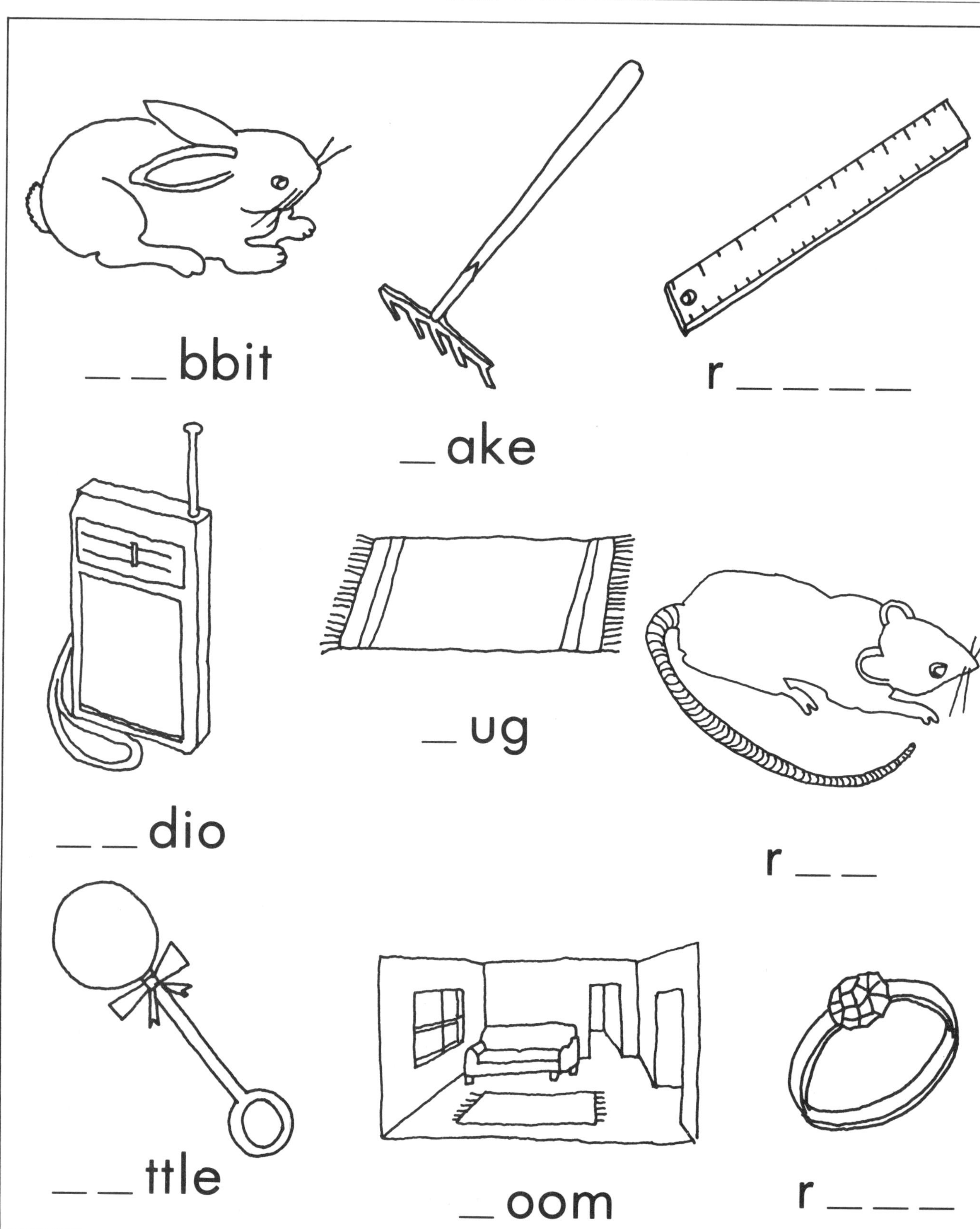

- Complete each word.

Spelling

SEATWORK 39

NAME ______________________________

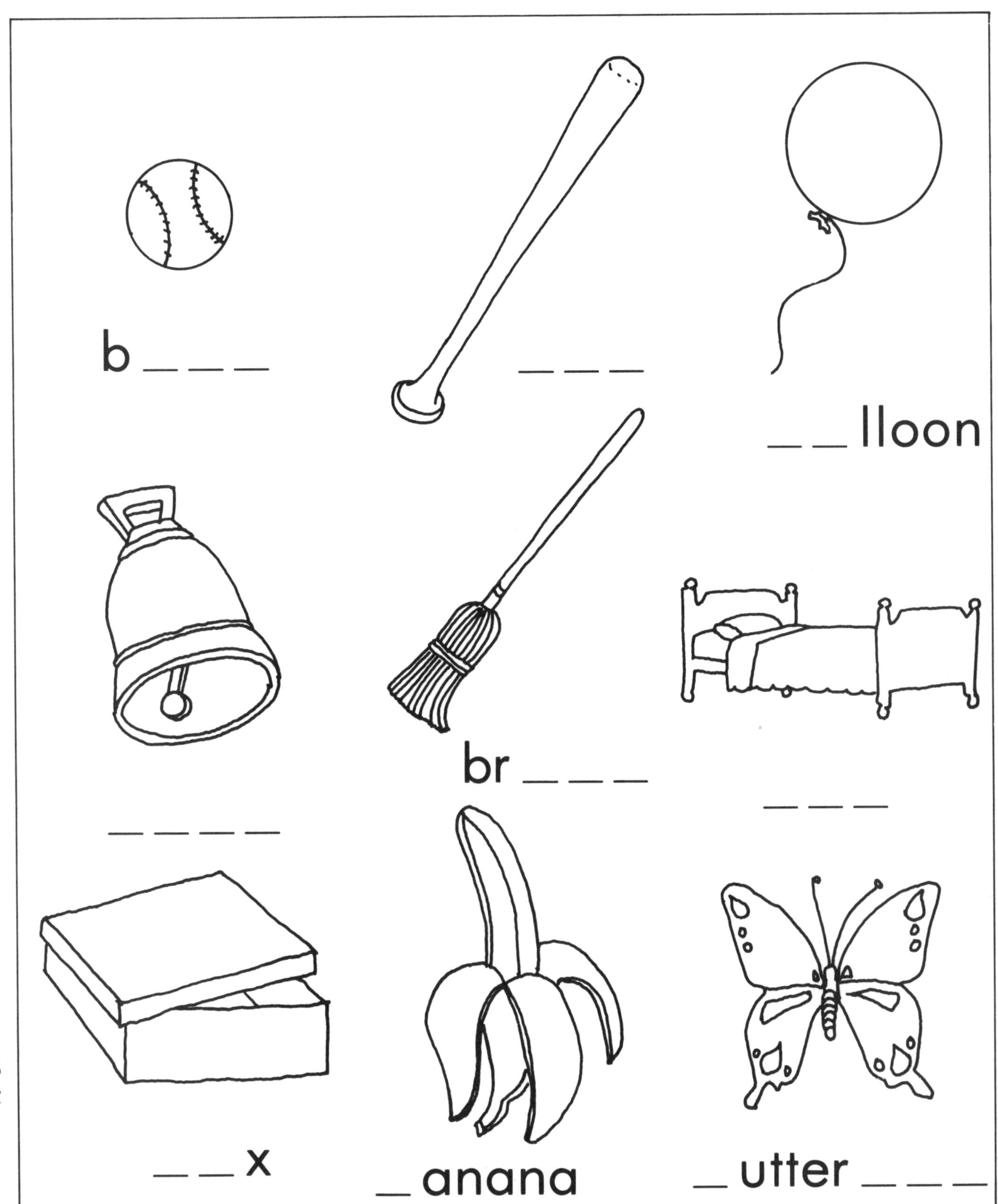

- Complete each word.

Spelling

SEATWORK 40

NAME ____________________

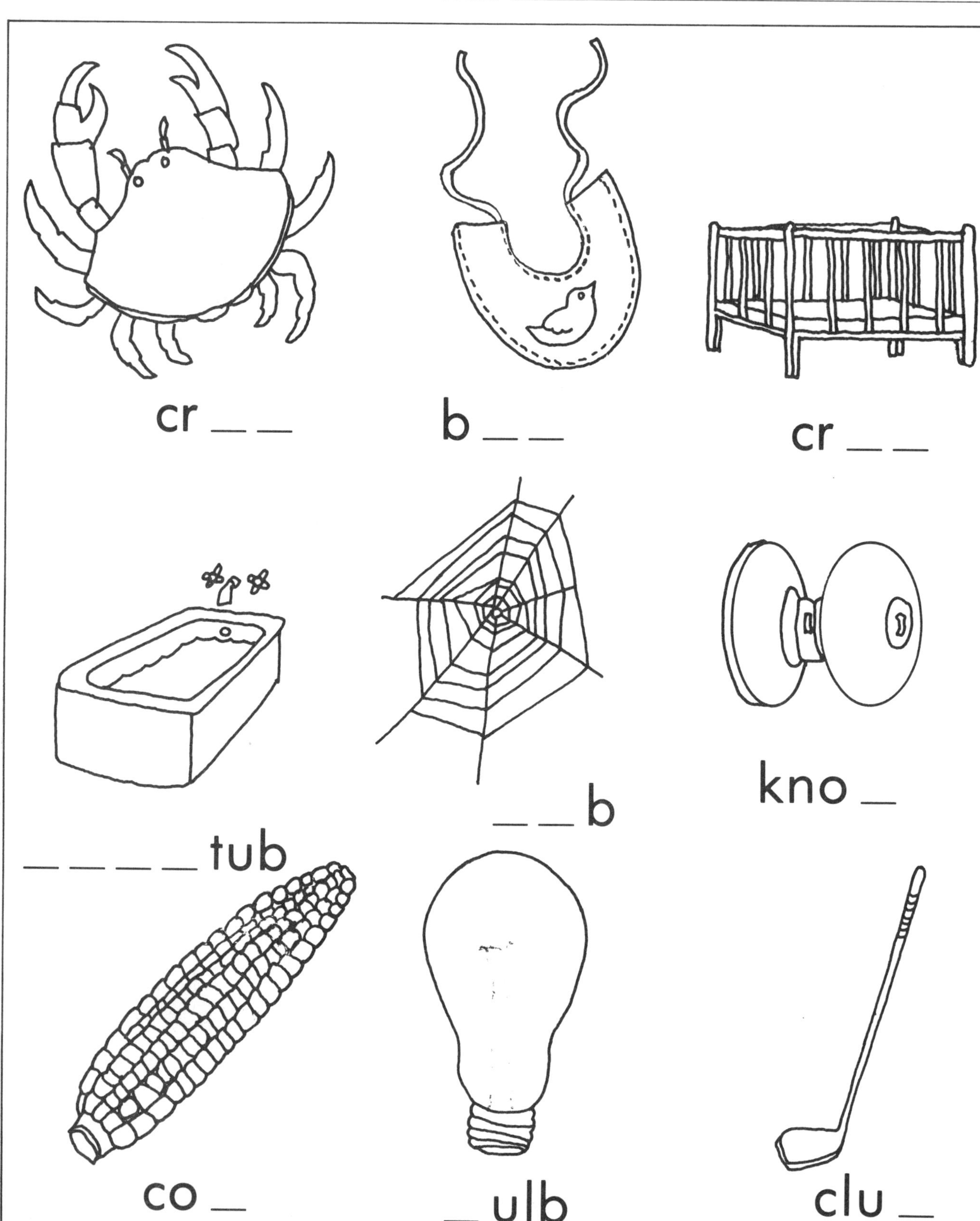

- Complete each word.

Spelling

SEATWORK 41

NAME ______________________

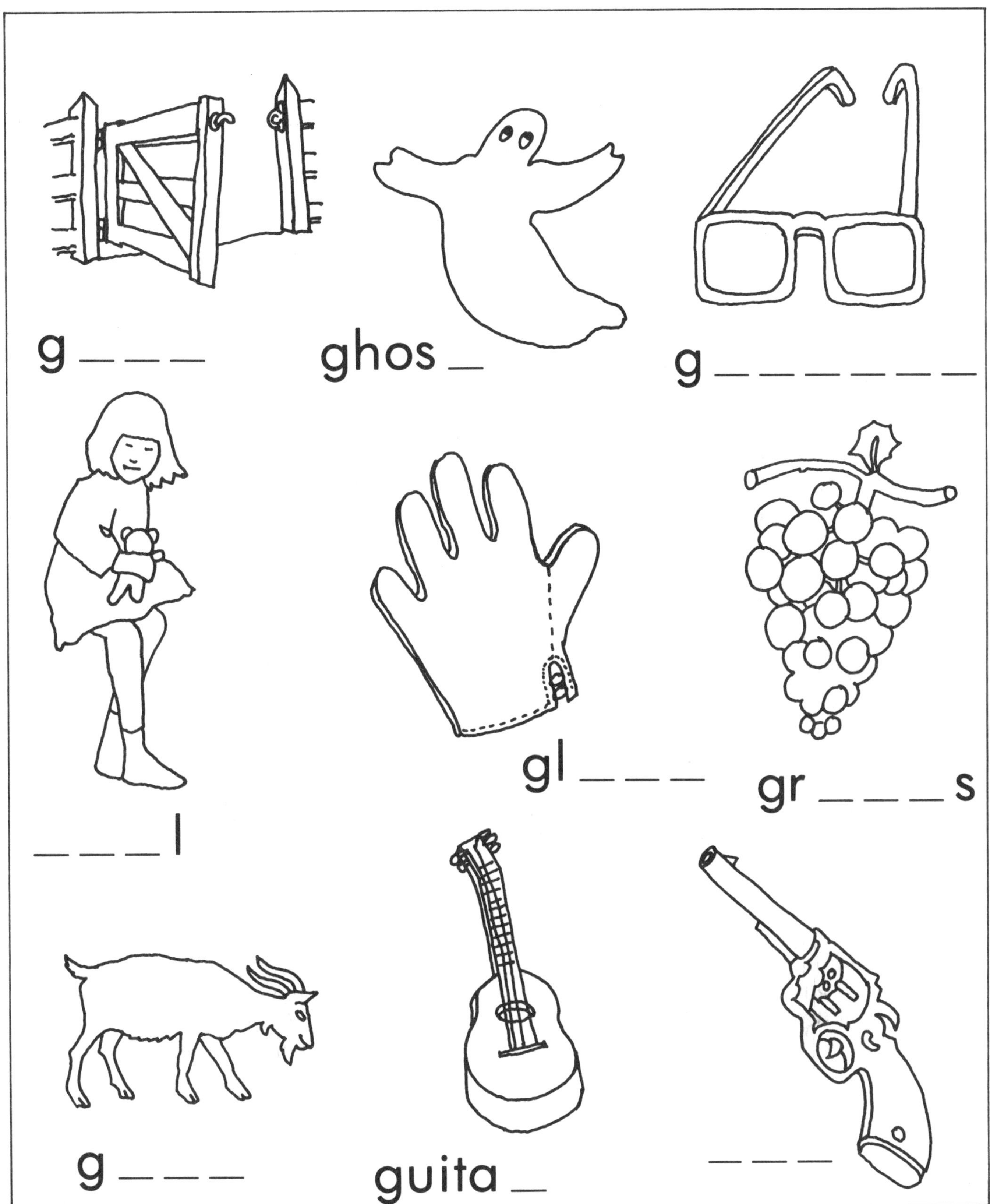

• Complete each word.

Spelling

SEATWORK 42

NAME ______________________________

- Complete each word.

Spelling

SEATWORK 43

NAME ______________________

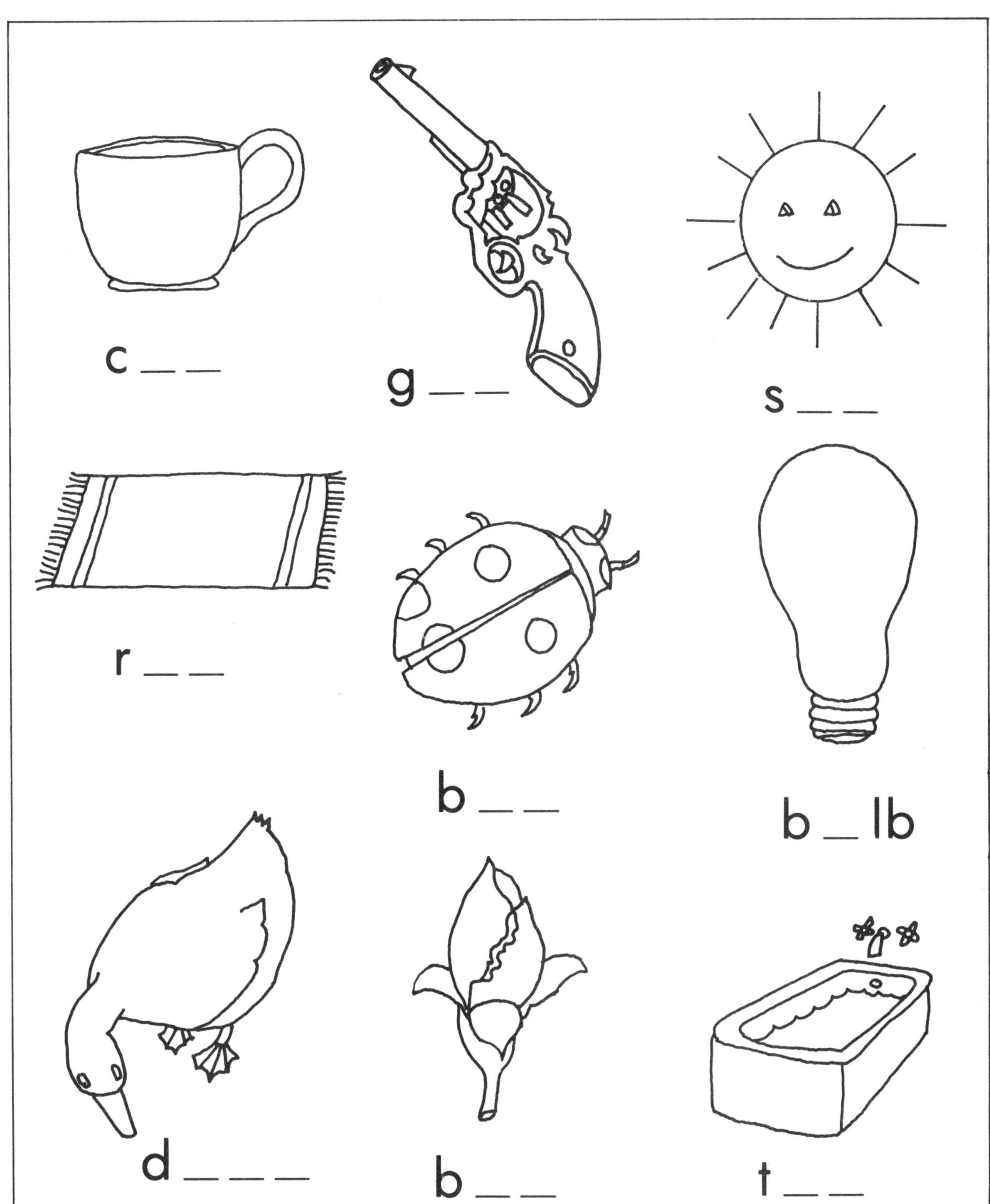

- Complete each word.

Spelling

SEATWORK 44

NAME ______________________________

- Complete each word.

Spelling

SEATWORK 45

NAME ______________________

- Complete each word.

Printing

SEATWORK 1

NAME ______________________

a b c d e f g h i j

k l m n o p q r s t

u v w x y z

A B C D E F G H I

J K L M N O P Q R

S T U V W X Y Z

1 2 3 4 5 6 7 8 9 10 11 12 13 14

15 16 17 18 19 20 21 22 23 24

25 26 27 28 29 30 31 32 33

Monday Tuesday Wednesday

Thursday Friday Saturday

Sunday

- Copy onto another paper.

Printing

SEATWORK 2

NAME ______________________

January	Jan.
February	Feb.
March	Mar.
April	Apr.
May	May
June	June
July	July
August	Aug.
September	Sept.
October	Oct.
November	Nov.
December	Dec.

- Copy onto another paper.

Printing

SEATWORK 3

NAME ______________________________

Printing

SEATWORK 4

NAME ____________________

a

a

a

a

a

• Trace letters and make additional letters.

Printing

SEATWORK

NAME ____________________

Answer Key

Reading

SEATWORK 1: Letter Recognition

NAME ______

a b c d e f g h

i j k l m n o p q

r s t u v w x y z

a b c d e f g h i

j k l m n o p q r

s t u v w x y z

• Trace the letters and print the missing letters.

Reading

SEATWORK 2: Letter Recognition

NAME ______

A B C D E F G

H I J K L M N

O P Q R S T

U V W X Y Z

A B C D E F G

H I J K L M N

O P Q R S T

U V W X Y Z

A B C D E F G

• Trace the letters and print the missing letters.

Reading

SEATWORK 3: Letter Recognition

NAME ____________

a b c d e f g h i
j k l m n o p q r
s t u v w x y z
a b c d e f g h i
j k l m n o p q r
s t u v w x y z
a b c d e f g h i
j k l m n o p q r
s t u v w x y z

- Trace the letters and print the missing letters.

Reading

SEATWORK 4: Letter Recognition

NAME ____________

A B C D E
F G H I J K
L M N O P
Q R S T U
V W X Y Z

- Trace the letters and print the missing letters.

Reading

SEATWORK 5: Plurals

NAME ____________

1 fan, 2 fans

1 fin, 2 fins

1 kit, 2 kits

1 fig, 2 figs

1 sip, 2 sips

1 bed, 2 beds

1 lid, 2 lids

1 cat, 2 cats

1 hat, 2 hats

1 mat, 2 mats

1 tap, 2 taps

1 hog, 2 hogs

1 van, 2 vans

1 dog, 2 dogs

1 log, 2 logs

- Write the plural of each word.

Reading

SEATWORK 6: Verbs Ending in S

NAME ____________

I sit. He sits.

I run. She runs.

I hop. He hops.

I eat. She eats.

I skip. He skips.

I play. She plays.

I stand. He stands.

I jump. She jumps.

I smile. He smiles.

I talk. She talks.

I turn. He turns.

I throw. She throws.

I sing. He sings.

I dance. She dances.

- Change the ending for each verb.

Reading
SEATWORK 7: Sentences

NAME ____________

dog I the see ⟶ I see the dog.

bat see the I I see the bat.

has ants Jill Jill has ants.

run hill I up the I run up the hill.

wet Sam's is hat Sam's hat is wet.

away dog runs the The dog runs away.

red the is van The van is red.

big is cat that That cat is big.

is wet not ball the The ball is not wet.

fills he can tin the He fills the tin can.

- Change the order of the words and print the sentence.

Reading
SEATWORK 8: Sentences

NAME ____________

can see ⟶ I see the can.

Answers will vary.

tin fill I will fill the tin.

met dog I met the dog.

she mad She made me mad.

ball hit I hit the ball.

hat see I see the hat.

cat dog I have a cat and dog.

man van The man has a van.

red hat I have a red hat.

- Make up and print a sentence including the given words.

Reading Test
SEATWORK 38

NAME ____________

1. cap / cat / **can**
2. ball / **bell** / bill
3. **mail** / rail / pail
4. peg / beg / **leg**
5. fight / **light** / sight
6. look / took / **book**
7. **pup** / cup / sup
8. **doll** / roll / toll
9. hike / **bike** / like
10. **box** / fox / lox
11. one / **two** / too
12. hut / **cut** / but

• Underline the word that matches the picture.

Reading Test
SEATWORK 39

NAME ____________

1. fall / call / **ball**
2. **bed** / red / fed
3. **pig** / dig / big
4. sell / tell / **bell**
5. rib / **bib** / fib
6. **gun** / pun / bun
7. dine / nine / **line**
8. cap / **cup** / cop
9. hall / hull / **hill**
10. **boy** / toy / soy
11. rail / **pail** / sail
12. rag / tag / **bag**

• Underline the word that matches the picture.

Reading Test
SEATWORK 40

NAME ______________________

1.  tin, ton, **ten**
2.  run, sin, **sun**
3.  can, **pan**, tan
4.  **tub**, hub, sub
5.  bunch, **lunch**, punch
6.  bag, **bug**, rag
7.  **hat**, bat, fat
8.  dog, fog, **log**
9.  wire, **fire**, hire
10.  **bat**, but, bit
11.  fun, **gun**, bun
12.  Nan, **Dan**, pan

• Underline the word that matches the picture.

Reading Test
SEATWORK 41

NAME ______________________

1.  hook, **book**, look
2.  **peg**, beg, leg
3.  mail, rail, **pail**
4.  bug, **bag**, big
5.  **house**, hill, hats
6.  pan, pun, **pin**
7.  **line**, lame, lone
8.  met, mad, **mat**
9.  ball, **bike**, bull
10.  fit, **fan**, fad
11.  pool, fool, **school**
12.  jug, **bug**, tug

• Underline the word that matches the picture.

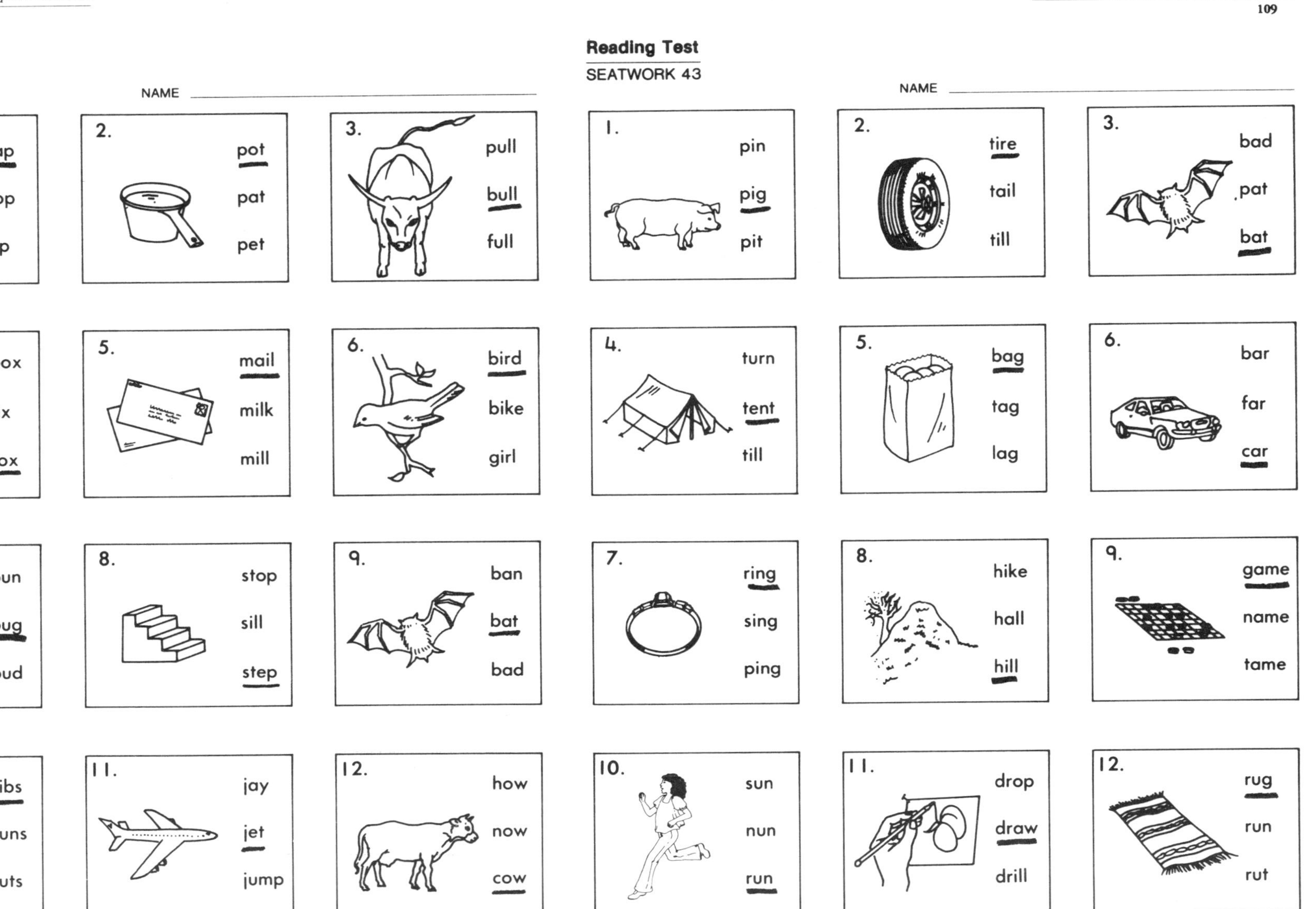

Reading Test

SEATWORK 42

NAME ____________________

1. tap top tip
2. pot pat pet
3. pull bull full
4. box fix fox
5. mail milk mill
6. bird bike girl
7. bun bug bud
8. stop sill step
9. ban bat bad
10. ribs runs ruts
11. jay jet jump
12. how now cow

- Underline the word that matches the picture.

Reading Test

SEATWORK 43

NAME ____________________

1. pin pig pit
2. tire tail till
3. bad pat bat
4. turn tent till
5. bag tag lag
6. bar far car
7. ring sing ping
8. hike hall hill
9. game name tame
10. sun nun run
11. drop draw drill
12. rug run rut

- Underline the word that matches the picture.

Reading Test

SEATWORK 44

NAME ____________

1. _ax_ ox box
2. cat _car_ can
3. cluck _clock_ click
4. step stop _star_
5. dill _doll_ ball
6. _frog_ from farm
7. tame tail _tire_
8. _night_ might right
9. down _gown_ gate
10. to _two_ too
11. mud sud _bud_
12. _tool_ fool took

• Underline the word that matches the picture.

Spelling

SEATWORK 1

NAME ____________

I	I	I	I	I
the	the	the	the	the
and	and	and	and	and
to	to	to	to	to
a	a	a	a	a

I see the cat and the dog.

I see the cat and the dog.

The dog ran to the boy.

The dog ran to the boy.

• Copy the words and sentences using the learning-to-spell routine.

Spelling
SEATWORK 2

NAME ____________

cat	cat	cat	cat	cat
cot	cot	cot	cot	cot
cup	cup	cup	cup	cup
can	can	can	can	can
cop	cop	cop	cop	cop

cat	pat	rat	mat	sat	bat
cat	pat	rat	mat	sat	bat

can	ran	man	pan	Dan
can	ran	man	pan	Dan

- Copy the words using the learning-to-spell routine.

Spelling
SEATWORK 3

NAME ____________

big	big	big	big	big
but	but	but	but	but
bet	bet	bet	bet	bet
Bob	Bob	Bob	Bob	Bob
bad	bad	bad	bad	bad

bet	pet	let	met	set	net
bet	pet	let	met	set	net
bad	mad	sad	lad	pad	dad
bad	mad	sad	lad	pad	dad

- Copy the words using the learning-to-spell routine.

Spelling
SEATWORK 4

NAME ____________

you of in we for
you of in we for
you of in we for
you of in we for

The cop saw Bob and the dog.
The cop saw Bob and the dog.
He likes the dog. He pats him.
He likes the dog. He pats him.
The cop likes Bob and the dog.
The cop likes Bob and the dog.

• Copy the words and sentences using the learning-to-spell routine.

Spelling
SEATWORK 5

NAME ____________

mat pet lot sit cut
mat pet lot sit cut
mat pet lot sit cut
mat pet lot sit cut

lot pot got not hot dot
lot pot got not hot dot
sit pit hit bit fit lit
sit pit hit bit fit lit
cut nut hut but rut
cut nut hut but rut

• Copy the words using the learning-to-spell routine.

Spelling
SEATWORK 6

NAME ____________

can can can can can
hen hen hen hen hen
pin pin pin pin pin
fun fun fun fun fun
Don Don Don Don Don

Don and Bob had lots of fun.
Don and Bob had lots of fun.
Don bet he could hit the ball.
Don bet he could hit the ball.
He won the bet. He won the bet.

- Copy the words and sentences using the learning-to-spell routine.

Spelling
SEATWORK 7

NAME ____________

it that is your have
it that is your have
it that is your have
it that is your have

The dog has a bad cut.
The dog has a bad cut.
He will go to the vet.
He will go to the vet.
The vet will fix the cut.
The vet will fix the cut.

- Copy the words and sentences using the learning-to-spell routine.

Spelling
SEATWORK 8

NAME ____________

bet	get	jet	let
bet	get	jet	let
bet	get	jet	let
bet	get	jet	let
bet	get	jet	let
bet	get	jet	let
net	pet	set	vet
net	pet	set	vet
net	pet	set	vet
net	pet	set	vet
net	pet	set	vet

• Copy the words using the test-study routine (for words with a vowel-consonant common ending).

Spelling
SEATWORK 9

NAME ____________

will	will	will	will	will
be	be	be	be	be
are	are	are	are	are
not	not	not	not	not
as	as	as	as	as

will bill hill fill kill pill sill

will bill hill fill kill pill sill

be he we me he we me

be he we me he we me

We will not be late today.

We will not be late today.

• Copy the words and the sentences using the learning-to-spell and the test-study routines (where appropriate).

Spelling

SEATWORK 10

NAME ________________

ban	can	fan	man	pan
ban	can	fan	man	pan
ban	can	fan	man	pan
ban	can	fan	man	pan
ban	can	fan	man	pan
ran	tan	van	Jan	Dan
ran	tan	van	Jan	Dan
ran	tan	van	Jan	Dan
ran	tan	van	Jan	Dan
ran	tan	van	Jan	Dan

- Copy the words using the test-study routine.

Spelling

SEATWORK 11

NAME ________________

bag	bag	bag	sag	sag	sag
tag	tag	tag	wag	wag	wag
beg	beg	beg	leg	leg	leg
peg	peg	peg	dig	dig	dig
fig	fig	fig	pig	pig	pig
wig	wig	wig	dog	dog	dog
fog	fog	fog	hog	hog	hog
jog	jog	jog	log	log	log
dug	dug	dug	hug	hug	hug
jug	jug	jug	mug	mug	mug
rug	rug	rug	tug	tug	tug

- Copy the words using the learning-to-spell routine.

Spelling
SEATWORK 12

NAME ____________

at	this	with	but	on
at	this	with	but	on
at	this	with	but	on
at	this	with	but	on

The pig and dog play in the mud.
The pig and dog play in the mud.
They dig up a big bag.
They dig up a big bag.
They tug at it and get it out.
They tug at it and get it out.

- Copy the words and sentences using the learning-to-spell routine.

Spelling
SEATWORK 13

NAME ____________

bad	bad	bad	Dad	Dad	Dad
had	had	had	mad	mad	mad
sad	sad	sad	bed	bed	bed
fed	fed	fed	led	led	led
red	red	red	Ted	Ted	Ted
bid	bid	bid	hid	hid	hid
lid	lid	lid	rid	rid	rid
cod	cod	cod	mod	mod	mod
nod	nod	nod	pod	pod	pod
sod	sod	sod	bud	bud	bud
dud	dud	dud	mud	mud	mud
sud	sud	sud	did	did	did

- Copy the words using the test-study routine.

Spelling
SEATWORK 14

NAME ______

at at

at at	no no	sit sit
a a	and and	see see
I I	fun fun	an an
an an	bit bit	has has
fat fat	pen pen	run run
in in	rat rat	me me
sat sat	as as	go go
pin pin	gun gun	the the

• Copy each word once using the learning-to-spell routine.

Spelling
SEATWORK 15

NAME ______

bin	bin	bin	bin
the	the	the	the
as	as	as	as
mat	mat	mat	mat
can	can	can	can
if	if	if	if
it	it	it	it
is	is	is	is
see	see	see	see
has	has	has	has
I	I	I	I

• Copy each word three times using the learning-to-spell routine.

Spelling
SEATWORK 16

NAME ______

yet	yet	yet	yet
I	I	I	I
see	see	see	see
vet	vet	vet	vet
wit	wit	wit	wit
kit	kit	kit	kit
on	on	on	on
jet	jet	jet	jet
the	the	the	the
is	is	is	is
go	go	go	go

- Copy each word three times using the learning-to-spell routine.

Spelling
SEATWORK 17

NAME ______

big	big	dip	dip
dig	dig	hip	hip
fig	fig	lip	lip
jig	jig	nip	nip
pig	pig	pip	pip
rig	rig	rip	rip
wig	wig	sip	sip
		tip	tip

- Copy each word once using the test-study routine.

Spelling

SEATWORK 18

NAME ____________

Answers will vary.

ad
sad

ad	in	o	at
sad	tin	so	bat
had	win	to	sat
an	et	am	it
can	set	jam	hit
fan	let	ham	sit
up	ed	en	ee
cup	red	ten	see
pup	bed	hen	bee

- Make up words using these endings.

Spelling

SEATWORK 19

NAME ____________

Answers will vary.

am
ham

am	et	at	it	an
ham	get	sat	sit	fan
dam	met	hat	hit	can
ram	wet	pat	bit	man
Sam	set	bat	fit	pan
ad	in	o	ip	ap
mad	fin	so	sip	map
had	win	to	tip	tap
bad	tin	go	dip	lap
sad	pin	do	hip	cap

- Make up words using these endings.

Spelling
SEATWORK 20

NAME ______

Answers will vary.

pan
fan
can

cat	pin	bet	tan	bad
sat	win	set	fan	had
mat	tin	met	man	sad
sit	bed	Sam	sap	Bob
bit	red	jam	tap	job
hit	fed	ham	map	mob
wig	gun	will	dot	sand
big	bun	mill	hot	hand
pig	sun	bill	tot	land

• Print other words with the same ending.

Spelling
SEATWORK 21

NAME ______

look look looking look look looking

see	see	seeing
ring	ring	ringing
cook	cook	cooking
sing	sing	singing
do	do	doing
bark	bark	barking
end	end	ending
turn	turn	turning

• Copy the word once, then again, adding *ing*.

Spelling
SEATWORK 22

NAME ____________

• Complete each word.

Spelling
SEATWORK 23

NAME ____________

table
ten
tv
teeth
tree
tack
towel
two
tent

• Complete each word.

Spelling
SEATWORK 24

NAME ____________________

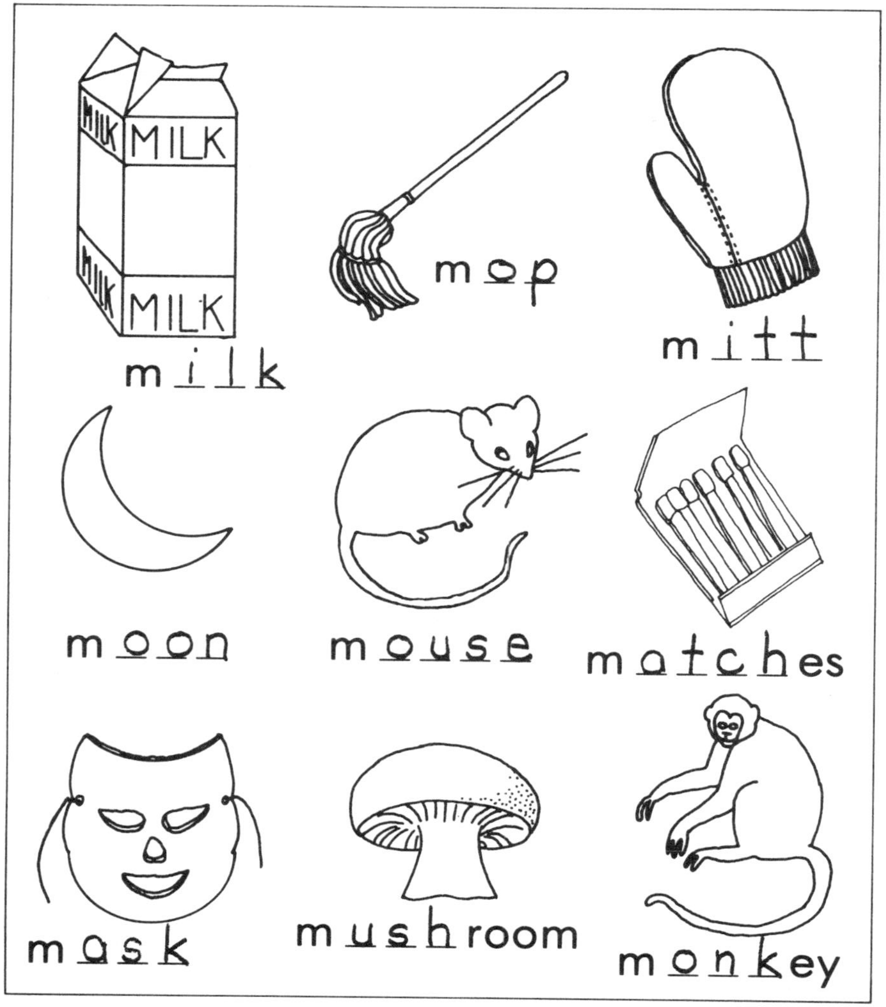
MILK
MILK
milk
mop
mitt
moon
mouse
matches
mask
mushroom
monkey

• Complete each word.

Spelling
SEATWORK 25

NAME ____________________

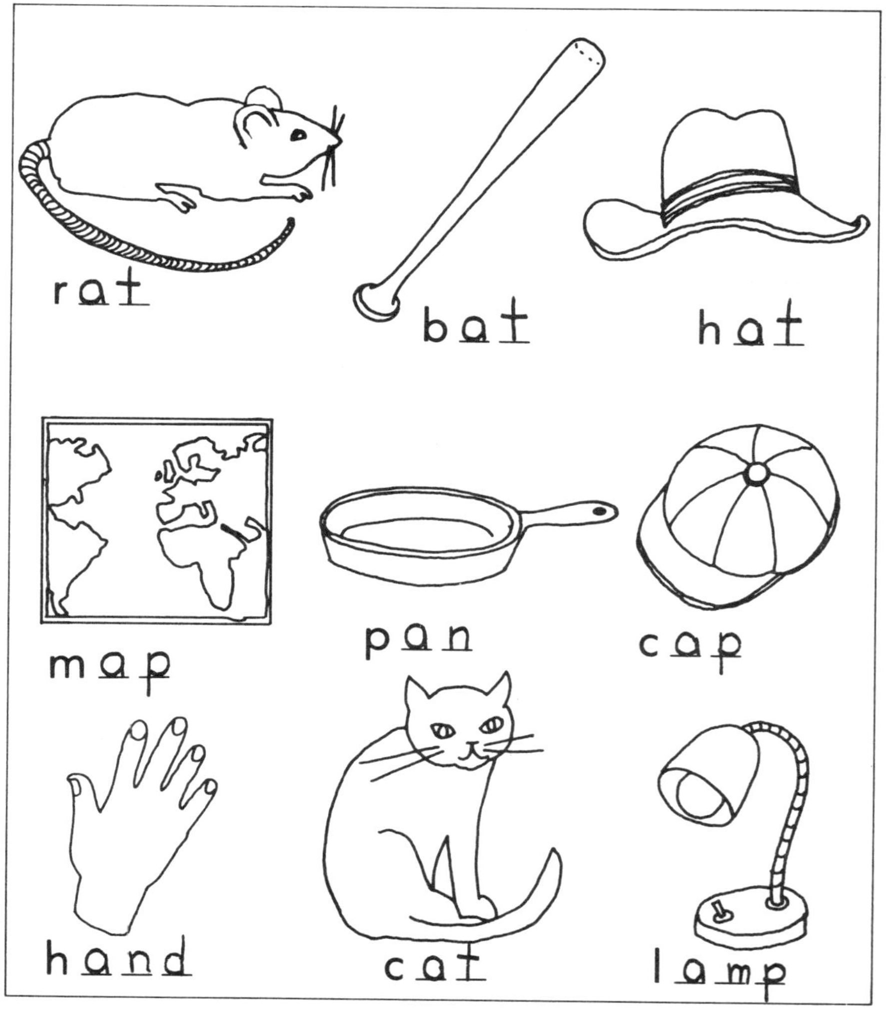
rat
bat
hat
map
pan
cap
hand
cat
lamp

• Complete each word.

Spelling

SEATWORK 26

NAME ____________________

• Complete each word.

Spelling

SEATWORK 27

NAME ____________________

coat
bat
boat
dart
cart
heart
hat
cat
rat

• Complete each word.

Spelling
SEATWORK 28

NAME ______________________

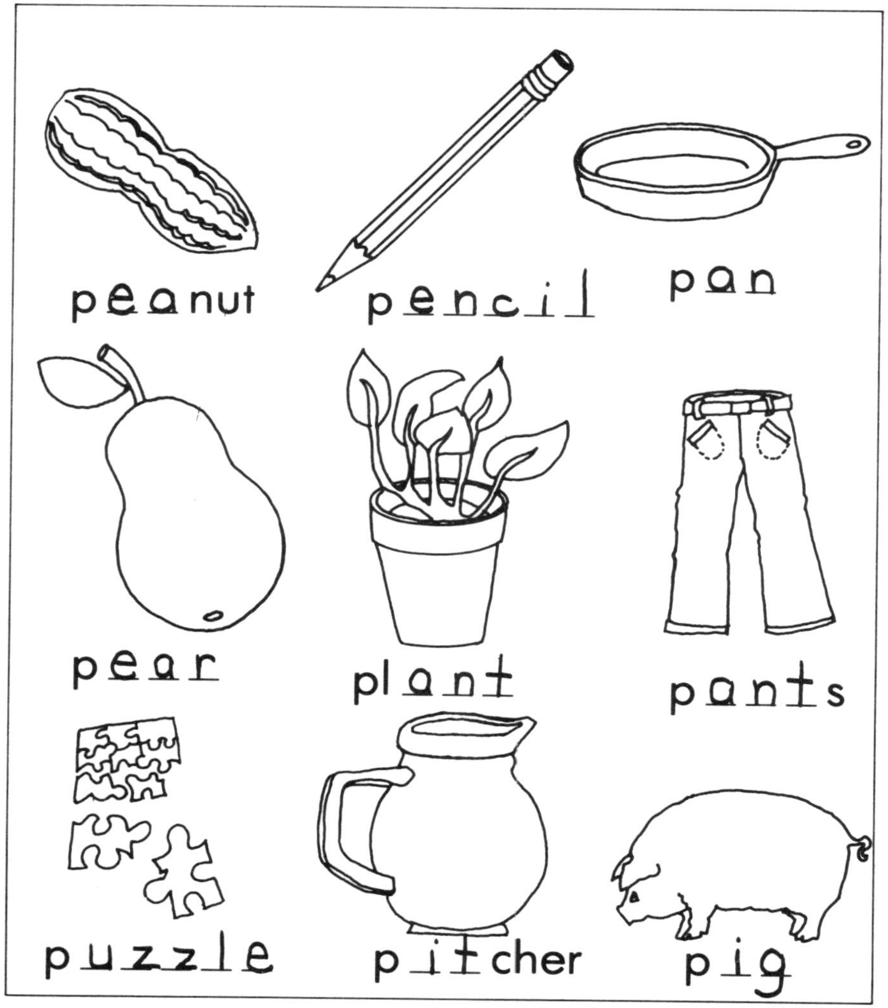
peanut
pencil
pan
pear
plant
pants
puzzle
pitcher
pig

• Complete each word.

Spelling
SEATWORK 29

NAME ______________________

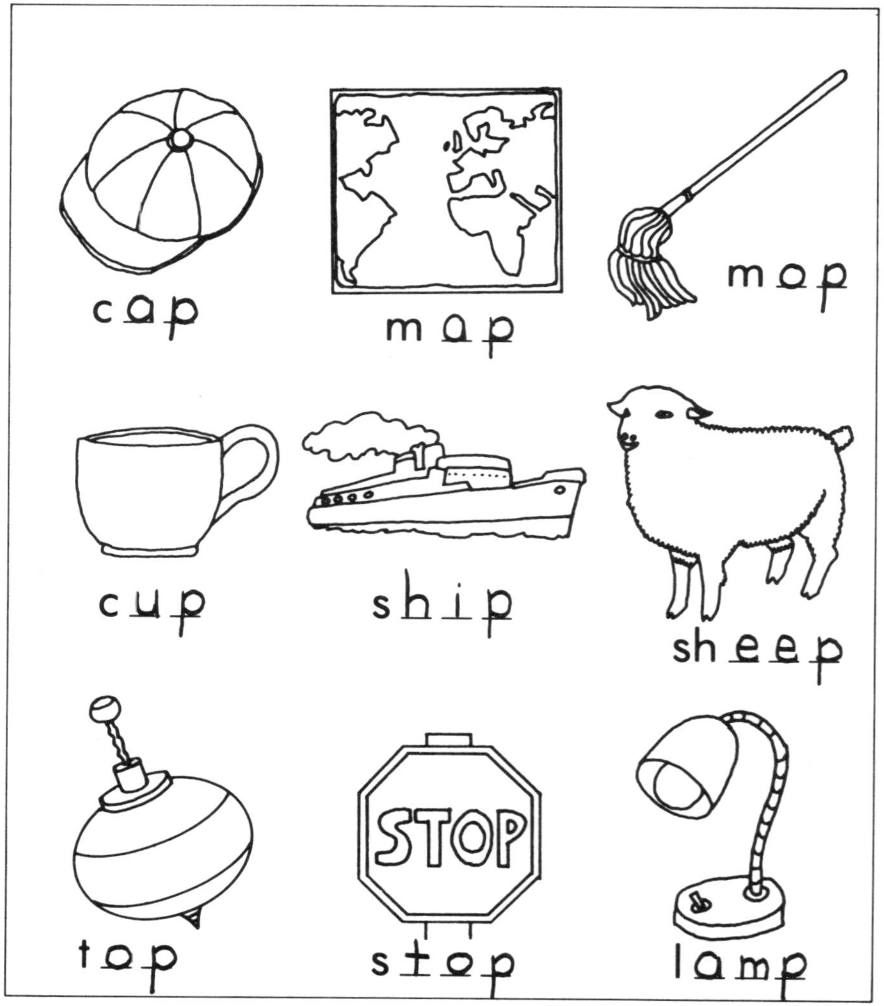
cap
map
mop
cup
ship
sheep
top
STOP
stop
lamp

• Complete each word.

Spelling

SEATWORK 30

NAME ______________________

doll mop top

bottle box clock

blocks lock sock

• Complete each word.

Spelling

SEATWORK 31

NAME ______________________

sun soldier 7 seven

sandwich sock Santa

sink 6 six saw

• Complete each word.

Spelling
SEATWORK 32

NAME ______________________

• Complete each word.

Spelling
SEATWORK 33

NAME ______________________

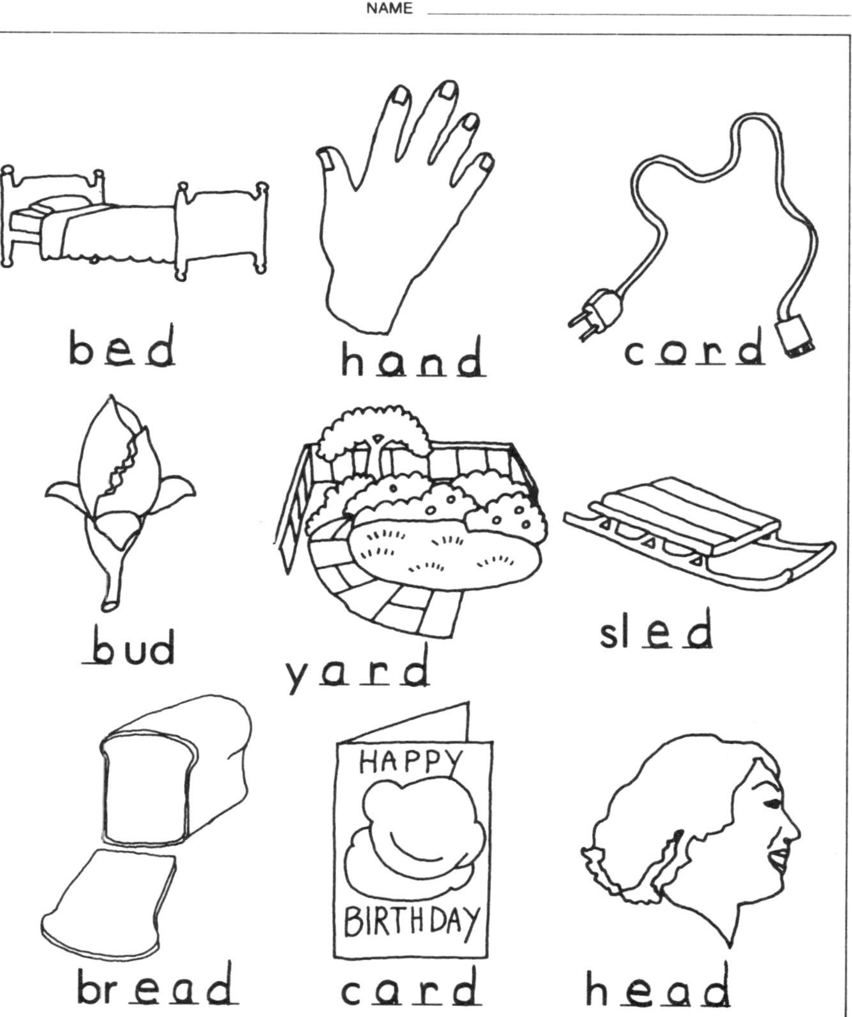

• Complete each word.

Spelling

SEATWORK 34

NAME ______________________

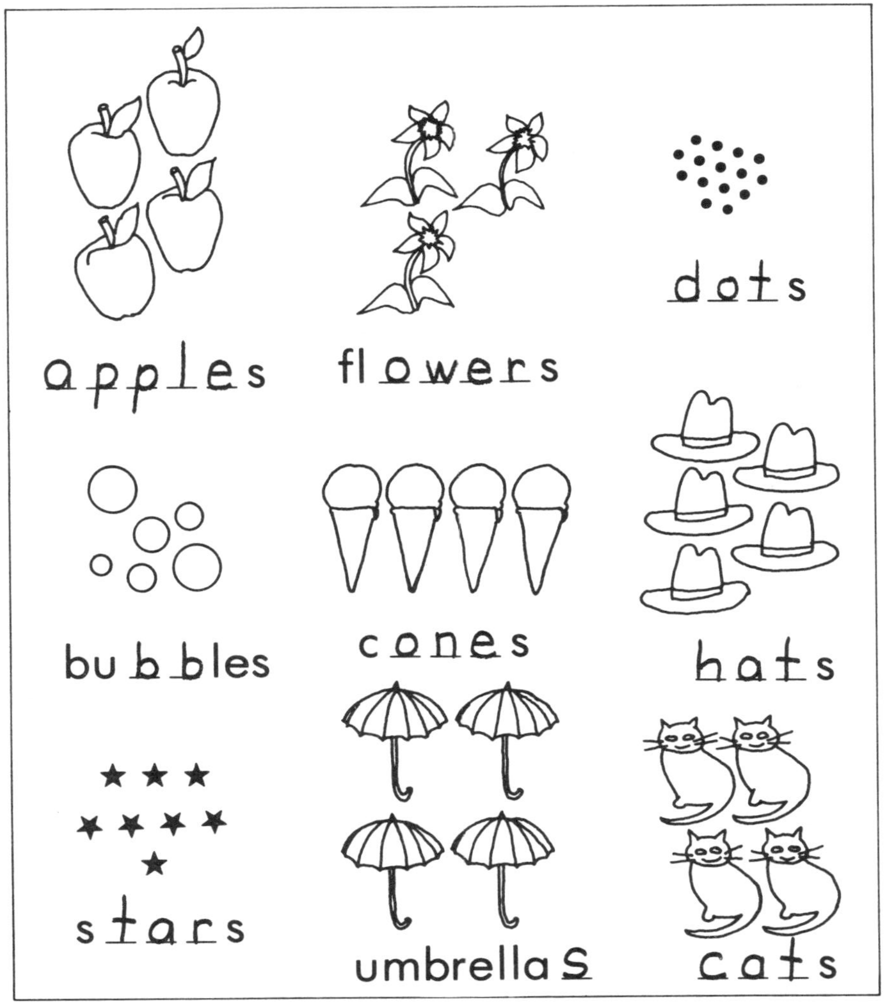
apples
flowers
dots
bubbles
cones
hats
stars
umbrellas
cats

• Complete each word.

Spelling

SEATWORK 35

NAME ______________________

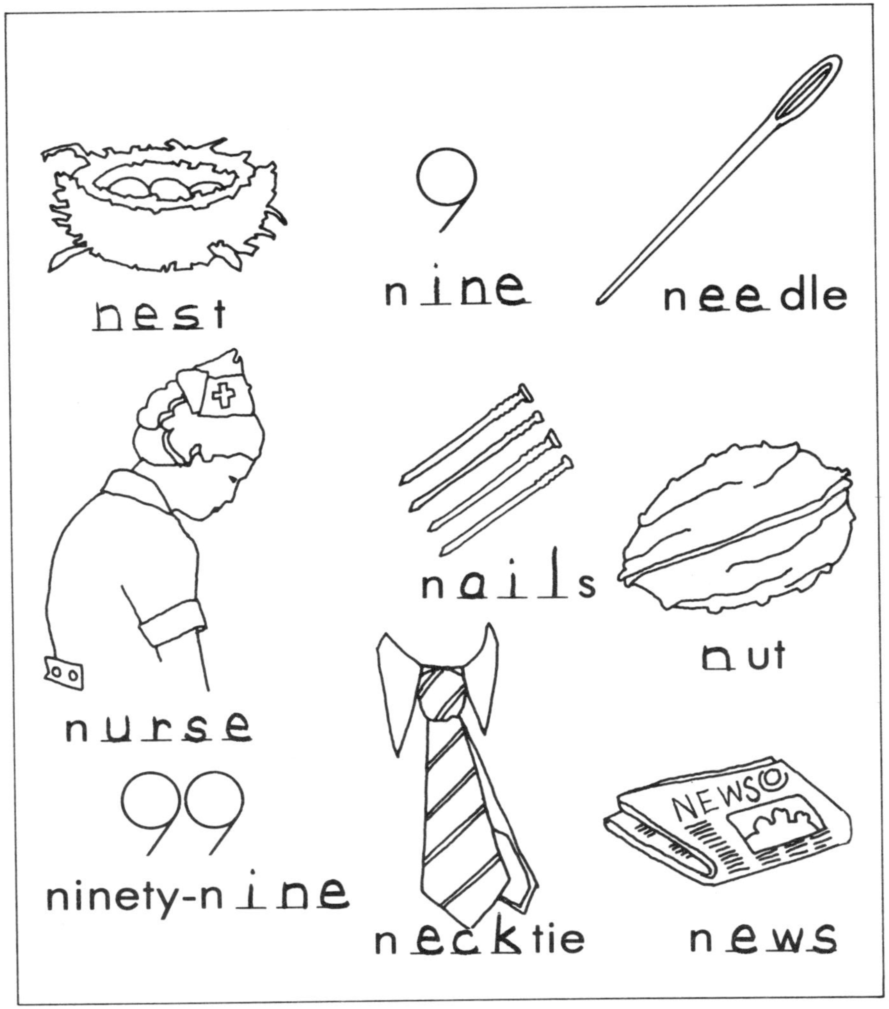
nest
9
nine
needle
nurse
nails
nut
99
ninety-nine
necktie
NEWS
news

• Complete each word.

Spelling

SEATWORK 36

NAME ______________________

• Complete each word.

Spelling

SEATWORK 37

NAME ______________________

bed
7
seven
pencil
sled
bell
bench
10
ten
tent
belt

• Complete each word.

Spelling
SEATWORK 38

NAME ____________________

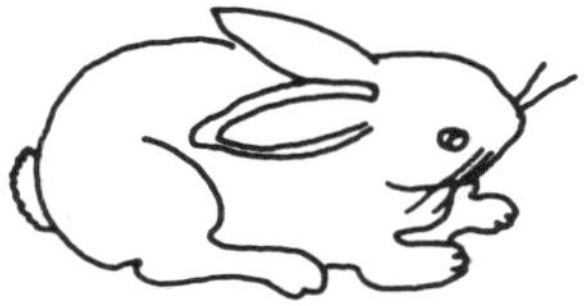

rabbit
rake 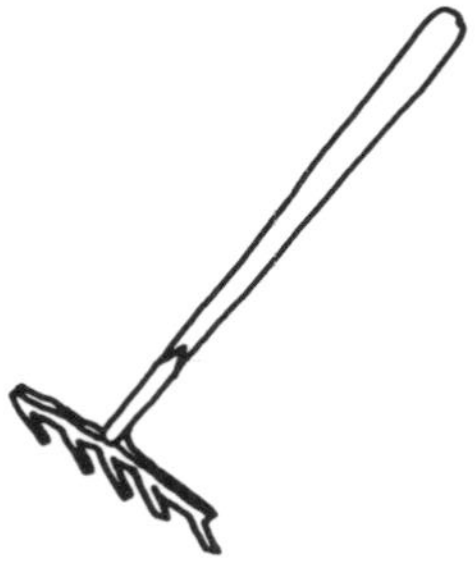
ruler 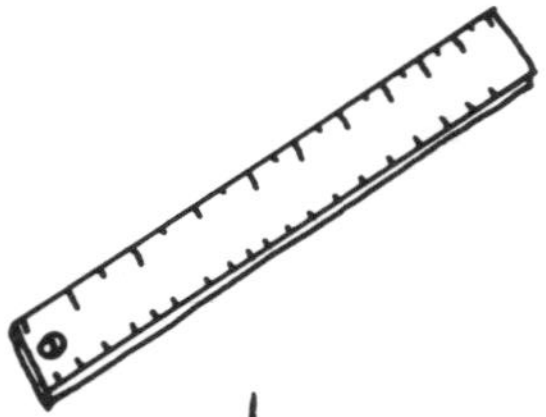
radio 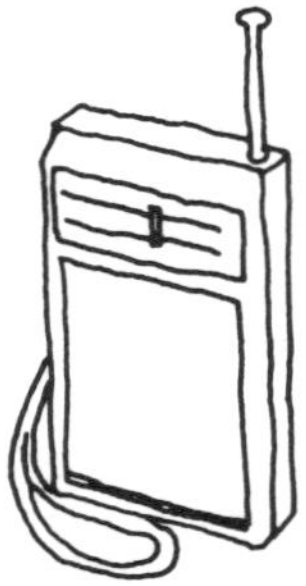
rug 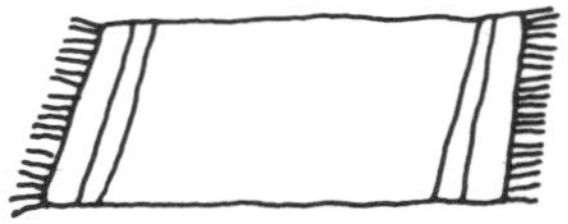
rat 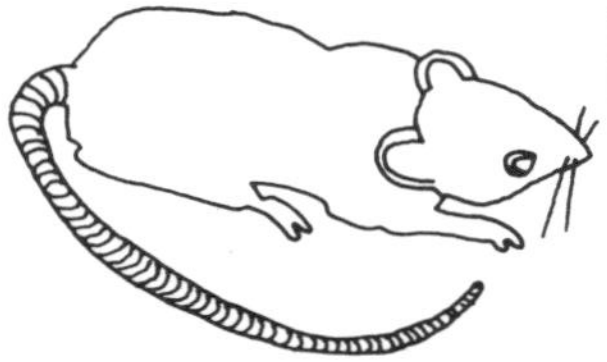
rattle 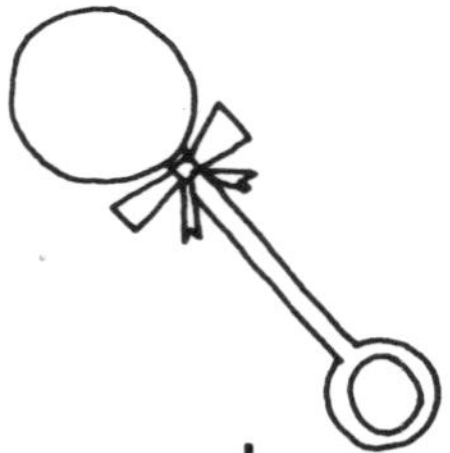
room 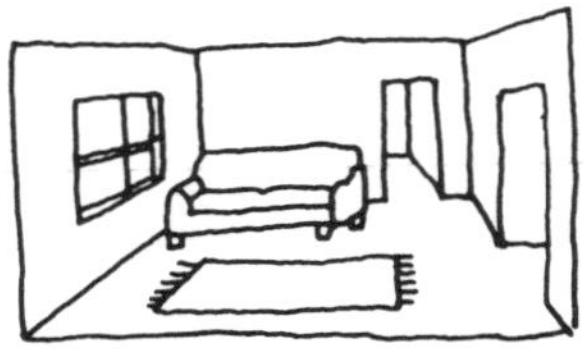
ring 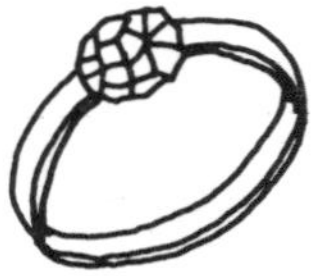

• Complete each word.

Spelling
SEATWORK 39

NAME ____________________

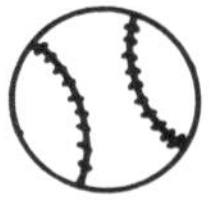

ball
bat 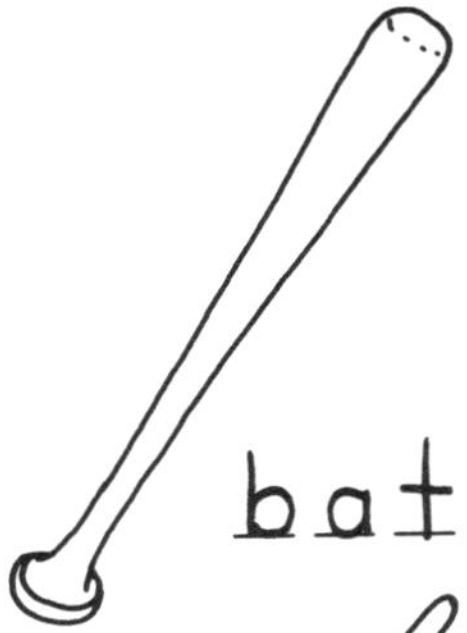
balloon 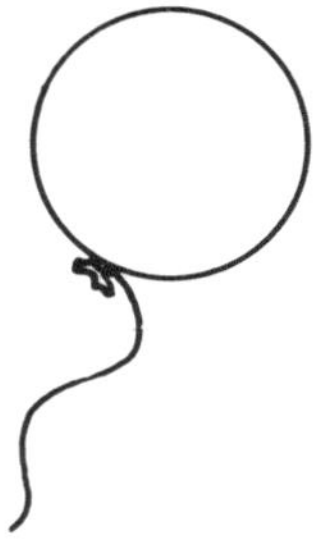
bell 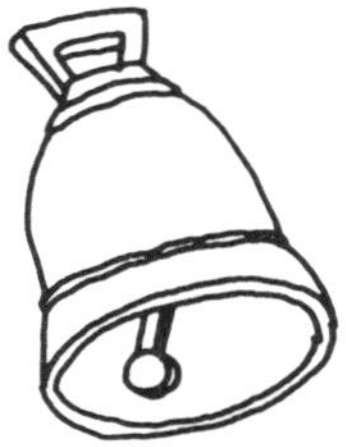
broom 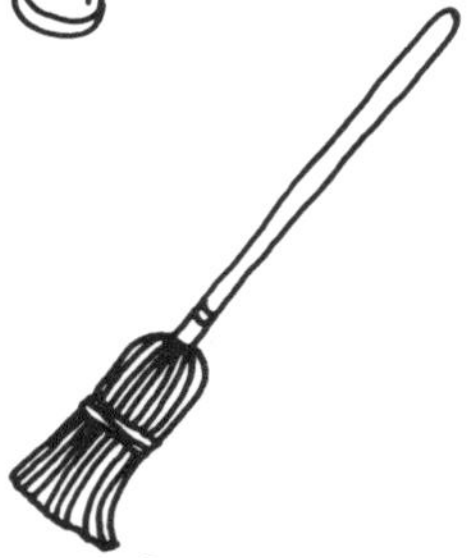
bed 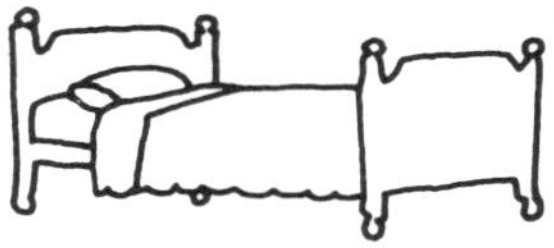
box 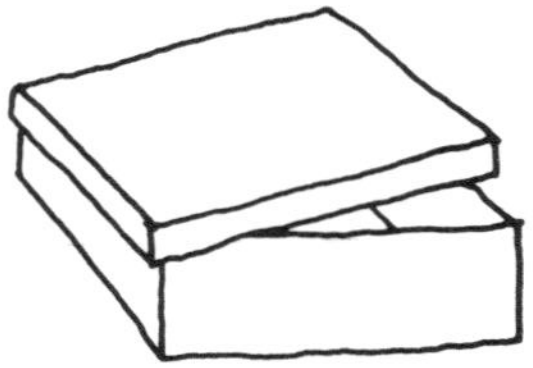
banana 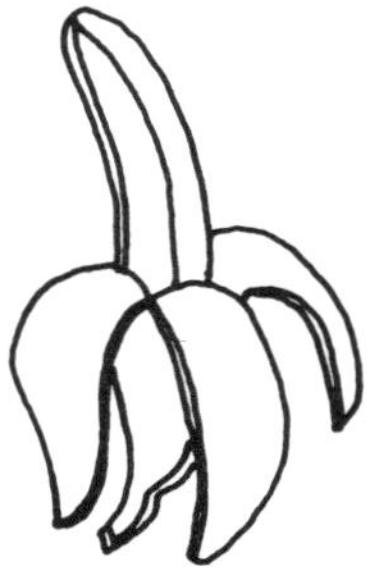
butterfly 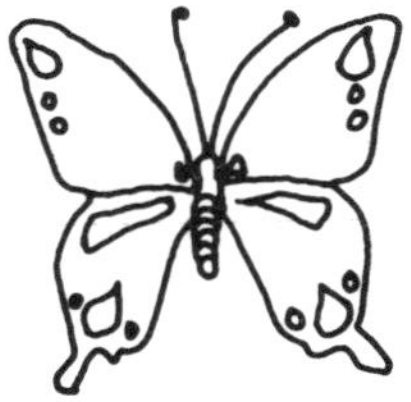

• Complete each word.

Spelling

SEATWORK 40

NAME ______________________

crab bib crib

bathtub web knob

cob bulb club

• Complete each word.

Spelling

SEATWORK 41

NAME ______________________

• Complete each word.

Spelling
SEATWORK 42

NAME ____________

bag tag pig

bug rug egg

flag dog frog

• Complete each word.

Spelling
SEATWORK 43

NAME ____________

cup gun sun

rug bug bulb

duck bud tub

• Complete each word.

Spelling

SEATWORK 44

NAME ______________________

ladder letter lock

lion lips line

leaf lid lamp

• Complete each word.

Spelling

SEATWORK 45

NAME ______________________

ax 6 six box

fox ox mix

sax 66 sixty-six WAX wax

• Complete each word.

Printing
SEATWORK 4

NAME ______________________

a

a

a

a

a

- Trace letters and make additional letters.